THE Horticulture GARDENER'S GUIDES
SHRUBS

Andrew McIndoe

HORTICULTURE
BOOKS
www.hortmag.com

A HORTICULTURE BOOK

Horticulture Publications, Boston, Massachusetts

First published in the US in 2005 ISBN 1-55870-748-4

Horticulture is a subsidiary of F+W Publications Inc. Company
Distributed by F+W Publications Inc.
4700 East Galbraith Road, Cincinnati, OH 45236
1-800-289-0963

Printed in Singapore by KHL Printing Co Pte Ltd
for Horticulture Publications, Boston, Massachusetts

Visit our website at www.hortmag.com

Commissioning Editor Mic Cady
Art Editor Sue Cleave
Production Director Roger Lane

Series Editor Sue Gordon, OutHouse Publishing
   Winchester, Hampshire SO22 5DS
Copy Editors Polly Boyd, Sue Gordon
Proofreader Alison Shakspeare
Indexer June Wilkins

American edition by
Craft Plus Publishing Ltd.
53 Crown Street
Brentwood, Essex CM14 4BD
Consultant Lynn M. Steiner, M.S. (Horticulture)

ORNAMENTAL PLANT OR PERNICIOUS WEED?

In certain circumstances ornamental garden plants can be
undesirable when introduced into natural habitats, either
because they compete with native flora, or because they act
as hosts to fungal and insect pests. Plants that are popular in
one part of the world may be considered undesirable in
another. Horticulturists have learned to be wary of the effect
that cultivated plants may have on native habitats and, as a
rule, any plant likely to be a problem in a particular area if it
escapes from cultivation is restricted and therefore is not
offered for sale.

PHOTOGRAPHIC CREDITS

The publishers would like to acknowledge with thanks all those whose
gardens are pictured in this book.

**ALL PHOTOGRAPHS WERE TAKEN BY ANDREW MCINDOE AND
JOHN HILLIER WITH THE EXCEPTION OF:**

David Austin® Roses: 113(Good Companions 3, 5), 115(Good
   Companions 3)
Eric Crichton: p14(lft)
Duncan & Davies: 51(*Acer palmatum* 'Burgundy Lace')
Garden Picture Library: pp (GC=Good Companions) 29(top lft)/J S Sira;
   49(GC 1) & back cover(top)/John Beedle; 49(GC 4)/Clive Nichols;
   52(top lft)/Philippe Bonduel; 52(top rt)/Mark Bolton; 56 & back
   flap/Clive Nichols; 63(GC 2)/J S Sira; 63(GC 5)/Sunniva Harte
   79(lft)/Mark Bolton; 85(GC 1)/Neil Holmes; 85(GC 3)/Jerry Pavia;
   90(top lft)/Vaughan Fleming; 93(GC 5) Neil Homes; 98(GC 3)/David
   Askham; 133(GC 1)/J S Sira; 136(top lft)/Neil Holmes; 154(GC 4)/
   J S Sira; 157(top ctre)/Didier Willery; 165(top rt)/Neil Holmes;
   175(btm rt)/Sunniva Harte; 177(ctre rt)/John Glover
New Leaf Plants: 43(Good Companions 4), 55(Good Companions 4)
Osberton Nurseries: 101(Good Companions 3), 105(Good
   Companions 3)

Contents

Introduction

In writing this book I have borne in mind the questions I am most often asked. I have also drawn on advice from other gardeners and on experience gained from successes and failures in gardens with which I have been involved.

This is not intended to be a definitive work on woody plants. That has already been written by the late Sir Harold Hillier, revised and updated by John Hillier VMH and Allen Coombes—*The Hillier Manual of Trees & Shrubs*. This book is a practical guide to choosing and using shrubs. As there is currently strong interest in traditional, English-style planting schemes, the emphasis is on plants that are appropriate for this type of garden. Many of the illustrations are of beautiful, old European gardens that exemplify this style.

Thirty years of garden center experience has taught me that most of us look at the individual plant, when what we should be doing is looking at the overall picture. We concentrate our efforts on assessing whether or not we like a particular plant, without considering how it will fit into our garden and what it will contribute.

Shrubs are the backbone of the English-style garden, and sometimes it is easy to forget the significance of their contributions. Some of our best shrubs are not glamorous, nor are they the plants of the moment, yet we have come to rely upon them and perhaps take their presence for granted.

A few years ago I moved from a small garden to a much larger plot, and I determined to garden accordingly: big, bold planting from the start, and no more messing about with little treasures that need close scrutiny to be admired. Yet I have to admit that I struggled—I was just as reluctant to make those bold decisions as the gardeners whom I have so often advised.

Interest in gardening is fostered and encouraged by success. This book is about helping you to attain success. A good garden has variety, and it has continuity of interest through the seasons. With container-grown plants now being the norm, we are able to select plants by season, at the time of year when they are performing at their best. As most of us are fair-weather gardeners, it is no wonder that our gardens tend to be at their most prolific in spring. With a little planning and thought, however, the interest can be spread over the whole year.

Most shrubs are good-value plants that will give many years of pleasure for a relatively small outlay. Because they may well be with us for a very long time, and are not plants that we choose every year, it is crucial that we select our shrubs wisely and grow them well. I hope this book helps you to achieve this.

Andrew McIndoe

Cornus kousa 'Gold Star'

THE SHRUBS IN THIS BOOK

In evoking the spirit of the English-style garden, we have focused on plants that mainly belong in this kind of setting.

Many of the species mentioned are commonly grown, but others are rarer and may not be easy to find. Some are new cultivars and others are traditional British varieties, which, if you can track them down, will add an air of authenticity to your design. The following sources of hard-to-find species should help you on your way to your English-style garden:

Cistus Nursery, 22711 NW Gillihan Road, Sauvie Island, Oregon 97231, tel (503) 621-2233

Gossler Farms Nursery, 1200 Weaver Road, Springfield, Oregon 97478-9691, tel (541) 746-3922

Heaths and Heathers Nursery, 631 East Pickering Road, Shelton, WA 98584, tel (360) 427-5318

Heronswood Nursery, 7530 NE 288th Street, Kingston, WA 98346, tel (360) 297-4172

Twombly Nursery, 162 Barn Hill Road, Monroe, CT 06468, tel (203) 261 2133

And for those in warmer zones, who want an idea of how to achieve an English-style garden with plants that will thrive in these areas:

Weston Gardens in Bloom, Inc., 8101 Anglin Drive, Fort Worth, TX, tel (817) 572-0549

USDA HARDINESS ZONES

Most species described in this book will thrive in temperate areas (zone 7 and thereabouts) and the seasonal changes described apply to these areas. Zones are indicated next to each species name, and cultivars are suitable for the same zones unless otherwise stated. Remember that a plant's site (whether windy, damp, or exposed) can also affect its hardiness.

Zone	Avg. annual min. recorded temp.	Zone	Avg. annual min. recorded temp.
1	Below -50°F	7	0°F to 10°F
2	-50°F to -40°F	8	10°F to 20°F
3	-40°F to -30°F	9	20°F to 30°F
4	-30°F to -20°F	10	30°F to 40°F
5	-20°F to -10°F	11	Above 40°F
6	-10°F to 0°F		

To find your zone, see the zone map on the back flap of this book.

INTRODUCING SHRUBS

Shrubs are woody plants with several branches arising from ground level. Some have showy flowers, others variegated or colorful foliage; some have attractive stems and bark, others aromatic leaves. Shrubs contribute to the garden picture at all levels, from the ground level to way above eye level. Some of the most important shrubs are just solid green but retain their foliage throughout the seasons. For centuries, people have planted them, shaped them, and used them to give structure to the garden.

Right: Le Jardin d'Angélique, Normandy, France

Shrubs in the English-style garden: a history

Ornamental horticulture has evolved over two millennia, with the most dramatic part of that evolution taking place in the past two centuries. Early gardeners had to choose from native plant material and a limited number of introductions from overseas. Since the golden age of plant hunting, instigated by the Victorians, gardeners have had a far greater wealth of plant material to work with. Since the very beginning, shrubs have played a vital role as structure plants in gardens. Today, their diversity of shape, form, color, and texture takes center stage.

The earliest-known gardens in Britain are those planted by the Romans during the 1st century A.D., attached to large villas and palaces such as Fishbourne, near Chichester in Sussex. It seems likely that these gardens consisted of a symmetrical planting of boxwood hedges, divided by gravel walks, alongside an open, landscaped space. There may well have been kitchen gardens, too, growing vegetables and fruits brought from the Continent. Sweet chestnut and walnut are thought to have reached Britain at this time.

Early gardens attached to monasteries cultivated a variety of trees and plants in orchards, kitchen gardens, and recreational areas. Most plants were aromatic or had medicinal properties.

IN A MONASTERY GARDEN

In the Anglo-Saxon period, which followed the end of the Roman era in Britain, the record becomes blurred, and little is known about horticulture at that time. During the Middle Ages, however, the spread of Christianity from continental Europe saw the establishment of monastic houses in Britain and, with them, a fostering of the tradition of cultivating plants. Aromatic plants and plants with medicinal uses—rosemary, thyme, sage, lavender—as well as any fruiting plants of food value, were brought over to be grown by the monks in their physic and kitchen gardens. The covered walks of the cloister surrounded an open green space, often with a central well.

Some medieval castles, too, had courtyard gardens, with paths crisscrossing flower beds in which native plants probably grew alongside those collected on religious crusades and missions abroad. Linking the garden with the surrounding landscape were mounds, which provided views over the castle walls.

THE PLANT SHAPERS

As the need for fortification became less intense and the medieval manor replaced the castle, gardens became a place for pastimes such as bowls or tennis. Attached to the house, gardens were generally enclosed by a hedge, often of boxwood or yew.

After the dissolution of the monasteries and the sale of monastic properties in the 16th century, the new landowners enclosed tracts of land for keeping deer or

Topiary and trimmed hedges at Cliveden, in Buckinghamshire, England. For many years trimming and shaping was the only way in which gardeners could enhance the variety of hardy plant material.

cattle and created formal gardens and terraces near the house, sheltered by hedges or walls, in which they grew ornamental flowers and herbs.

By now, the influence of the Italian Renaissance was beginning to show itself in the gardens of grand English houses. Geometrical layouts mirrored the alignment of the house, featuring sundials, fountains, and statues. This period saw the rise in popularity of the Tudor knot garden—an intricate pattern of low hedges.

In the 1600s wealthy Stuart monarchs took inspiration from the French, rather than the Italians, and they introduced broad avenues of trees, often in conjunction with rectangular ornamental parterres of formal low hedges, best viewed from a mount, raised terraces, or the upper floors of the house. The spaces between the hedges were often filled with herbs, low shrubs, or annual flowers. King James I's head gardener, Mollet, used topiary extensively, making it fashionable. It was also popular in Dutch-style gardens, along with water features, trees, and bulbs, including, of course, tulips.

THE LANDSCAPERS

The formality of the Italian Renaissance garden gave way to a more natural look in the 18th century. William Kent's garden for Lord Burlington at Chiswick House, London, with its temples and classical ornaments in open parkland with trees, became hugely influential. Kent's pupil and son-in-law Lancelot "Capability" Brown

continued his work, making the house an integral part of the landscape. Formality was taking a break: no hedges, no clipping, and a different type of control of the plant material. Humphrey Repton followed in Brown's footsteps as a landscape gardener, but reintroduced terraces and flower gardens adjoining the house.

ACROSS THE ATLANTIC

The 17th-century British colonists in America took the gardening tradition with them. Their first priority was growing food, but before long New England cottage gardens were flourishing with the seeds and bulbs of favorite plants from home. In the New York area the Huguenots, too, brought their love of gardening, and by the late 1660s clipped evergreens were found alongside the roses, tulips, and crown imperials of Dutch and French gardens. The first commercial nurseries began importing trees, shrubs, and herbaceous plants from Europe. When William Penn founded Pennsylvania he envisaged a "greene towne," with each house having a good-sized garden. His own property was later to become the site of the world-famous Longwood Gardens.

The expansion of trading in the 18th and 19th centuries brought great wealth to America, as well as to places along the trade routes, such as Madeira.

The gardens of Quinta do Palheiro, in Madeira, Portugal, originally laid out in the 18th century. Gardens on international trade routes, such as these, became rich in plant material from all over the world.

Shipbuilders, merchants, and sea captains built houses in fashionable Continental styles, and gardens followed suit. As cargoes moved across the seas, so too did plants. The wealthy liked the variety that the new plants brought to their gardens; gardeners enjoyed greater prestige.

THE PLANT HUNTERS

The Victorian era saw the emergence of a new passion for plants. Bedding plants made their debut in a big way, raised in greenhouses and planted out for exotic summer color. Public gardens, parks, and open spaces brought horticulture to the masses, in styles varying

This magnificent plant is the original specimen of *Rhododendron maccabeanum*, collected by Frank Kingdon-Ward in the Far East and planted at Trewithen Gardens, near Truro, in Cornwall, England, .

from formal to wild. The fruits of the labors of plant hunters and collectors started to make their impact.

Plants from China, Japan, the Himalayas, and the Americas swelled the nursery catalogs manyfold. British gardens could not have been better placed to appreciate this influx of new plant material. A wealthy population, a long gardening history, and a love of plants were contributory factors, but most significant was the country's climate: temperate, with plenty of rainfall—broadly similar to that of the main regions of the world that were so rich in good garden plants.

Plant hunting was nothing new. The John Tradescants, elder and younger, had brought plants back from Europe and Virginia to Britain in the 17th century. However, it was during the late 18th and early 19th centuries that collecting began in earnest, with hunters such as John Fraser and David Douglas seeking out plants in North America, Philipp von Siebold in Japan, and William Lobb in Chile and California.

The late 19th century and early 20th century proved to be the golden age of plant hunting. Wealthy private gardeners and the nurseries that served them sponsored expeditions: Robert Fortune in China and Japan, John Gould Veitch in Japan, William Hooker in the Himalayas, Charles Maries in China and Japan, E.H. Wilson and George Forrest in China. The era came to a close in 1958 with the death of Frank Kingdon-Ward, who collected widely in China, Burma, and Tibet.

Gardeners will recognize the names of these plant collectors, immortalized in many of our most popular garden plants. The gardener of today is often surprised to learn how recent many of these introductions are: some of our popular shrubs have been in our gardens for less than 100 years.

NEW PLANTS, A NEW STYLE

In the late 1800s and early 1900s William Robinson advocated permanent planting in place of bedding, combining exotics and bold-foliage plants in a native wild garden setting. Gardens began to look something like ours. Robinson's contemporary Gertrude Jekyll, regarded as the 20th century's most influential gardener, took the new palette of plant material a stage further by building on color schemes and using plants as a material to integrate the house into the garden and the surrounding landscape.

Ann's Grove Gardens, in County Cork, Southern Ireland, exemplifies the informal style of William Robinson, with exotic and native species interplanted in the natural landscape.

A little later in the 20th century, Vita Sackville-West, at Sissinghurst Castle in Kent, and the American-born Lawrence Johnston, at Hidcote Manor in the Cotswolds, combined formal and informal planting, integrating different styles of gardening with notable success.

On a more domestic scale, the growth of the suburbs saw a proliferation of small plots requiring hardy, easy-to-grow plants that tolerated the smoky atmosphere. While gardening at the grander end of the scale

Lanhydrock, near Bodmin in Cornwall, England, where the legacy of the Victorian plant collectors sits in a woodland setting alongside the formal bedding schemes that were so typical of the era.

still celebrated the introduction of new plants from the far corners of the world, the smaller domestic garden popularized a chosen few.

WHERE DO SHRUBS FIT IN?

The majority of ornamental shrubs have arrived in our gardens in the last 200 years, and mostly in the 20th century. Yes, of course, there were woody plants in gardens—indigenous species and those introduced subsequently from Europe and beyond—but it is only in the past century that the English gardener has learned to use the various types of plant together.

The shrub provides the permanent structure in the middle layer of the landscape: it occupies the layer beneath the canopy of trees, while providing permanent height and body to the layer of herbaceous plants and smaller subjects below. Of course, sometimes tall shrubs may creep into the higher layer, and many dwarf shrubs are important in the lower layer.

PLANTS OF GARDEN ORIGIN

Fifty years ago the flowering shrubs found in the average garden were few in variety: forsythia, roses, ribes, syringa, philadelphus, spiraea, cotoneaster, berberis, cytisus, and a handful more. Since then, many of the introductions made by the plant hunters have become widely available, vastly increasing the range of material available to gardeners.

Even greater than the number of plants returned by the plant hunters, however, is the influx that has resulted from selection and hybridization. Variation arises in plants that grow in the wild as well as in plants that are cultivated, and over the years gardeners have selected and propagated the best forms of naturally occurring species. Fired by the quest for such improvements as larger flowers, a longer flowering season, more compact growth, and higher disease resistance, they have also learned to select and modify plants through hybridization.

As far as shrubs are concerned, the hybridization process—from seed to flowering, to selection, trials, and commercial propagation—is a long one. In the case of a new hybrid rose, more than ten years elapse from the time the original cross is made to the launch of the new variety. Herbaceous perennials and annual bedding plants reach maturity more quickly, so the process is quicker—but many disappear as fast as they arrive.

All plant types have their phases of popularity, but shrubs remain the essential ingredient in any garden, and a good plant endures, however long it takes to reach us.

Shrubs are an essential element in most gardens. Today's gardener has access to a wide range of hardy shrubs that form the essential structure in the garden and link it to the natural landscape.

Speaking botanically

Latin names, as opposed to common names, may be frightening at first, but they are essential when it comes to accurate communication. A plant's common name may vary from one area to another. And when it comes to using common names in a different country, the confusion is greater still, even when the same native tongue is used.

PLANT CLASSIFICATION

FAMILY In plant classification the flowering plants are divided into a number of families. Each of these families contains a number of genera that have similar characteristics. For example, the rose family, Rosaceae, includes not only the genus *Rosa* but also a number of other genera, including *Potentilla*, *Cotoneaster*, *Malus*, and *Pyracantha*. A plant's botanical name consists of the genus and the species.

GENUS The generic name is something like our surname. It always starts with a capital letter and is always a noun. It is often derived from names found in an ancient language, such as Latin, Greek, or Arabic. *Daphne*, for example, is named after the daughter of the ancient Greek river god. Other generic names commemorate real people—in some cases the person who discovered the plant: *Deutzia*, for example, is named after J. Deutz; *Fuchsia* after Leonard Fuchs.

SPECIES The specific name, or epithet, is more like our first name, except that it is written after the genus and always starts with a lower-case letter. It cannot stand alone as a name and is not specific to that plant. As a Latin adjective, the specific name takes the gender of the generic name, so its ending agrees with the noun (although, as in any language, there are exceptions). The specific name is usually descriptive, giving us some information about the plant.

> **Specific names fall into four main categories:**
>
> - **Describing origin:** by continent, country, region—e.g., *sinensis, -e*, from China.
>
> - **Describing habitat:** from mountains, woods, fields, water—e.g., *montanus, -a, -um*, of mountains.
>
> - **Describing the plant or a feature of the plant,** such as its size, habit, leaf shape, flower color—e.g., *fastigiatus, -a, -um*, erect growing.
>
> - **Commemorating a botanist, plant collector, famous horticulturist, patron**—e.g., *davidii*, after Armand David, 19th-century plant collector.

SUBSPECIES, VARIETAS, AND FORMA These are the botanically recognized subdivisions of a species

where distinct forms occur in the wild. These are variously known as subspecies (ssp.), varietas or variety (var.), and forma or form (f.). For example *Skimmia japonica* ssp. *reevesiana*.

CULTIVAR A cultivar is a distinct form of a species that has been selected from wild or cultivated stock and has then been maintained in cultivation by vegetative propagation. In other words, all offspring come from one original plant or clone. The cultivar name is written with an initial capital letter within single quotation marks, and follows the specific name. For example, *Acer palmatum* 'Bloodgood'.

In gardening nomenclature, "cultivar" and "variety" are interchangeable. Also, the term "form" is used in a general way to refer to a variety, subspecies, or cultivar.

CLONE To all intents and purposes, a clone is the same as a cultivar: a selection of single individuals maintained in cultivation by vegetative propagation. All offspring are identical to the original.

GROUP A group lies somewhere between a cultivar and the subdivision of a species. A cultivar shows little or no variation, having originated from one individual. Members of a group can show variation, but not enough to separate them botanically. So the *Acer palmatum* Atropurpureum Group includes forms of *Acer palmatum* with purple foliage that are not named as cultivars.

HYBRID Species are collected from the wild, but hybrids are usually born in gardens. Over the years, gardeners have hybridized species and, in some cases, genera. Where a hybrid has originated from a cross made between two species, the new "hybrid epithet" is preceded by a multiplication sign. For example *Elaeagnus* × *ebbingei* is a hybrid between *Elaeagnus macrophylla* and *Elaeagnus submacrophylla*.

Sometimes, when two genera are closely related, it is possible to create a hybrid between them. In this case the multiplication sign comes before the generic name. For example × *Halimiocistus sahucii* is a hybrid between *Halimium umbellatum* and *Cistus salvifolius*.

NAME CHANGES

The naming of plants using botanical nomenclature is an ongoing process. As their knowledge increases, botanists find it necessary to make changes to nomenclature. It is important to remember that the numbers of plants introduced into cultivation in the last 200 years is vast, and it sometimes becomes apparent that plants that at first appeared similar are in fact sufficiently different to require separate classification. Hence changes in nomenclature. Old names, when they are well known, are often shown in parentheses after the new name. For example, *Brachyglottis* 'Sunshine' (*Senecio* 'Sunshine').

SELLING NAMES

Normally a plant is identified by its cultivar name, which is shown inside quotation marks. Sometimes a plant may be better known under a selling name, or trade description, than its original name. This is usually registered as a trademark. The selling name is written without quotation marks. For example, *Prunus caroliniana* 'Monus', Bright 'N Tight™. It is evident that the selling name in this instance is infinitely more appealing than the cultivar name and will impact on the commercial success of the plant.

PLANT BREEDERS' RIGHTS

Certain plants may not be propagated for sale without royalties being paid to the registered breeder. Wherever such plants are offered for sale, the letters P.P. or P.P.A.F. must follow the plant's name but precede the selling name. For example, *Rosa* x 'Radrazz' P.P. Knock Out™.

Two internationally accepted codes control all plant nomenclature. The botanical names (in other words, the generic and specific names) are covered by the International Code of Botanical Nomenclature. This is applied to wild and cultivated plants. The cultivar names and nomenclature, which are used in addition to the botanical name, are covered by the International Code of Nomenclature for Cultivated Plants. This relates only to garden plants.

PLANT NAMES ARE FUN

Whether the gardener is a natural linguist or not, botanical Latin is a satisfying language. Just as a feel for plants grows the more you work with them, so a feel for plant names develops over time. Not only are the names in a language that can be used anywhere in the world; they also provide immediately accessible information about the plant to which they refer. A few examples:

Specific epithet	Meaning	Example
alatus, -a, -um	winged	*Euonymus alatus*
fruticosus, -a, -um	shrubby	*Phlomis fruticosa*
littoralis, -e	of seashores	*Griselinia littoralis*
mollis, -e	soft	*Hamamelis mollis*
praecox	early	*Cytisus praecox*
sanguineus, -a, -um	blood red	*Cornus sanguinea*
stellatus, -a, -um	starry	*Magnolia stellata*
sylvaticus, -a, -um	of woodland	*Fagus sylvatica*

The fascinating subject of plant names and their meanings is fully explored in Horticulture's *Plant Names Explained*.

Buying shrubs

Choosing shrubs is easy: the gardener has access to an enormous range of hardy plants through mail order catalogs, nurseries, and garden centers. Most shrubs are purchased after visiting a plant retailer and personally selecting the plants; because of modern production techniques, there are plenty of high-quality plants to choose from.

Today, most shrubs are "container-grown". That is, the plant has been grown in a pot since it was propagated. Most shrubs are propagated either by taking cuttings or by grafting. A young rooted plant is grown-on in a small pot to what is called the liner stage. Usually it is then potted into the final pot, in which it will be sold. The roots are kept intact and undisturbed at each potting, and it is important that they remain so when, finally, it is planted in the ground.

Some shrubs grow better in the open ground than they do in pots. These are lifted from the field and are potted in the fall. If they are planted within a few months of potting, the compost may fall away from the roots because the plant has not had time to get established in the pot. These "containerized" plants need extra care after planting, until they are established.

It used to be that all deciduous shrubs were sold "bare-root". Today, some hedging is still sold in this way during the winter. Plants are lifted from the field in the dormant season and are sold with little or no soil around their roots.

"Balled and burlapped" plants are field-grown and are lifted during the dormant season, with the ball of soil around the roots preserved and the root system kept intact. This is the traditional way of supplying evergreens and large specimen shrubs, particularly those with a fibrous root system, such as rhododendrons, Japanese maples, and magnolias. The rootball is often wrapped in burlap to keep it intact. In most cases, this should be left in position and allowed to rot away in the planting hole. If you are unsure about this, be sure to ask the nursery staff for advice: their recommendation will depend on what material has been used.

BUYING TIME

Sometimes plants are offered in more than one size. Buying bigger usually means buying time. But is that a good idea?

Today shrubs are normally measured by the size of pot in which they are grown. A plant sold in a quality nursery or garden center should be well rooted around in its pot, so the size of pot is an indication of the plant's maturity. Sizes refer to the volume of the pot.

POT SIZE?	PLANT SIZE
6in. or. ¼ gallon 	Starter shrubs—that is, the first stage after propagation; sometimes offered for sale during the fall and spring. This is a good way to buy young evergreen shrubs for mixing with seasonal bedding plants in a container. It is also a good way to plant hedging economically—as long as you are patient.
½ and ¾ gallon 	The standard size of shrubs sold by garden centers and used for amenity planting—usually a year on from the smallest size. This is the best size to choose for general planting. There should be a healthy root system all around the outside of the rootball. However, you should still be able to see some potting mix. Even to the inexperienced eye, it is obvious if the plant is potbound, or choked with roots, and growth has been impaired as a result.
2 and 2½ gallon 	Small specimen shrubs, popular for quick impact—often one year more advanced than the standard product. This is a way of buying time. The plants are, of course, more expensive, but it is worth the investment in the case of key plants and those that are slow to grow in the early stages. In a new planting scheme, it is worth buying some of these larger plants to achieve a degree of maturity at the outset. Remember, however, that a small plant, if given good growing conditions, often catches up with a larger one.

specimen. A properly grown young shrub branches well from the base; this is achieved by cutting back at the liner stage, while the plant is in the nursery. A well-grown shrub has strong growth and a generally healthy appearance. This is the plant to buy.

Bear in mind that some shrubs do not look good early in life—the stage at which you are most likely to see them offered for sale in the garden center. These are highlighted in the plant descriptions in this book.

Container-grown plants (above) enable the gardener to buy and plant at any time of the year, even when shrubs are in flower.
The perfect shrub (left) has good branch framework, healthy foliage, and a well-developed root system.

SUBSTITUTES

When you are looking for a specific plant, perhaps one recommended by a friend or one that you have seen in a book, be prepared to consider a close substitute. New varieties are being introduced all the time, in many cases improvements on established favorites.

By insisting on the exact variety you went out to buy, you may end up turning down a better plant: *Spiraea japonica* 'Goldflame', for example, has been superseded by *Spiraea japonica* 'Firelight', a superior variety that does not revert. 'Goldflame' will still be recommended by those who are not aware of 'Firelight'.

Buying container-grown plants means that you see what you are getting. You can buy a container-grown plant in leaf and flower, in season. Illustrated labels give a very good idea of what the leaf and flower look like.

WHAT IS A GOOD PLANT?

Shrubs vary enormously in shape, size, and habit. However, in most cases it is possible to spot, at an early stage, a plant that will develop into a well-shaped

Growing conditions

If you have deep, fertile, well-drained soil that does not dry out and has no perennial weeds, you cannot go wrong. However, most of us do not enjoy such conditions, and a little effort is required. The establishment and subsequent growth rate of all garden plants are affected by the quality of the environment in which they are planted. Good preparation reaps rewards.

KNOW YOUR SOIL

Soil is a complex mixture of animal, vegetable, and mineral matter, living and dead, with the addition of air and water. The proportions of the constituents vary.

Normally the basic mineral content comes from the underlying rock, as a result of erosion. So if you know what the underlying rock is, you have a good idea of the type of soil.

Indigenous trees and plants are a clue to the underlying soil type. Birch trees grow on virtually any soil, but bracken growing with them is a good indication that the soil is acidic.

Organic matter decomposes and mixes with the mineral content. This adds to the nutrient content and provides the sticky, glutinous substance known as humus, which keeps the mineral particles apart but also sticks to them, holding on to water and nutrients for plants to absorb.

All soils need plenty of organic matter, and they are improved by the addition of more, especially in an intensively cultivated area such as a garden.

ACID OR ALKALINE?

You can tell a lot about your soil just by looking at it and then by looking at existing plants in your garden and in neighboring gardens, and at indigenous trees and plants in the local area.

It is important to know the pH of your soil. This is the measure of acidity or alkalinity, on a scale of 0 to 14. Soils with a low pH are acid; those with a high pH are alkaline, rich in lime. The ideal is a neutral to slightly acid soil (7.0pH), which successfully supports the widest range of plants.

If your garden is in an area surrounded by pine trees, oak trees, healthy rhododendrons, and camellias, then your soil is acid. There is no need to bother with a soil test.

If the surrounding fields are flecked with fragments of limestone, your grass is fine and short, the soil is shallow, and beech trees thrive, you are on alkaline soil. Do not bother to check. If you want to grow lime-hating, acid-loving plants, put them in containers of lime-free ericaceous soil mix.

Limestone and flints indicate an alkaline soil, often dry and well-drained.

A pH meter is easy to use. Water the soil thoroughly beforehand.

If soil has been imported, or if you are between soil type areas, it is worth doing a pH check. Either use a soil pH check kit or, better still, buy a pH meter, which is easier to use and is a good way of checking all parts of the garden.

COMPOSTING—THE KEY TO SUCCESS

Whatever kind of soil you have, your garden is an area of intense cultivation. To keep soil in peak condition, it is vital to add organic matter. Compost your garden and household waste, and return it to the soil.

FROST WARNING

When planting in the fall, avoid bulky organic manure unless it is very well rotted. Fresh manure contains readily available nitrogen, and this can stimulate soft new growth, which is easily damaged by frost. This is particularly a problem with certain evergreens, including hebes.

INCREASING FERTILITY

Most soils carry an adequate supply of plant nutrients for growth, but for the best results, supplement this with a balanced fertilizer in slow-release form. A general, slow-release fertilizer, containing the major plant nutrients as well as trace elements, can be used for all plants except the alkaline-intolerant ones (that is, ericaceous and acid-loving plants). Acid-loving subjects are fussy, light feeders and need a specific formulation.

IMPROVING CLAY SOIL

When preparing clay soil for planting, dig in the fall. Leave the surface rough to allow frost to penetrate during the winter months. The freeze-thaw action of the weather does much of the cultivation. The application of lime to newly dug soil in winter works miracles. This changes the charge on the clay particles, making them stick together in groups forming larger particles; the result is a soil with more open, crumbly texture. This raises the soil pH, so is not good for alkaline-intolerant plants. Adding coarse horticultural grit and plenty of organic matter further improves heavy clay soils.

FEEDING PLANTS

Resist the temptation to overfeed, particularly at the time of planting.

Water and nutrients enter the plant through its root hairs. For this to happen, the solution of "salts", or nutrients, in the soil water has to be weaker than the solution in the root hair cell. If it is stronger, water is drawn out of the root, the plant cannot then take in water through its roots, and it wilts. This is referred to as scorching: in dry, warm weather, especially if there is a light wind, the plant goes crisp.

Fertilizer used at time of planting should be high in phosphorus, or phosphate, as it is usually called. This is the nutrient used for root growth and formation, and aids establishment.

Slow-release general fertilizers supply all the nutrients that plants need during a growing season. There is rarely a need to feed with anything else.

Controlled-release fertilizers are those little spherical granules used by nurseries in container mixes. They release nutrients only when the soil is moist enough and temperatures are high enough for plant growth. The granules need to be applied only once a year. They are an excellent choice for plants in containers and are also a good option for dry situations, where other types of fertilizer could cause problems if the level of moisture in the soil drops. Liquid and soluble fertilizers are not for shrubs, unless they need a boost.

Chelated iron is not a complete fertilizer but is an excellent tonic for yellowing ericaceous, acid-loving plants. This yellowing, known as chlorosis, is usually caused by iron deficiency. A liquid tonic, chelated iron supplies iron in an easy-to absorb-formulation.

UNDERSTANDING FERTILIZERS
The major nutrients

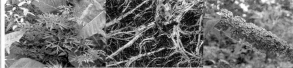

| **N**—nitrogen, for leaves and shoots | **P**—phosphorus (phosphate), for roots | **K**—potash (potassium), for flowers and fruit |

Trace elements Nutrients essential for healthy growth, but needed in small amounts, trace elements are the vitamins and minerals of the plant world. Examples include iron, magnesium, and manganese.

The nutrient content of all fertilizers, and the ratio of these nutrients to one another, is indicated on the packaging.

Successful planting

Except when you are making a brand-new garden, you are most likely to be planting individual subjects in existing beds, either to extend a border or to replace a plant that has been removed. Container-grown plants can be planted at any time of the year and in theory are easy to establish. In practice, getting them started in the garden can present problems, unless you follow certain guidelines.

A young container shrub has led a sheltered existence in the nursery. It has probably been under glass or polyethylene, being watered regularly, kept free of pests, and in nice, cuddly, warm potting mix, and it will have been fed a balanced diet of controlled-release fertilizer with the occasional addition of a liquid supplement.

If the new plant is to establish quickly in your garden, its new growing environment has to be at least as appealing as that of the pot. A small hole chipped out of solid, cold, wet clay, which is about to bake hard in the summer sun, is simply not inviting. The roots will stay firmly in the original soil ball, and the plant will sit still in protest.

A happy plant is an attractive plant that will grow and give pleasure without having to struggle to survive. We tend to choose what we like, but in fact the best choice of plant has to be what will grow well in the situation it is chosen for. If we choose a plant for a location that is not ideal for it, we will have to battle to get it to thrive.

LOCATION, LOCATION

Choosing the right plant for the right spot is as much about what will grow well in a particular situation as what will look right.

The plant's native habitat dictates what growing conditions it will require in the garden. For example plants with gray and aromatic foliage often hail from the Mediterranean region, so they like plenty of sunshine, relatively dry conditions, and good drainage.

The more contact the gardener has with plants, the more he or she gains a feel for their requirements. We are fortunate today in that we can draw on a large pool of experience and knowledge, but this need not deter the adventurous gardener from breaking new ground or from finding out by trial and error whether or not a plant that is generally considered to be for a "hot, dry, sunny" site will, in fact, tolerate shade and moist soil.

PROVIDING SHELTER

Some plants, particularly evergreens from warmer climates, suffer in the winter, from wind chill as well as from cold. In a drying wind, the plant loses water from its leaves, but if the ground is frozen, the roots are unable to draw water from the soil. This can result in damage to the plant, or even its death.

Another problem is that freezing can rupture the vessels that carry water up the plant. The damage does not show until the weather warms up, when the leaves and stems are no longer receiving a water supply.

Give a plant that is not fully hardy a greater chance of survival by planting it in the shelter of a wall, near the house, or where other shrubs or garden structures provide shelter from the wind. During severe weather, protect delicate plants with a floating row cover, a light fabric that is placed loosely over the plant. Attach the fabric carefully, so that it stays in place but does not cause damage. Never use polyethylene sheeting; this will cause condensation and extreme fluctuations of temperature, which will do more harm than good.

1 FIRST DIG A HOLE

The planting hole should be at least twice the size of the plant's rootball. Using a spade and a fork, break up the base of the hole to ensure good drainage and successful root penetration. Mix plenty of good garden compost, well-rotted farmyard manure, recycled green waste, or proprietary planting mix both with the soil in the bottom of the hole and with the soil that has been dug out. Sprinkle a slow-release fertilizer over the soil that is to be returned to the hole and a good handful in the base of the hole. Mix in with the fork. Replace the soil mixture to leave the hole slightly deeper than the rootball of the shrub.

2 GET YOUR LEVELS RIGHT

Before you knock the new shrub out of its pot, check that the potting mix is wet through. It is very difficult to wet a dry rootball once it is buried.

Knock the plant out of its container and place the rootball in the center of the hole. The surface of the potting mix should be just below the natural soil level.

As long as the shrub is not pot-bound, do not tease out or damage the roots. To do so would defeat the object of container planting. Any strong roots that separate themselves from the bottom of the rootball can be spread out in the planting hole, but do not interfere any more than that.

3 FIRM FOOTING

Replace the soil around the plant, mixing it well with the slow-release fertilizer and the compost. Then gently firm the soil around the rootball with your heel. Firm from the outside of the hole toward the rootball. Do not compress the rootball by pushing down on it with your foot.

Replace more soil to about ½in. (1cm) above the surface level. Ideally you should make a dish of the soil surface so as to direct rainfall, or irrigation water, into the rootball. Water well.

WATERING

- In the early stages of a plant's life, while the root system is developing, it is really important to have a supply of water always available and to water frequently.

- The peat, or peat substitute, that is used in potting mixtures is usually harder to wet than the soil, so when water is applied it will stay in the spaces in the soil rather than penetrating the rootball. The result: dry plant, poor growth (if any), no establishment.

- On dry soil, a slow trickle is better than a torrent. Water applied quickly often runs off without penetrating the surface. Water applied slowly has time to find the spaces in the soil and so wet the particles.

- Ericaceous plants, such as rhododendrons and azaleas, have particularly dense, fibrous root systems, which are very difficult to wet once they dry out. A very slow-dripping hose is effective or, on larger areas of planting, a soaker hose.

Pruning

In today's gardens, it is pruning more than anything else that robs plants of their finest hour. Pruning is the one gardening task we never forget to do. But, sadly, both our timing and our technique are often wrong; the most destructive pest in the garden is the gardener.

Gardening is founded on snipping, trimming, neatness, and order: hedges, topiary, lawns. In the days before we had such a plethora of plants to fill our gardens, it was only by shaping plants that the gardener could create variety. Far be it from him to allow a plant to achieve its potential or to grow naturally; he must be in control.

Some great gardeners, including Vita Sackville-West and Gertrude Jekyll, combined informality with formality. Could it be that providing the gardener with structural hedges to trim was their way of ensuring that the most treasured plants were protected from the hand pruners?

Spring in the garden is a time of cultivation and planting. Emerging weeds divert our attention. The grass grows quickly and needs cutting. There are tubs to fill, hanging baskets to plant, seeds to sow, vegetables to plant. Shrubs are safe: there is no time for pruning anything (except, perhaps, the roses).

Fall, on the other hand, leaves the deciduous shrubs naked and vulnerable. It is garden cleanup time: leaves to collect, herbaceous plants to cut back, bedding plants to grub out, compost to make. And, while we are at it, how about "tidying up" those shrubs? Before we know it, they are half their original height. Nice and tidy. And after all, they will grow again next year—a bit like a bad haircut, but with more devastating results.

Gardeners are generally nervous about pruning, until they get armed and dangerous. Then nerves turn into aggression and they set to with hand pruners, loppers, and chain saws, hell-bent on destruction. There are just a few rules to learn before you cut.

A clipped peacock at Cliveden, in Buckinghamshire, England. The desire to control plants does not rule out creativity, or even humor, in the garden.

WHEN TO PRUNE?

In the warmer zones, the time to prune is just after flowering. If you have to prune, and want to prune, do it immediately after flowering. The new shoots that are made after pruning then have time to grow, ripen, and produce flower buds for the following year. Further north, it may be prudent to leave pruning until spring. See pages 23–25.

THE GOLDEN RULES

- You do not have to prune. Pruning is a garden thing. In nature, "pruning," if it happens at all, is a natural process. It is not an essential stage of the plant's life cycle. Many gardeners seem to think that every plant needs pruning to achieve results. This is not the case.

- The harder you prune, the more vigorous will be the growth afterward. Plants are "intelligent," and hormones will respond to your amputations by stimulating vigorous growth to replace what has been removed.

- Light pruning produces light lateral growth and a bushier plant. If the plant is one that flowers or fruits on this type of growth, go ahead and "snip," but do it in a logical, controlled way.

There is a logical exception to the rule. Plants that are grown for fruit should not be pruned after flowering (or there will be no fruit). Prune selectively after the fruit has appeared. Yes, you may lose some of next year's flowers, but as long as you know what these buds look like, you will know where to cut.

WHY PRUNE?

TO CONTROL SHAPE Some plants—hedges, topiary, trimmed and trained plants that provide formal structure —are pruned regularly to control their shape. Familiar examples are boxwood, and bay. Frequent light trimming produces plenty of young, fresh growth on the outside of the plant—bushy growth, with lots of lateral branching.

However, this type of pruning is disastrous when practiced on other ornamental shrubs, especially the deciduous ones. The plant is robbed of its natural habit and ends up looking artificial and ugly. So often are plants subjected to this treatment, they are frequently not recognizable for what they are.

These boxwood balls provide structure among informally planted shrubs and herbaceous perennials. With their size and shape controlled, they become a focal point, in contrast to the irregular shapes of other plants.

Selective pruning to control the shape of the plant works if thought is given to how the plant will react when the growth is either cut back or removed. Removal of competing branches, to promote an open structure, is beneficial to both the growth habit and the health of the plant. It lets light into the leaves and allows air to circulate through the plant.

Plants growing together in a border should be pruned in relation to each other, rather than being made to stand alone as individual subjects. Shrubs that may have been planted a little too closely can often be integrated by selective removal, to ground level, of some of the branches.

TO CONTROL SIZE If a plant has gotten to a point where drastic pruning is required to control its size, ask yourself whether it is in fact too big for the location. If pruning has to be done on a regular basis, leaving the shrub more disfigured after each pruning, ask yourself whether it might be better to replace it with a less vigorous subject.

The key to success is to take action sooner, rather than later. Too often a shrub is allowed to get far too big for the space it occupies.

The next question is "How much can I cut it back by?" Each year, starting at an early stage, take a good look at the shrub, try to foresee next season's growth, and prune accordingly. Keeping a shrub under control is a manageable task if it is done in easy stages. In other words, if you are going to have to prune at some point, start at an early stage, and do it regularly. This applies particularly to the evergreen, structure shrubs and, of course, to anything grown as a trimmed hedge.

This ornamental elder is cut back or pollarded to the same point in early spring each year. Because the annual growth is always approximately the same, the height achieved is the same each year, and size is restricted.

TO CONTROL PESTS AND DISEASES The first thing to remove when you prune is any diseased or damaged wood. This is essential to prevent dieback and the spread of disease to new growth.

TO PROMOTE FLOWERING AND FRUITING We prune roses and fruit trees both to promote the growth that will produce flower buds and to prevent the plant from putting all its energies into vegetative growth.

- Many of the modern hybrid roses need hard pruning to stimulate the vigorous new growth that will produce flower buds.
- Many of the old roses respond better to lighter pruning, to stimulate twiggy growth and side branches that will bear flowers.
- Many apples and pears produce their flowers, and therefore their fruit, on small side branches called spurs. Pruning aims to build up the numbers and quality of these spurs to increase fruit production. The same is true of wisteria.

Wisteria, normally a climber, can be grown as a shrub if pruned carefully. Pruning back the long shoots creates spurs, which carry the flower buds.

CORRECT PRUNING

- Always use a good-quality, sharp pair of hand pruners and a pruning saw; clean cuts heal well and minimize the chance of infection. Never leave "snags."
- Cut to just above a node, with a slanting cut sloping away from the bud. This, theoretically, directs any rainwater away from the growing bud.

- Where possible, cut to an outward-facing bud, as this promotes an open structure. Use your common sense and look carefully before each cut. Once you develop an eye for this, it is obvious which way the bud will grow when you have removed the growth above it.
- Remember that pieces of stem left without any growth buds will die back, promoting the spread of disease.

A SIMPLE GUIDE TO PRUNING THE VARIOUS TYPES OF SHRUB

This is a simple rule-of-thumb guide; there are always exceptions.

DECIDUOUS SHRUBS FLOWERING IN EARLY SPRING

e.g., forsythia, ribes

Prune after flowering. Cut out wood that has flowered, back to where vigorous new shoots are emerging. This is done selectively, paying attention to the overall shape. It is not essential every year, but should be done frequently.

DECIDUOUS SHRUBS FLOWERING IN LATE SPRING AND EARLY SUMMER

e.g., deutzia, lilac, philadelphus

Prune after flowering. Cut out wood that has flowered back to where vigorous new shoots are emerging. Take out some branches to ground level each year on mature shrubs that are overcrowded in the center. The new growth produced will flower the following year.

DECIDUOUS SHRUBS FLOWERING IN LATE SUMMER

e.g., *Hydrangea paniculata*, buddleia, perovskia, caryopteris

Prune hard in late winter. This stimulates vigorous growth that will ripen during the summer and flower later in the year. As a rule of thumb, all these examples are cut back by two-thirds.

EVERGREEN SHRUBS

e.g., *Viburnum tinus*, *Prunus laurocerasus*, aucuba, choisya, photinia

Prune in late spring. This is a time of active growth; cutting back will stimulate a rapid flush of replacement growth.

ACID-LOVING PLANTS

e.g., camellias, rhododendrons, azaleas

Pruning is not necessary, but do it immediately after flowering if you must.

Camellias respond well to pruning, as do many rhododendrons. Deciduous azaleas must be pruned with great care to preserve the branch framework.

SILVER-FOLIAGE PLANTS

e.g., brachyglottis, santolina, helichrysum, lavender

In the warmer zones, prune straight after flowering—or before, if you prefer, in the case of undesirable yellow flowers of santolina and brachyglottis.

Pruning by the end of summer allows the plants to produce a generous flush of new silver growth before winter. Always cut back to where you can see new growth buds emerging. If you cut back into bare wood, regeneration cannot be guaranteed.

If you live further north, these plants should be trimmed back in mid-spring, when the danger of frost damage has passed.

Shaped silver-leaved plants that are not being grown for flowering require regular trimming throughout the summer.

A SIMPLE SEASONAL GUIDE TO PRUNING

Whatever the time of year, if in doubt, leave the plant alone and consult a good pruning guide.

MIDWINTER

Prune roses. Floribundas and Hybrid Teas: cut down to three buds above ground level. New English and shrub roses: remove any dead wood and prune lightly to promote lateral growth, which will produce flower buds.

LATE WINTER

Cut back caryopteris, perovskia, and ceratostigma by two-thirds or more. It is easy to see the growth buds, which will produce next year's shoots and flowers, on the lower part of the stem—cut back to here.

Hard prune buddleia and *Hydrangea paniculata*. Cut mature plants back to about 3ft. (1m), young plants to 2ft. (60cm). This promotes vigorous arching branches.

Hard prune young plants of *Sambucus racemosa* cultivars to promote vigorous growth and good leaf color.

EARLY SPRING

Hard prune *Cornus alba* and other subjects grown for winter stems. Cut half of the stems back to ground level each year.

Lightly prune photinia to encourage more new growth shoots of good color.

Prune hydrangeas (except *paniculata;* see above), removing old flower heads back to fat buds (which will flower later). On old plants, remove some older stems each year, to ground level.

MID-SPRING

Prune forsythia, ribes, and any early-flowering deciduous shrubs after flowering. Cut out the older stems that have flowered, allowing new growth to come through.

Prune hebes by mid-spring. Overgrown and straggly plants can be cut back to where new shoots are emerging lower on the stems.

LATE SPRING

Prune camellias, if necessary to control size.

Cut out any winter damage in evergreens such as choisya and aucuba.

Prune evergreen shrubs to control size and shape, if desired.

EARLY SUMMER

Prune lilacs after flowering. They can be cut back hard; even old branches can be pruned, if done selectively. The vigorous new growth will flower next year.

Deadhead rhododendrons as the flowers fade, allowing new growth shoots to develop more freely.

Deadhead roses that repeat flower. Rather than just removing the flower head, cut back to an emerging, strong shoot lower down the stem.

MIDSUMMER

Prune back large-flowered abutilons by about a third. This allows enough time for new growth that will flower next year to appear.

Prune philadelphus, deutzia and weigela after flowering. Cut some of the older growth that has flowered back to the base, thinning other flowered stems to allow new shoots to grow through gracefully.

LATE SUMMER (WARMER ZONES ONLY)

Cut back silver-foliage shrubs such as lavender, santolina, and helichrysum after flowering. Cut back to where you can see new shoots emerging deep in the plant. This leaves them time to produce a flush of new growth that will stay silver all winter.

EARLY FALL

Deadhead and tidy roses as the flowers fade, except for those varieties that produce winter hips.

MID-FALL

Tidy herbaceous plants as they die back, but preserve the seed heads and stems of those that remain decorative in the winter.

LATE FALL

Prune vines (*Vitis*) once the leaves have fallen. This must be done before midwinter, or the plants will bleed.

EARLY WINTER

Winter-prune fruit trees; the same applies to ornamental crab (*Malus*), to control shape and disease.

Planting for structure

Whatever the size of the garden, the hardest thing to get right is the basic structure. It is something that frightens most of us. We worry that what we plant will get too big, cast shade or interfere with the foundations of the house. Our concerns are boundless. Often this is all due to an underlying fear of the unknown and an inability to visualize what the garden will look like in years to come, when our young plants have grown to maturity.

It may be that we find structure difficult because it is not a part of the design process that we are used to dealing with. When it comes to the house, the structure is normally already there for us. We may make alterations as time goes by, but there is usually something to start with. The same is true when we take on a mature garden.

In the house, we decorate, furnish, and add finishing touches to our own taste. In garden design, this is the easy part: adding bulbs, bedding, alpines, and seasonal color and interest. We can buy on impulse and fit our acquisitions into the gaps without changing anything permanently. Nice, safe decisions.

However, gardens simply do not work without structure. Hard landscaping may provide some of this, in the form of paving, walling, pergolas, arches, and garden buildings, but these elements come to life only when structural planting is added.

DESIGN GUIDELINES

The objective is to create an attractive picture to look at from the house and a comfortable space to live in outdoors.

To please the eye, gardens need the right proportion of space and planting. As a rule of thumb, this should be one-third planting and two-thirds space. The latter can be made up of grass, paving, gravel, water, or even low, ground-cover plants. Most gardens tend towards a higher proportion of space, with insufficient planting.

Any garden should fit with the property to which it is attached and with the surrounding landscape. The

---

GIVE THEM SPACE

- When planning planting areas, avoid borders that run parallel to the fence line around the edge of the garden.

- Most people make their borders too narrow. The minimum depth for a border is 3ft. (1m); 6ft. (2m) is barely adequate; 10ft. (3m) is better.

- Go out and measure the spread of an average, mature shrub—for example, choisya or ceanothus. The rule with borders is fewer, but deeper.

- To see what your garden will look like, lay a hose down on the ground to mark the edge of the proposed bed. Be bold: envision the area full of plants.

- If you start off with straight, narrow borders, barely wider than the plants you put into them, in no time you will be out there with a spade making them wider so as to allow the mower to pass without damaging the growing plants. Worse still, you will be bringing the pruners into action, trimming those new shrubs into neat, but ugly, shapes.

style, mood, and design of the garden must be in keeping with the house. This is also true of the plants; these should suit the style of garden.

In a contained space, the choice can be individual. In more open situations, look at any trees, large conifers, or shrubs in neighboring gardens or in the surrounding countryside and take them into account as part of the full garden picture. Use them to expand the landscape.

Deciduous shrubs, cultivated forms of native species, are appropriate for many gardens. Hollies, yew, and small-leaved evergreens work well, and white- and silver-variegations seem to fit. Use yellow foliage with care. Exotics and conifers, if used at all, need careful placing.

Town gardens need solid, evergreen structure to balance the weight of masonry around them. Strong colors, yellow foliage, and bold yellow variegations can work in shady situations.

VERTICAL INTEREST

Most gardens are too flat. Height is essential, to give scale to the rest of the garden and to make the space three-dimensional. The oft-requested "tree that grows to six feet and then stops" is simply inadequate. Height need not mean heavy tree cover; light, airy trees such as birch and mountain ash will deliver. Bold, upright shrubs, such as abutilon, may do the trick. For even stronger vertical accents, use climbers on pergolas and arches.

PLANT LAYERS

Successful gardens have three levels of planting:
1 Above eye level: trees, tall shrubs and climbers.
2 At eye level: shrubs and tall herbaceous plants.
3 Below eye level: dwarf shrubs, herbaceous perennials and ground cover.

A border at Le Bois des Moutiers, near Dieppe, in Normandy, France, exemplifies the successful use of different levels of planting.

It is important that the structural framework provided by plants works all year round.

Trees provide the canopy above eye level. The winter silhouette of a deciduous tree provides structure just as effectively as the solid mass of any evergreen tree. Some tall shrubs contribute here, too, but it is really in the eye-level landscape that they play a leading role.

Evergreens and deciduous shrubs with a strong branch framework come into their own in the middle planting layer, at eye level. Smaller-leaved, lighter-growing plants, such as pittosporums, provide structure without weight. Large-leaved evergreens—for example, fatsias—contribute more solid structure and a dark background that sets off the color of the planting in the foreground.

The lower layer is often the most scrutinized: low-growing shrubs, herbaceous perennials, bulbs, and seasonal bedding plants are found here. This is where gardeners are apt to concentrate most of their effort. It is readily accessible, so it is relatively easy to rectify planting mistakes here.

CHOOSING AND POSITIONING STRUCTURAL PLANTS

Choose structure plants carefully. They are a valuable source of variety in color and texture, as well as being architecturally useful. Give careful consideration to the positioning of plants and how they relate to their neighbours. Bear in mind color, shape, leaf form, and texture. Get it right, and the individual contribution from each plant will increase manyfold.

Newly planted areas should initially look very sparse, with plenty of space for the permanent plants to grow and mature. In the early years, gaps can be filled with annuals, bulbs, and temporary herbaceous planting.

TIMESCALE

We are all impatient, and plants do not give instant results. Most of the disasters that occur in the garden are the result of trying to resolve this conflict. All too often, those who plant, or inherit, a hedge of × *Cupressocyparis leylandii*, for example, live to regret it.

Shrubs planted for structure take time to mature. Eventually some may get too big, and perhaps after five to ten years some of the planting will need to be removed or replaced. That is part of gardening. However, it is important not to plant something that is going to present serious problems in the future.

Structure plants need not be heavy, or plain green. The light, silver-variegated form of *Pittosporum* 'Garnettii' provides height and shape without weight.

Basic evergreens

Plain evergreens and their variegated forms contribute solid structure to mixed borders of deciduous woody and herbaceous plants. Without them, planting lacks body, and planting areas can become a void during during the winter months. These shrubs provide the basic framework of the garden. They are the foundations upon which the rest of the planting is built.

Arbutus unedo

Arbutus unedo (zone 8–10), the Killarney strawberry tree, is a beautiful small evergreen tree with reddish brown, peeling bark when mature. A member of the family Ericaceae, it is unusual in tolerating alkalinity. The white, pieris-like flowers appear at the same time as the strawberry fruits in the fall. As a young plant, it makes a valuable bushy shrub, wind-tolerant and good by the coast. The variety **Arbutus unedo 'Compacta'** is smaller and has an interesting growth habit. **Arbutus unedo 'Elfin King'** has a great abundance of attractive, brightly colored fruits. **Arbutus 'Marina'** is very suitable for pruning and maintaining as a large rounded bush.

Arbutus makes a good alternative to photinia where the requirement is for a slower-growing, denser plant, which has smaller foliage.

Buxus sempervirens (zone 6–9), or common box, grows to make a large shrub or small tree with masses of small, round, dark green leaves. It is found all over southern Europe, northern Africa and western Asia. It is naturalized through southern England, but it is not clear whether it is a British native or was introduced by the Romans.

Box has been a quintessential element of garden structure throughout Europe and parts of North America for centuries. Its positive response to clipping and shaping has resulted in its use for hedging and topiary of all kinds. Its hardy nature and its longevity make it indispensable for the construction of parterres. Indeed, there are some formal gardens where it is the only plant used.

There are many cultivars, all with different rates of growth and growth habits. Some of the variegated forms are particularly fine (see page 57).

Buxus sempervirens 'Suffruticosa', or edging box, is the very dwarf form commonly used for formal edging to paths and beds. Leaves are medium, ovate, and a bright shiny green. This plant is slow growing, and therefore easily controlled, and is ideal for making the lowest of hedges. It can be grown in modern, gravel parterres and clipped to

Box at Bourton House Garden, England.

make interesting raised shapes—true vegetable masonry! *Buxus microphylla* 'Faulkner' (zone 5–9) is an alternative to *Buxus sempervirens* 'Suffruticosa', and also widely grown. It is compact, with a more spreading habit.

Contemporary minimalist garden design makes extensive, and creative, use of box both for topiary in containers and for "cloud" beds and hedges—a reflection of the endurance and adaptability of this plant in our gardens.

Box is easy to grow and generally needs little attention. Although it is a hardy plant, the new growth can be hit by frost, but the plant soon grows

Buxus sempervirens 'Suffruticosa'

BOX BLIGHT

In recent years, box blight has become a problem. Initially this can be mistaken for nutrient deficiency, but the disease quickly progresses to patchy dieback, with the foliage becoming yellow, dry, and parchmentlike.

Treatment: cut out the affected growth and burn it. Keep the plant watered and fed with a balanced soluble feed. The less stress the plant suffers, the greater its chance of recovery. Spray with Bordeaux mixture or a traditional copper fungicide.

through any damage. Box is extremely susceptible to nutrient deficiency, especially when grown in containers or on light, well-drained soils. Potassium deficiency shows itself as bronzing of the foliage, particularly in winter. Potassium is very soluble and quickly washed away by winter rainfall, but the problem can be rectified by applying a general, slow-release fertilizer.

Elaeagnus × ebbingei (zone 7–11) is a hybrid between *Elaeagnus pungens* from Japan and *Elaeagnus macrophylla* from Korea and Japan. This is a big, fast-growing, vigorous shrub that will deliver screening and shelter while serving as an attractive feature in the garden. The mature leaves are fairly large, dark green on top and silver beneath. The new shoots are gray-olive with russet down. Its most surprising attribute is the fragrance of its flowers, produced under the foliage in early winter. Visually, the appearance of the tiny, creamy-white flowers does not transform the bush, but the fragrance is unmissable, often sending the gardener in search of some exotic bloom in the undergrowth.

It was only in 1929 that *Elaeagnus × ebbingei* was introduced into British gardens, so perhaps it is no surprise that it is not more extensively planted in North America. It is used in sites where quick results and wind resistance are required. It is excellent by the sea.

The silvery underside of the foliage and a tolerance of dry conditions make this an plant ideal for providing structure in mixed planting that has a high proportion of silver and gray foliage. Its subtle color makes it a good mixer; it is easy to accommodate and provides a sympathetic backdrop to any foreground scheme.

Elaeagnus responds well to pruning, though this should be done carefully if the bony frame of the plant is not to become more of a feature than the foliage. Selective hard pruning of stems is more

Elaeagnus × ebbingei

Ilex aquifolium 'J.C. van Tol'

desirable than cutting back moderately. It also responds well to clipping if this is done from an early stage, so it makes an excellent hedge. It is easier to cut than laurel because the leaves are smaller.

The waxy dust that covers the leaves can be irritating to the nose when handling the plant, so take precautions.

Ilex aquifolium (zone 6–9), the native English holly, has been revered for its shiny, dark, evergreen leaves since ancient times. Early people marveled at its powers. While other trees shed their leaves and creatures hibernated during the frozen days of winter, holly shone green and, what is more, produced fruit and reproduced, defying the elements and celebrating the birth of life itself with its shiny red berries. Holly was regarded as a plant with magical powers. Branches were used to surround livestock pens—not only did its spiny leaves repel predators; its magical powers warded off any evil spirits. Holly planted by the cottage door kept witches away. Noone dared fell a holly tree.

Holly has medicinal uses. Writing in the 17th century, the English physician, Nicholas Culpeper claimed that red holly berries brought relief from colds and clammy phlegm, while yellow berries relieved phlegm brought on by excess alcohol. A medicinal tea was made from the leaves.

In the garden, the cultivars of *Ilex aquifolium* are superb, stately structure plants. They take time to reach maturity but are worth the wait.

The variegated forms of ilex (see Plant Profile, page 62) are more widely planted than the plain green. Of the green cultivars, *Ilex aquifolium* 'J.C. van Tol' is the most sought-after. Shiny, dark green, almost spineless leaves contrast with abundant red berries. This cultivar is self-pollinating, so can be planted singly.

Ilex aquifolium 'Ferox' (hedgehog holly) is male, so produces no berries. It is interesting for its small, very spiny leaves; the spines grow not only from the leaf edges but also from the upper surface. It is lower and slower-growing than others and, having resided in English gardens since the 17th century, is thought to be the oldest holly variety still in cultivation.

Ilex crenata 'Convexa' (zone 5–7) is a superb form of the Japanese holly. The leaves are like those of box but larger, much darker, and glossier. It has a dense, bushy habit and, although it makes only a small shrub, is an imposing structure plant. Ideal to trim and shape, it is a good alternative to box for a low hedge It freely produces shiny, black fruits in the late fall.

Ilex × meserveae 'Blue Girl'

Ilex × meserveae 'Blue Prince'

Ilex × meserveae (zone 5–8), the blue hollies, were raised in New York to cope with the severe winters of eastern North America. They are bushy shrubs, up to 6ft. (2m) high, with black-purple shoots and softly spined leaves that are smaller than other varieties. The glossy foliage is dark blue-green, providing a welcome change from the emerald greens of most other hollies. Female varieties have scarlet fruits. **'Blue Angel'** and **'Blue Girl'** are female, **'Blue Boy'** and **'Blue Prince'** male. Their hardiness has made them popular in continental Europe as well as North America. The blue hollies are an excellent choice for structural plants in modern schemes, combining well with metal and slate.

Laurus nobilis (zone 8–9), the bay laurel, is the true laurel. The first recorded date of cultivation in Britain is 1562, but it is probable that this plant was introduced long before then. It played a significant part in the culture of ancient Rome—it was the leaves of the bay laurel that were used to adorn dignitaries and heroes—and it is likely that the Romans took it to Britain with them. The aromatic leaves are widely used for their culinary qualities and feature extensively in dishes across the Mediterranean region, where the plant is widespread.

Left unpruned, *Laurus nobilis* makes a dense pyramid. The foliage is dark and matte, the perfect background for other plants. It can be susceptible to frost damage in extreme conditions, but tolerates the salt air of coastal areas. It is good on shallow alkaline soils, enjoying the good drainage and low nutrient content. The small, yellowish-green flowers appear in April, clustering the branches of plants that have not been repeatedly clipped.

KEEPING A BAY IN TRIM

Trained bay is easily maintained by pinching, as long as this is done when the new, soft shoots first flush. Pinch each shoot back to two leaves and buds, paying attention to maintaining the shape of the plant.

A high percentage of bays used in gardens are trained, often as "lollipops" or pyramids. *Laurus nobilis* responds well to clipping and training, so was embraced by continental European and, later, British gardeners for this purpose. Belgium is the center for high-quality trained bay, with large nurseries dedicated to this purpose.

Left untrained, *Laurus nobilis* makes an excellent informal structure plant; its vertical growth habit makes it very useful for screening. There is a good golden form: *Laurus nobilis* 'Aurea' (see page 42).

The large-leaved Japanese and Chinese **privets** are not often used as big structure plants, although they have excellent qualities. *Ligustrum japonicum* (zone 7–10) is a dense, medium-sized shrub with olive-green leaves, similar to those of a camellia. It has white flowers in late summer and is a good hedge or screen. The best variety is *Ligustrum japonicum* 'Macrophyllum', with dark foliage and broader leaves. *Ligustrum japonicum* 'Rotundifolium' is an interestingly architectural shrub with rounded, thick, dark leaves. It is very slow and compact, and usually grows into an interesting shape.

Ligustrum lucidum (zone 7–10), the Chinese privet, is much larger-growing, often making a small tree. With long, pointed leaves, it resembles a

---

PLANTING PARTNERS

Both the yellow-fruiting holly *Ilex aquifolium* 'Yellow Berry' (z. 6–9) and the bronze-yellow cultivar *Ilex aquifolium* 'Amber'(left) complement yellow-variegated evergreens such as *Elaeagnus pungens* 'Maculata' (z. 6–9).

Viburnum tinus 'Robustum' (z. 8–9) has large heads of white flowers and is strong growing. It combines well with white-variegated shrubs such as *Pittosporum* 'Variegatum' (z. 9–10).

The purplish new growth of *Weigela* 'Wine and Roses' (z. 5–9) complements golden-foliage deciduous shrubs, particularly *Sambucus racemosa* 'Sutherland Gold' (z. 3–7).

Ligustrum lucidum

Osmanthus × burkwoodii

Myrtus communis

Phillyrea angustifolia

large version of the hedging privet. Its habit is symmetrical and in the fall it has conspicuous panicles of white flowers. It is a good choice where a large background shrub is needed quickly.

Myrtus communis (zone 8–9), the common myrtle, is a Mediterranean shrub, which was introduced over 150 years ago. It is hardy in milder zones, particularly by the coast, and grows well in the shelter of a sunny wall. In ideal conditions it will reach 13ft. (4m), growing successfully on any well-drained soil, including limestone. The pretty foliage is shiny and rich dark green. The white flowers are produced in summer and may be followed by purple-black berries. Because of its traditional and medicinal connections, it associates well with herbs and aromatics. It is an appropriate choice to have by the house as a symbol of health and well-being.

A compact form, *Myrtus communis* ssp. *tarentina*, has small narrow, dark green leaves, pink-tinged flowers in the fall, and white berries.

Osmanthus are hollylike evergreens, good structure plants that grow on virtually any soil. The variegated forms are perhaps the best known, but there are some excellent plain green forms, well worth remembering when it comes to choosing easy-to-grow evergreens.

Osmanthus decorus (zone 7–9), previously known as *Phillyrea decora*, deserves to be planted more often than it is. Forming a large, broad dome, it is a good, tough, and easy-to-grow plant with large, leathery, shiny leaves and small fragrant white flowers in spring.

Osmanthus × burkwoodii (zone 6–8) is the best-known osmanthus. Previously offered as × *Osmarea burkwoodii*, it has been in our gardens since 1930. It is hardy and compact, with upright growth, light tan stems, and neat oval, dark green, leathery leaves. It produces profuse white, very fragrant flowers in late spring. This useful shrub can be grown in sun or shade, and it can be trimmed to shape in more formal schemes.

A very useful alternative to a green holly, ideal for smaller gardens, *Osmanthus heterophyllus* 'Gulftide' (zone 6–9) looks like a small, dark green holly, with leaves often twisted, very spiny, and glossy. Growth is compact; the plant rarely gets large.

Phillyrea is a genus that offers some excellent evergreen structure plants. It is a pity it is not more widely known. *Phillyrea* are handsome creatures of the olive family, closely related to osmanthus.

Phillyrea angustifolia (zone 7–8) is the most attractive species, although hard to find. It has neat narrow, shiny, dark green leaves. Although a compact, rounded shrub, it has a wonderfully loose quality, with elegant sprays of foliage that are useful for cutting. The flowers are like those of box: creamy yellow and carried on the fine stems, in May and June. It is a good coastal plant. Its finest quality is its gentle movement in the breeze; it lacks the stiffness of so many structural evergreens.

Phillyrea latifolia (zone 7–8) has broader leaves and is larger-growing than *Phillyrea angustifolia*. Often confused with the holly oak, *Quercus ilex*, it offers a useful alternative where *Quercus ilex* would grow too large. The leaves are small, neat, and dark green; white flowers are produced in spring. It becomes looser in habit as the plant matures and the branches become weighed down by the fine foliage.

Viburnum tinus (zone 8–9) deserves a mention here (see pages 186–87 for a fuller account). Although not widely planted, *Viburnum tinus* gives solid, year-round structure on any site, in almost any conditions except very waterlogged soil. It responds well to trimming—the main problem is deciding when to trim, as the plant has such a long flowering season. Pruning is best done in spring as the flowers are fading, though this will sacrifice the blue-black berries on plants that produce them.

Lighter and brighter evergreens

Not all evergreen shrubs need to be solid and heavy. The evergreen shrubs described here provide structure in the garden while remaining light and bright in character. They can also be particularly useful for enlivening a dark, shady corner. Small leaves, shiny foliage, and different shades of green provide lighter, brighter highlights than heavier evergreens.

Choisya ternata (zone 8–10), the Mexican orange blossom, is an extremely useful, medium-sized shrub, making a neat rounded bush and needing no attention. The trifoliate leaves are shiny, dark green, and strongly aromatic when crushed, characteristic of the family Rutaceae, to which it belongs. The family includes citrus and the herb rue.

Choisyas flower best in an open position but will grow in sun or in shade, on any soil. They are happiest in zones 8–10, but may thrive in zone 7, in a sheltered site. The white, scented flowers are carried in clusters in the leaf axils through late spring and early summer and again in the fall. In fact, some plants are rarely out of flower.

Choisyas need no pruning, but you can trim them after flowering if you need to control size. Ideally, do this from an early age, as plants that have been cut back hard into the old wood, after they have been allowed to grow too large for their situation, rarely recover.

Choisya ternata is everyone's ideal shrub: easy to grow, with a long season of flowering, evergreen, scented, and trouble-free. If it has one drawback, it is that it can be slow to get started, so patience is required for the first few years.

One of the few evergreen shrubs unpalatable to deer and rabbits, choisya is invaluable for those living in areas where these animals are a problem.

The yellow-leaved cultivar **Choisya ternata 'Sundance'** does not flower as freely as *Choisya ternata*, but it compensates with the brilliance of its young, yellow foliage. The tips can be subject to frost damage, but this is easily rectified by trimming in early spring. See also page 40.

Griselinia littoralis (zone 8–9) is a native of New Zealand, notable for its rounded, glossy, apple-green leaves. The upright, yellowish stems and ocher tint in the foliage are reminiscent of seaweed and are an acquired taste. Care is needed when siting this plant; the variegated forms may be easier to accommodate than the plain, but can look out of place in a traditional garden.

However, griselinias offer lighter alternatives to heavy evergreens, such

Griselinia littoralis

Choisya ternata

as laurel, and mix well with golden-variegated plants. They grow quickly, make a good screen, and respond well to trimming, so they make excellent hedging plants. They are very useful in coastal locations (*littoralis* means "of sea shores"). These shrubs are not for cold areas and do not thrive in alkaline conditions. See also page 61.

Pittosporum tenuifolium

Pittosporum tenuifolium (zone 9–10) is a native of New Zealand. Considered an exotic species when it was first introduced, it is now naturalized in parts of California. The plant is a columnar shrub of neat habit. Small, pale green undulate leaves are carried on dark twigs; although there are masses of leaves, the shrub has the effect of being solid without being dense and is well clothed to the ground. Tiny, chocolate, honey-scented flowers are produced in spring; although they are not showy, they make a pleasing contrast to the foliage, and the fragrance is noticeable in the garden. *Pittosporum tenuifolium* normally does well in seaside gardens. Although it prefers good drainage, it seems happy on heavy clay. The foliage is widely used in floristry, so it is a shrub that flower arrangers appreciate. The plant responds well to clipping, so its shape and size are easily controlled and it makes an excellent hedge.

There are many cultivars, with white- and gold-variegated and purple foliage. (See pages 49, 64).

Photinia × *fraseri* (zone 7–9) is best known as a lime-tolerant substitute for pieris. (For pieris, see pages 63, 109.) The popular photinia is a large, vigor-

ous, evergreen shrub. The glossy, leathery dark green leaves are similar to those of the Portugal laurel but have a serrated edge and are more upright along the branches. They resemble individual, large rose leaflets—a clue to the family this plant belongs to: Rosaceae.

The new growth is an attractive coppery red and is the feature for which the plant is best known. The clusters of white flowers, very similar to those of hawthorn but larger, are pretty in the spring. The popular forms of the plant are very hardy, and even the soft new growth is fairly frost-resistant—certainly much more so than that of pieris.

Photinia is a large, easy-to-grow shrub that thrives on any soil, unless conditions are very wet. Color is better when there is a reasonable amount of sunshine, but the plant is shade-tolerant.

Photinia × *fraseri* 'Red Robin' is the best-known clone, and probably the most spectacular. It was raised in New Zealand but is hardy in the southern parts of zone 8 southward. The new growth is bright red and is considered equal to pieris in the brilliance of its display.

Photinia × *fraseri* 'Indian Princess' is equally useful. It is even more hardy and vigorous, with coppery red new growth.

Young container-grown photinia plants often look weak and lax in habit, but their appearance belies their later performance. Hard pruning after planting helps to promote vigorous growth and good branch structure from the base.

Photinias make excellent screening plants and mix well with other large evergreen and deciduous shrubs to provide an effective visual or sound barrier. They respond well to pruning and trimming, so they are ideal as a hedge or for training as a standard. In this form, they make a useful and showy evergreen tree. Trimming results in a flush of new growth.

DOUBLE FLUSH

To get the maximum red foliage from your photinia, trim it twice a year, in spring and again in summer. The second of the two flushes of new growth that result from trimming normally lasts all winter.

Photinia × *fraseri* 'Red Robin'

Bold-foliage evergreens

Evergreen shrubs with large, glossy leaves make a bold statement in the garden and provide a welcome contrast to small, fine green and variegated leaves. Too many small-leaved plants can look fussy and lack impact. Large-leaved plants have great presence against them, providing contrast in the structure planting.

Aucuba japonica (zone 7–10), the spotted laurel, is the unsung hero of the garden. These evergreen, shade-loving shrubs grow in just about any soil or situation, however sunless. They have the ability to compete with the roots of trees such as beech and horse chestnut. Even in such adverse conditions, they perform well, their bold, glossy foliage making them a very attractive feature of the garden. The variegated forms bring a little sunshine to the darkest corners.

As the name suggests, *Aucuba japonica* originate from Japan. Being remarkably hardy plants, they are often grown in continental Europe as container plants for winter decoration. They survive unscathed on the sidewalks of Amsterdam and Brussels in the freezing, windy conditions of midwinter. They are also very resistant to atmospheric pollution, so suit urban areas. At the other end of the scale, they make sturdy indoor plants and are ideal for drafty hallways and lobbies where more tender subjects would die.

The flowers are insignificant, small and reddish-purple, produced in April. On female plants, attractive red berries follow. To fruit well, female plants need plentiful sunshine and a male pollinator.

The first form to be introduced to North America from Japan, in 1783, was *Aucuba japonica* 'Variegata' ('Maculata'). It has yellow-speckled leaves and is female. See pages 57 for the variegated aucubas.

Of the plain green aucubas, *Aucuba japonica* f. *longifolia* is well worth looking for. *Aucuba japonica* f. *longifolia* 'Salicifolia' ("leaves like a willow") has very narrow leaves on sea-green stems and is particularly prolific in its fruit production.

Aucuba japonica 'Rozannie' is a true bold-foliage evergreen with broad, toothed, dark leaves. It is a compact female form that berries well when pollinated.

The aucubas make rounded bushes 6–10ft. (2–3m) high and are good solid structure plants. They require no pruning, but if you do want to cut the plants back, to reduce size, do it carefully, with hand pruners. Clipping with shears results in unsightly remnants of disfigured leaves.

Sometimes aucubas show blackening of the new shoots in winter. This is not due to frost damage but is the effect of drought during the previous summer. Cut out the damaged growth, and the plant quickly recovers.

Fatsia japonica (zone 8–9), castor oil plant, is the ultimate big, green, glossy evergreen. It is exotic in character, yet it fits well into many planting schemes, particularly more modern designs.

A native of Japan, fatsia is quite hardy once established. It grows well in any well-drained soil and tolerates any aspect. It is at its best in shade or semi-shade, when the foliage is rich dark green; in full sun, the foliage is harder

Fatsia japonica

Aucuba japonica f. *longifolia* 'Salicifolia'

and more olive in color. The leaves are palmate and on a happy plant are remarkably large. Fatsia flowers in late fall and early winter, producing a creamy-white inflorescence, like a giant ivy flower, arising from the apical bud. It looks particularly striking against the backdrop of deep green foliage.

Fatsia is an excellent choice for a pot and also for coastal gardens. Left to thrive, it will make a large shrub of spreading habit.

The variegated form *Fatsia japonica* 'Variegata' (zone 8–9) is now also available and, being less vigorous than the plain form, is an excellent plant for the small garden. It tends to be a little more tender, so a sheltered spot is ideal. It looks superb underplanted with a small-leaved, white-variegated ivy.

PRUNING FATSIA

After several years in a container, fatsia can sometimes get leggy and bare at the base. In this situation, hard pruning, down to 1ft. (30cm), will result in vigorous growth and healthy new foliage.

Magnolia grandiflora (zone 7–9) is a magnificent evergreen traditionally grown as a wall shrub in colder zones. Known as the southern magnolia, it is a native of the southeastern United States but is widely grown as a specimen tree in many southern gardens. It makes an excellent, open-ground, large shrub if given shelter and full sun. The huge, creamy, deliciously fragrant flowers are produced in summer and early fall on mature plants. Some cultivars flower early in life; choose one of these if you are growing the plant for flowers as well as foliage. See also pages 134–35.

Magnolia grandiflora 'Edith Bogue' is the most popular variety. It is one of the hardiest selections. The very large flowers are produced from an early age. *Magnolia grandiflora*

Magnolia grandiflora

'Bracken's Brown Beauty' is a very hardy variety and makes an excellent formal structure plant. The dark leaves are reddish-brown on the underside, making a superb backdrop for the huge, fragrant flowers. *Magnolia grandiflora* 'Victoria' is another very hardy variety selected in Victoria, British Columbia. The leaves are an exceptionally rich brown beneath.

Magnolia grandiflora 'Little Gem' appeals to those who have a small garden and a strong desire for this beautiful evergreen. However, it is a tender plant and very slow growing in the early stages of its life.

Magnolia grandiflora needs sun and good drainage. It resents being planted too deep and reacts by standing still, even on the finest soil. It will grow on limestone, so long as the soil is deep and plenty of organic matter is added.

The New Zealand flax, which is not a shrub in the true sense but is generally treated as if it were, is an invaluable structure plant and belongs with this group of shrubs. *Phormium tenax* (zone 8–10) is often overlooked in favor of its more colorful relations (see pages 55, 66, 125); the plain green species, however, is tough, with magnificent sword-shaped leaves, which can reach a height of 6ft. (2m). It suits contempo-

Phormium tenax

rary schemes, and is a valuable architectural plant to balance heavy masonry. In summer, established plants produce statuesque, antlerlike flower spikes, bronze-red in color, reaching at least 4m (13ft). *Phormium tenax* stands up to exposed conditions and is excellent by the sea. It grows on any fertile soil and in any situation, looking as good beside water as it does in the desert.

Prunus laurocerasus (zone 6–8), the cherry laurel, is from eastern Europe and southwest Asia and is widely used in landscape planting in the southeastern United States. It is true that this is probably the most tolerant shrub when

Prunus laurocerasus 'Rotundifolia'

PRUNING LAUREL HEDGES

Because of its large leathery leaves, any cherry laurel used as a hedge or a shaped subject should be clipped early in the year. New growth will then quickly hide the damaged leaves. If you cut it any later, you will be left with unsightly chopped leaves spoiling the appearance for the rest of the season. Cut smaller specimens with hand pruners for best effect.

---

it comes to colonizing shade and areas that are overhung by trees, but in the garden it should normally be regarded as a screening plant.

Cherry laurels grow quickly, attaining a height of 20ft. (6m) if left unchecked. They make excellent broad hedges and were loved by the Victorians, including Gertrude Jekyll, for this purpose.

The variety *Prunus laurocerasus* 'Rotundifolia' (zone 6–8) has shorter, rounder leaves and is highly suited to clipping, so is perfect for hedging or for making into solid shapes in the border. *Prunus laurocerasus* 'Marble Dragon' (zone 6–8) has glossy and variegatedfoliage; green that is touched with gold and apricot.

Its ease of cultivation means that many cultivars are often selected as low-maintenance landscape plants. The shiny, dark green foliage of the low,

compact *Prunus laurocerasus* 'Otto Luyken' (zone 6–8), once widely grown as a garden shrub, is the perfect foil for its showy, upright spikes of white flowers. Unfortunately, however, shot-hole virus, which affects the new growth at the end of the branches, often spoils the foliage. This virus can affect all prunus, deciduous and evergreen, but especially the less vigorous types.

Prunus lusitanica (zone 7–9), the Portugal laurel, can make a beautiful specimen tree if it is allowed to grow to maturity. It is normally seen as a rounded bush, and suits clipping and training. The dark green leaves are thinner and finer than those of the common cherry laurel, carried on attractive red stems and leaf

Prunus lusitanica

stalks. It is surprisingly hardy and it tolerates limestone. This plant deserves wider consideration as a structure plant.

Viburnum davidii (zone 7–9) was introduced by plant collector Ernest Wilson from western China as recently as 1904. The versatility of this wonderful evergreen gives it a wide variety of uses in many different types of garden. It grows on any soil, in sun or shade, and its continuous visual appeal can make it an excellent permanent subject for the confines of a pot.

Viburnum davidii

Often referred to as good ground-cover, it is far more than this. Left to reach its potential, it spreads to form a mound up to 3ft. (1m) high and 5ft. (1.5m) wide. Growth is neat and compact.

The large, perfect, leathery oval leaves are conspicuously veined along their length. They are glossy above, deep raven green, and lighter beneath. The leaf and flower cluster stalks are often red; the dull white flowers are usually produced in late spring and early summer. On female plants, these are followed by small, egg-shaped, blue-black fruits that persist through winter. A male pollinator is required if a female plant is to fruit; planting in groups is desirable. The way to be sure of getting a female plant is to buy it in fruit.

Viburnum davidii's bold form suits contemporary and oriental schemes and works well with gravel, pebbles, and rock. It contributes structure to a shade planting of pulmonarias and vincas.

FOLIAGE EFFECTS

Flowers will come and go, but the contribution made to the garden picture by leaves is long lasting. It is the color and texture of foliage that should form the basis of any planting scheme. While structure shrubs create a solid green framework, different-colored foliage sets the tone: cheerful yellow, dramatic wine, uplifting gold or silver variegations, and ethereal silver. A dull garden is a garden that lacks variety. Shrubs that are well chosen for their foliage effects are the foundation of

RIGHT: *Cotinus coggygria* 'Velvet Cloak' in combination with an orange hemerocallis

Yellow and gold

The last two decades of the 20th century saw the introduction of many golden-leaved variations of familar shrubs; other yellow plants were also much loved. Since then, however, yellow has become less popular in the garden, while purple- and silver-variegated foliage and pastels have come to the fore. Daffodil sales have fallen as hyacinth and crocus sales have soared. Marigolds are neglected, while impatiens and petunias are snapped up for pots, baskets, and borders.

Golden-yellow foliage is a sure way to brighten up the garden. Since yellow attracts the eye, its positioning needs careful consideration. Use it where you want to draw attention—such as a gateway, an entrance, or a focal point—and avoid planting it where it will distract from the focus of the design.

Some yellow-leaved plants scorch in sunlight, so try not to plant them in open situations. Most yellow foliage loses some color in shade and reverts to a light lime green, which is less striking. The majority of golden-leaved plants tend to be at their best in late summer, and they always complement the oranges and reds of early fall.

GOLDEN EVERGREENS

The heavy spotting and variegation of some of the **aucubas** give an overall effect of a yellow-leaved shrub. The yellow-splashed foliage of *Aucuba japonica* 'Marmorata' (zone 7–10) is particularly strong, making this plant a natural choice where a golden-leaved evergreen is needed for a shady site. Aucubas also make superb structure plants (see also pages 35, 57, 96, 122).

Many consider *Choisya ternata* 'Sundance' (zone 8–10) to be one of the finest yellow-leaved evergreens, and for a patch of sunshine in the shrub border all year round, it is hard to beat. Although not as free-flowering as

Golden foliage and yellow flowers blend to create a sunny picture.

MIXING AND MATCHING

For best effect, aim to include sufficient solid green and yellow-variegated foliage in the scheme to dilute the yellow and allow the individual plants to shine.

The lime green of *Alchemilla mollis* (z. 4–7), softens yellow and links it with solid greens. The bronze-purple of *Foeniculum vulgare* 'Purpureum' (z. 5–8), bronze fennel, provides a foil for the yellow and adds depth and interest.

Choisya ternata (see page 33), this plant makes up for the lack of flowers with a spectacular display of glossy golden leaves throughout the year. Sometimes the growing tips can be clipped by frost, but if you nip these back in early spring, the plant will quickly recover. Its solid structure is ideal with lighter deciduous shrubs—for example *Philadelphus microphyllus* or *Spiraea* 'Arguta'. Avoid planting with pink shrubs—the combination of colors is not pleasing.

The newer, golden-leaved **Choisya 'Goldfingers'** (zone 8–10) has finer foliage, and the color is softer yellow. The golden-leaved form of *Choisya* 'Aztec Pearl', it can be slow at first, with a horizontal growth habit when young. It improves with age, but for faster and more robust effect, choose **'Sundance'**.

Although not widely available, **Coleonema pulchellum 'Sunset Gold'** (zone 9–10) can be found for sale in spring, when it is covered with small white, starry flowers. It is very much like a heather but with more arching, horizontal growth, and rather tarnished golden foliage. It is tender and needs neutral or acid soil, and is also very susceptible to drying out. For a similar foliage effect from a plant that succeeds

At Denmans, in Sussex, England, *Escallonia laevis* 'Gold Brian' (right) draws the eye to a focal point, the blue seat.

more easily, choose one of the infinitely superior golden forms of *Erica arborea*.

Erica arborea (zone 7–8), the tree heath (see page 132), is native to southern Europe, southwest Asia, and north and east Africa. Although it will form a medium to large shrub, once established it can be pruned hard after flowering to promote long sprays of flowers the following season. The fragrant, tiny round flowers are profuse in early spring; they produce clouds of pollen when shaken. *Erica arborea* **'Albert's Gold'** is a vigorous grower with bright yellow young foliage; **'Estrella Gold'** is smaller, and has bright yellow new growth.

Choisya ternata 'Sundance'

Erica arborea 'Albert's Gold'

Choisya 'Goldfingers'

Escallonia laevis 'Gold Ellen'

WHERE TO GROW TREE HEATHS

Although recommended for acid soils, these shrubs are more lime-tolerant than many of the callunas. They will grow successfully on clay soils if the pH is not too high. Tree heaths are excellent subjects for bridging the gap between conifers and broad-leaved shrubs in mixed plantings.

Escallonia laevis (zone 8–10), which originates from Brazil, boasts two cultivars that are regarded as golden-foliage evergreens: *Escallonia laevis* **'Gold Brian'**, with yellow foliage, becoming dark green with age; and *Escallonia laevis* **'Gold Ellen'**, with green leaves that are broadly margined with yellow, giving the overall effect of a golden shrub. Both cultivars have the characteristic sticky, aromatic, lustrous foliage and straight horizontal branches of escallonia. Both produce deep pink flowers; to some the combination with the golden leaves is unattractive. Although these plants are reasonably hardy, they are not suitable for cold, exposed situations and do best in full sun on light soils. They combine well with phormiums and grasses.

Although there are no broad-leaved hebes bearing golden-yellow foliage, **Hebe ochracea** (zone 7–9), one of the

Ilex crenata 'Golden Gem'

Laurus nobilis 'Aurea'

Lonicera nitida 'Baggesen's Gold'

so-called whipcord hebes, has foliage with a distinct ocher-gold tarnish. This color is otherwise confined to conifers. Its habit, too, is similar to that of a prostrate juniper—a low, irregularly layered star shape. Small white flowers appear in summer but are of secondary importance to the foliage, which makes more of an impact in other seasons, particularly during the winter. **Hebe ochracea 'James Stirling'** is an excellent, popular cultivar. Combined with conifers and heathers, it makes a good addition to the front of a yellow-themed planting scheme. (See Good Companions, below.)

A golden-leaved form of the Japanese holly, **Ilex crenata 'Golden Gem'** (zone 5–7) is a small, compact shrub with a flattened top and yellow leaves. The color is at its best during the winter and spring, so it can be used to bring color to the rock garden or winter containers. It is slow-growing and needs little attention. As a female holly, it is able to produce berries, but rarely flowers.

The golden-leaved bay laurel, **Laurus nobilis 'Aurea'** (zone 8–9), is thought by many gardeners to be an ugly duckling of a plant. As a young container-grown shrub, it can be

straggly, and appears chlorotic with its uneven yellow foliage. As a large, mature shrub, however, it has the same statuesque, dense pyramidal habit as the green-leaved bay laurel, but with a lighter character. In low winter sunshine the leaves are particularly golden and glorious. It is an excellent alternative to a large yellow conifer. It can be clipped and pruned to shape. Do this in spring, as the foliage starts to green, and just before new shoots appear. If there is space, allow it to reach its potential.

California privet, **Ligustrum ovalifolium** (zone 5–9), is used mainly for hedging (see page 122). It is easy to grow on any soil and is a tolerant plant, shedding its leaves only in cold conditions. Its wide use as a suburban hedge in the latter part of the 20th century has caused privet to be overlooked as a shrub suitable for general garden use. The golden privet, **Ligustrum ovalifolium 'Variegatum'**, will grow to make a large, graceful shrub of up to 10ft. (3m). Upright and arching, the thin branches produce bright, rich yellow leaves, sometimes with a green center. The habit is more open and sparse in shade, making it a useful shrub to lighten a dark corner. Its white flowers are strongly fragrant.

Lonicera nitida 'Baggesen's Gold' (zone 7–9) is an amazingly versatile plant, used variously as a winter container plant, an evergreen shrub, and a hedging plant. *Lonicera nitida* (see page 122) is a dense, small-leaved, dark

GOOD COMPANIONS

Plant *Fuchsia* 'Genii' (1) (z. 7–9) with other yellow-leaved plants, such as *Hosta* 'Golden Tiara' (z. 4–8) and the grass *Carex elata* 'Aurea' (2) (z. 5–9) or, for a striking contrast, with a purple heuchera such as *Heuchera* 'Plum Pudding' (3) (z. 4–8).

Hebe ochracea 'James Stirling' (4) (z. 7–9) complements *Spiraea japonica* 'Firelight' (5) (z. 3–8) and contrasts well with *Euonymus fortunei* 'Emerald 'n' Gold' (6) (z. 5–8).

Osmanthus heterophyllus 'Goshiki'

Pittosporum tenuifolium 'Warnham Gold'

evergreen shrub with straight twigs. It ultimately reaches 6ft. (2m), and has been used for hedging because of its quick growth and positive response to clipping. In some gardens it has occasionally been used successfully as a faster growing, easily accommodated substitute for box.

If it is left unclipped, *Lonicera nitida* 'Baggesen's Gold' (zone 7–9) grows into a graceful plant, with leaves that turn from yellow during summer to yellow-green in the fall. The tiny leaves makes this a very attractive shrub.

When the plant is in shade, the foliage color is a yellow-green throughout the year; on poor soil the color is a paler, almost primrose yellow on occasions.

Osmanthus heterophyllus 'Goshiki' (zone 6–9) is normally regarded as variegated, but the overall effect is certainly more of a soft yellow shrub than one with conspicuous variegation. The small, hollylike leaves are mottled with yellow and are bronze-tinted when young. The color tends to be lighter and more yellow in full sun. This is a superb evergreen shrub of compact habit and a

uniform, mounded shape. It is a very good choice for a container as an alternative to box, and is an excellent structure shrub in mixed plantings. The soft color sits easily with a wide range of plants and is gentler on the eye than many gold or variegated plants.

For stronger foliage effect, consider *Osmanthus heterophyllus* 'Ogon', (zone 6–9) which has dark green foliage and bright, deep gold young growth. This is a bold shrub, and a good choice for the foreground when planted with gold-variegated evergreen shrubs.

A superb yellow-leaved shrub for structure is *Pittosporum tenuifolium* 'Warnham Gold' (zone 9–10), with greenish-yellow young foliage that matures to golden-yellow. The leaves are softly wavy and loose in habit, but they achieve dense cover. In winter the color intensifies to soft old gold, which looks delightful against dark evergreens or clear blue winter skies. As the plant matures, it makes a tall, narrow cone.

YELLOW AND GOLD PLANT COMBINATIONS

The Yellow Border at Le Clos du Coudray, Normandy, in France. This perfectly illustrates how stunning combinations are created when golden-leaved trees, such as *Robinia pseudoacacia* 'Frisia' (z. 3–8), *Gleditsia triacanthos* 'Sunburst' (z. 3–9), or *Ptelea trifoliata* 'Aurea' (z. 3–9), are mixed with attractive golden-leaved shrubs and yellow-flowering herbaceous plants.

DECIDUOUS SHRUBS WITH GOLDEN FOLIAGE

All maples are highly valued for their most attractive foliage (see also pages 50–51). If you decide you would like an *Acer shirasawanum* 'Aureum' or *Acer japonicum* 'Aureum' (zone 5–8) in your garden, plant it as soon as possible. Growth is slow, and it takes some time to reach its potential. However, even when the plant is not much more than a small twig, the stunning acid-yellow color of the foliage is an eye-catcher. The shrub's elegant, spreading habit is distinctly oriental. The leaves are rounded and sharply toothed, changing from yellow to orange-red in the fall. A shrub for dappled shade and shelter, this acer does not like drought, and the foliage will scorch in full sun. It associates well with hostas, grasses, ground-cover plants, and pebbles in an uncluttered scheme. This is not a shrub to mix with flowering subjects.

A recent lack of interest in **berberis** has led to a decline in the popularity of *Berberis thunbergii* 'Aurea' (zone 4–8). However, it is very striking when the wonderful bright yellow new growth appears—a shade that suits the small round leaves, carried on wandlike branches; this color changes to pale green as the season progresses. The foliage can scorch in strong sun. This problem is not suffered by the recent cultivar *Berberis thunbergii* 'Bonanza

Acer shirasawanum 'Aureum'

Gold' (zone 4–8), with orange-red new shoots that turn yellow-green.

Caryopteris (zone 7–8) are good plants for sunny positions on well-drained soil, and thrive on lime. The aromatic leaves are usually a soft gray-green, which blends well with the fluffy blue, late-summer flowers. *Caryopteris* × *clandonensis* 'Worcester Gold' has golden-yellow, flushed foliage. While the combination of yellow leaves and blue flowers is not unappealing, it does not mix well with some autumn-flowering herbaceous plants. It is unattractive with sedum and echinacea, for example, but works well with rudbeckia.

The virtues of the red stems of *Cornus alba* 'Aurea' (zone 2–8) are

Cornus alba 'Aurea'

extolled in the section on shrubs for winter (see pages 177–78). It is a plant that works hard year-round, however, for there are few yellow-leaved plants with such soft grace as this one. The large, well-spaced leaves are an almost translucent shade of yellow, and they complement variegated or green shrubs, without shouting. As another

Berberis thunbergii 'Aurea'

Caryopteris × clandonensis 'Worcester Gold'

LATE-SUMMER BLUES

All golden-leaved subjects look stunning in association with blue flowers. Remember that there are some excellent late-summer blues: caryopteris, ceratostigma, perovskia and the autumn-flowering ceanothus. These shrubs bloom when many gold-foliage plants are at their best.

Cotinus coggygria 'Golden Spirit'

subject. The habit is upright, with red shoots and leaves that are lime-yellow in sun, lime-green in semi-shade. The flowers are small for a hybrid fuchsia, with a violet corolla and cerise calyx—a pleasing contrast to the yellow of the foliage. *Fuchsia* 'Genii' works well with other yellow-leaved plants, such as hostas and grasses, and is striking with purple heucheras, which combine beautifully with the flowers (see Good Companions, page 42).

Philadelphus coronarius 'Aureus' (zone 4–8) is a widely planted deciduous yellow-leaved shrub. The leaves are bright acid yellow when young, maturing to greenish yellow. In semi-shade the leaves are more lime yellow and contrast superbly with purple-leaved shrubs such as the elder *Sambucus nigra* f. *porphyrophylla* 'Eva' (formerly 'Black Lace', see page 54). The new foliage is at its eye-catching best when the late tulips are in flower (see Good Companions, page 47).

Philadelphus coronarius 'Aureus' is generally a tough, tolerant plant that withstands poor, dry soil, although its leaves may scorch in hot sunshine. It is a medium-sized shrub; and although not as free-flowering as most philadelphus, it produces plenty of fragrant, single, creamy white flowers. Prune immediately after flowering, cutting out some of the old wood that has flowered and leaving the vigorous new shoots.

bonus, the leaves turn a wonderful salmon color in the fall, before falling to reveal the winter stems. Selective pruning of half of the stems to ground level each year ensures well-colored new wood, and keeps the shrub light and open in character. It is very useful for sun or shade, on any soil, and is particularly tolerant of wet conditions.

Cotinus coggygria 'Golden Spirit' (zone 4–8) is a relatively new introduction that is proving to be an excellent plant. It grows well and, like all the more familiar purple-leaved smoke bushes (see page 54), has excellent leaf form. This is a large shrub, reaching about 6ft. (2m) in height and spread. It responds well to pruning, and the long, straight sprays of foliage produced after it has been cut back are among its attractions. This plant is useful in a large pot, so long as it is pruned hard each spring. After a hot summer, it has sensational orange-salmon autumn color, even in shade.

Fuchsia 'Genii' (zone 7–9) is a dwarf shrub that develops its best color in full sun and does not scorch. It is surprisingly hardy, and in mild zones it can be regarded as a permanent garden

Philadelphus coronarius 'Aureus'

45

Physocarpus opulifolius 'Dart's Gold' (zone 2–7) is a compact shrub that thrives anywhere. Its flowers are white, tinged pink, and appear all along the branches in early summer. The leaves are similar in shape to those of *Ribes*, (flowering currant) but are bright yellow, staying this color for a long period, and are much more scorch resistant. (See Good Companions page 93.) This is less often seen than the dark-leaved *Physocarpus opulifolius* 'Diabolo' (see page 54).

Ribes sanguineum 'Brocklebankii' (zone 6–7) is smaller and slower-growing than most flowering currants. The leaves are attractive in form and color (a rich golden-yellow), but tend to scorch and jar with the pink flowers, produced at a time when most people find the contrast of yellow forsythia and

Ribes sanguineum 'Brocklebankii'

Rubus cockburnianus 'Golden Vale'

pink cherry blossom more than enough. *Rubus cockburnianus* (zone 6–7) is a strong-growing bramble, with arching purple stems and white blooms. *Rubus cockburnianus* 'Goldenvale' has the same white stems, exposed in winter, but this cultivar is blessed with brilliant golden-yellow, fernlike leaves in summer. This variety is not nearly as invasive as the species, and can be

pruned hard at the end of winter to keep it in control. This is truly a plant for all seasons, happy in sun or shade, and deserves wider planting.

A golden form of the purple-berried elder, *Sambucus racemosa* 'Plumosa Aurea' (zone 3–7) is one of the most graceful yellow-leaved shrubs. It is a medium-to-large shrub with deeply cut golden foliage, conical rather than flat

PLANT PROFILE

Spiraea

Spiraeas are hardy shrubs, easy to grow on any soil and requiring little care. Prune these foliage types in early spring, before the new growth really gets going, as light or as hard as you wish. Because they stay looking good for a long period, spiraeas are excellent garden center plants. Unfortunately, this has led to overplanting, but with their pleasing habit and attractive foliage, they are useful low-growing shrubs for many planting schemes. Some plants, such as *Spiraea japonica* 'Goldflame' (z. 3–8), will produce reverted green shoots; cut them out as soon as they appear to retain their golden color.

Spiraea japonica 'Candlelight' (z. 3–8) is a compact shrub with foliage a clear yellow that gradually deepens. It does not revert, and has good autumn leaf color. The pink flowers contrast with the foliage, but this is not a subtle combination.

Spiraea japonica 'Firelight' (z. 3–8) has orange-red young foliage and a graceful, arching habit. The autumn color is fiery red. (See Good Companions, page 42.)

Spiraea japonica 'Goldflame' (z. 3–8) is a very popular dwarf shrub. It has upright growth and deep rose red

flowers. The young leaves are bright reddish orange on tan-barked stems. They eventually become rich yellow, then green. (See Good Companions, right.)

Spiraea japonica 'Golden Princess' (z. 3–8), of dwarf habit, has bronze-red foliage that gradually turns a brilliant yellow and, in the fall, red. Its flowers are deep pink.

Spiraea japonica 'Magic Carpet' (z. 3–8) has a spreading habit and bright red new foliage, turning yellow. The compact flower heads are deep pink. It is a good plant for ground cover and containers.

MORE YELLOW AND GOLD SHRUBS *Acer negundo* 'Kelly's Gold' • *Calluna vulgaris* 'Beoley Gold' • *Ceratostigma willmottianum* 'Desert Skies' • *Cornus mas* 'Aurea' • *Corylus avellana* 'Aurea' • *Erica carnea* 'Aurea' •

Sambucus racemosa 'Plumosa Aurea'

flower heads, which crowd the branches in mid-spring, and clusters of scarlet fruits, which in this golden form are insignificant. It is best in light shade, as it is likely to scorch in full sun. Another golden cultivar, **Sambucus racemosa 'Sutherland Gold'** (zone 3–7) is not as fine and graceful, but is scorch-resistant and therefore more useful. Prune in late winter, selectively cutting back some older branches to healthy buds near the base of the plant.

There are several varieties of weigela with golden-yellow foliage. **Weigela 'Looymansii Aurea'** (zone 5–9) is an old variety, found as a seedling in 1873. The foliage is light gold and is best in partial shade: in full sun, the color is

Sambucus racemosa 'Sutherland Gold'

Weigela 'Briant Rubidor'

harsher and the leaves scorch. A disadvantage of this plant is that the gold foliage clashes with the pink flowers. Today, the cultivar **Weigela florida 'Briant Rubidor'** (zone 5–9) is a better alternative. The leaves are yellow or green, with a broad yellow margin, and the flowers are a dark carmine-red, which looks better with the foliage.

GOOD COMPANIONS

Philadelphus coronarius 'Aureus' (z. 4–8) makes a wonderful backdrop to *Tulipa* 'Black Parrot', 'Queen of Night', or 'Black Hero' (1) (z. 4–9).

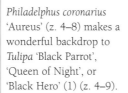

Underplant a spiraea that has orange-red new growth, such as *Spiraea japonica* 'Goldflame' (2) (z. 3–8), with early-flowering dwarf bulbs *Scilla siberica* (z. 5–8) or a blue *Anemone blanda* (3) (z. 5–8).

Ilex aquifolium 'Flavescens' • *Kolkwitzia amabilis* 'Maradco' • *Leycesteria formosa* 'Golden Lanterns' • *Ligustrum lucidum* 'Golden Wax' • *Ptelea trifoliata* 'Aurea' • *Ribes alpinum* 'Aureum' • *Viburnum opulus* 'Aureum' •

Purple and plum

The Red Border at Hidcote Manor Garden, in Gloucestershire, England.

Wild, hot colors become stronger and richer when blended with deep plum, wine, and bronze—tones that exist in plants at all levels, from the leafy canopy of trees such as acer to the ground-cover carpeting of ajuga or heuchera. Purple is often planted as a contrast to yellow. It stands bold and beautiful against orange and gold, while, with its ingredient colors of red, blue, brown and pink, it has a softening and melting effect on bright shades of yellow.

MIXING AND MATCHING

Shrubs with purplish red foliage mix well with many other colors of leaf and flower, but each combination produces a very different effect.

Purplish red foliage provides a strong contrast to yellow, which works where dramatic effect or a focal point is required but can be overpowering. Usually a yellow-leaved shrub against a purple-leaved shrub is too much: two solid masses competing. For example, imagine *Cotinus coggygria* 'Royal Purple' (z. 4–8) alongside *Choisya ternata* 'Sundance' (z. 8–10).

However, if the partners are at different levels in the planting scheme—if they are different in form, or if one is much lighter in structure than the other – the effect can be stunning: purple cotinus beneath golden gleditsia, 'Black Parrot' tulips against golden philadelphus, or perhaps purple heucheras under golden spiraeas.

The addition of purple foliage adds weight and depth to any planting of silver, blue, and pink. It contributes a richness that makes a scheme more interesting and eye-catching. Purple-leaved deciduous shrubs, such as *Sambucus* (elder, z. 5–7) and *Corylus* (hazel, z. 4–7), combine particularly well with cottage garden favorites such as herbaceous geraniums, artemisias, delphiniums, and lavenders. They also make dramatic supports for climbers such as *Clematis texensis* (z. 4–9) and *Clematis viticella* (z. 5–8), the deep velvet background of the purple foliage complementing the embroidery of the clematis flowers.

Wine red foliage is a dramatic complement to hot colors. Try adding the chocolate-leaved varieties of those exotic summer visitors—cannas, dahlias, and begonias. Structural, red-leaved plants such as berberis, cotinus, and pittosporums look stunning with *Dahlia* 'Bishop of Llandaff'. In late summer, any of these will serve as the perfect backdrop for crocosmias or heleniums.

EVERGREEN PURPLES

There are very few purple evergreens. The purple *Pittosporum tenuifolium* 'Purpureum' (zone 9–10) has shiny, crinkle-edged leaves of deep bronze-purple in fall and winter, carried on wiry, upright stems. The new spring growth is fresh, bright apple-green, and the darkness intensifies gradually through the year. This is a shrub with a spindly habit, and is rarely offered for sale because it has such an unappealing form while in a container. However, once the plant is established, its light, bony form is an attractive addition to any scheme, and it is useful for cutting.

A shorter, smaller, more compact cultivar is *Pittosporum tenuifolium* 'Tom Thumb' (zone 9–10). The density and intensity of its foliage in winter is stunning, which makes it the ideal partner for the glowing winter stems of cornus (see pages 177–78), or the pretty, nodding blooms of *Helleborus orientalis* (zone 5–8). It is also an excellent long-term subject for a container: a glazed oriental pot is the perfect foil for the color and texture of the leaves. This shrub was originally raised in New Zealand but proves to be very hardy in the northern hemisphere.

On a lighter note, the hard-to-find *Pseudowintera colorata* (zone 9), also from New Zealand, likes a little shelter and dislikes shallow limestone. It is excellent in semi-shade, in a pot containing ericaceous soil mix. The leaves are gray-olive in the center but flushed pink and edged and blotched with Merlot purple. A pleasing low mound of a shrub, this is a good choice to plant with azaleas and low-growing rhododendrons for interest year-round.

Salvia officinalis 'Purpurascens' (zone 5–10), the purple-leaf sage, is the perfect mixer (see Good Companions, right). It has made the move from the herb garden to the flower border and

Pittosporum tenuifolium 'Tom Thumb'

Pittosporum tenuifolium 'Purpureum'

Pseudowintera colorata

has become one of our best-loved dwarf shrubs. The dusky purple foliage, which becomes richer in summer and grayer in winter, is perfect for softening paving, as a container plant, for the front of a border, or to combine with gray foliage. Delightfully aromatic, the leaves of sage can be used in cooking. It is therefore a suitable partner for rosemary and thyme

in hot, dry planting schemes. Like most Mediterranean plants, this sage prefers good drainage and relatively dry soil, but it is surprisingly accommodating and will even survive heavy clay, provided it is not waterlogged. However, it is short-lived on heavy soils—replace plants approximately every three years. *(Continued on page 52.)*

GOOD COMPANIONS

Make a purple and silver cameo with *Hebe* 'Mrs. Winder' ('Waikiki') (1) (z. 8–10), *Salvia officinalis* 'Purpurascens' (2) (z. 5–10), *Lavandula stoechas* ssp. *pedunculata* ('Papillon') (3) (z. 7–8), and *Santolina chamaecyparissus* (4) (z. 6–9).

Acer

The Japanese maples are the aristocrats of the deciduous red-foliage shrubs or small trees. In spring the feathery scarlet leaves unfurl, like tiny fishing flies resting on the branches. The soft foliage then shimmers gracefully through the summer months, until the display of fiery autumn tints sets the plant ablaze, putting its more introvert companions firmly in the shade.

Japanese maples make excellent subjects for containers for sheltered positions. Their architectural form and mature character suit minimalist schemes, where the individual beauty of the plant can be appreciated.

Global interest in Japanese maples has resulted in a myriad named cultivars. As a rule of thumb, the *palmatum* types are fairly upright and normally carry their branches in attractive layers. The cut-leaf types (the Dissectum group) are generally lower growing, forming a mound. Most of the upright, red-leaved varieties are derivatives of the *Acer palmatum* Atropurpureum group. These make large shrubs of graceful habit.

Sometimes considered delicate (zone 6–8), these maples are susceptible to wind damage; in exposed surroundings, shelter them with hardier neighbors. They enjoy the dappled shade from taller trees, but if deprived of too much sunlight they lose color, and the rich burgundy foliage becomes a muddy green. Grow them in non-alkaline, loam-based soil mix, and water well throughout the growing season.

Acer palmatum types prefer moist, well-drained, loamy soil, and grow best in neutral to acid conditions. The stronger-growing varieties succeed in alkaline soil and are surprisingly tolerant of inhospitable conditions.

In all cases, pruning of Japanese maples should be necessary only to rectify damage or to remove dead and diseased wood. Trimming can ruin the plant's natural shape and beauty. Do not prune in winter, as branches cut during the dormant season tend to let disease into the plant. For more on acers, see pages 66–67, 168–69.

Acer palmatum 'Fireglow' with *Tulipa* 'Queen of Night'.

Acer palmatum 'Bloodgood' (z. 6–8) (right) is an excellent form, widely grown for its deep reddish purple foliage, which turns red in fall. The winged fruits, conspicuous on mature plants, are also attractive. Acer palmatum 'Fireglow' (z. 6–8) is similar but more vigorous and generally considered to be an improvement on 'Bloodgood'.

Acer palmatum 'Burgundy Lace' (z. 6–8) is broad-spreading, forming a mound of feathered foliage, wider than it is high.

Acer palmatum 'Trompenburg' (z. 6–8) has deep purplish red young leaves that turn greener later in the season, before putting on a good display of bright red autumn color. The leaves are deeply divided, with narrow lobes and rolled margins. This is a very tough acer.

Acer palmatum var. dissectum 'Crimson Queen' (z. 6–8) is a cut-leaf type, with rich reddish purple foliage that holds its color well. The downward-swept branches and deeply cut foliage resemble the plumage of an exotic bird.

Acer palmatum 'Corallinum' (z. 6–8), a slow-growing cultivar with small, deep-cut leaves that open salmon pink.

Acer palmatum 'Beni-maiko' (z. 6–8) has delicate leaves on fine branches, giving wonderful movement. The young leaves are fiery red, later pink, then greenish red. All shades appear on the plant at the same time, creating the effect of an Impressionist painting.

Acer palmatum var. dissectum 'Inaba-shidare' (z. 6–8) has large purple leaves with red stems. This is a strong-growing cultivar that retains its color throughout the season before turning red in the fall.

Hebe 'Amy'

Hebe 'Caledonia'

Cut back the flower spikes of the purple-leaved sage in summer, after the flowers fade, to encourage new growth. Plants can also be trimmed in late spring to promote bushiness. Ideally, plant as small, young plants in groups of three. If one fails, others will fill the space. (See Good Companions, pages 49, 83.)

The **hebes**, mostly originating from New Zealand, include some purple-leaved evergreens. (For cultivation of hebes, see page 76). *Hebe* '**Mrs. Winder**' ('**Waikiki**') (zone 8–10) is a popular hebe. A shrub of rounded habit, it grows to about 3ft. (1m). The small shiny, purple leaves combine well with the bright blue flowers in summer and fall. A robust hybrid, this hebe usually makes a good recovery if damaged by bad weather. Combine it

LOOKING AFTER HEBES

If you need to prune your hebes, to control their size or to promote bushiness, do so after the danger of severe frost has passed. Cut the branches back to a point where new green shoots are emerging. Cutting back hard into bare wood is risky, and there is no certainty that the plant will recover.

Larger-leaved hebes may suffer from leaf-spot diseases, particularly after mild, damp winters. Treat this by cutting back and treating the new growth, as it emerges, with a systemic fungicide.

with lavenders and gray-leaved subjects (see Good Companions, page 49).

Hebe '**Amy**' (zone 8–10) has long, large, oval, pointed leaves. Purple when young, they become dark green as they mature, but the whole plant always has a purple hue. On a sheltered site, winter color is good. The small, violet-purple bottlebrush flowers appear through summer into fall on upright stems, making a small rounded bush. Another reliable purple-leaved evergreen is *Hebe* '**Caledonia**' (zone 8–10), a dwarf, compact, rounded shrub with plum-tinted foliage and violet flowers from late spring into fall.

Hebe '**Pascal**' (zone 8–10) is a new variety, so may be hard to find. Compact and upright in habit, it has stunning, deep burgundy foliage in winter and spring, which becomes bronze-green in summer; it has mauve flowers in summer and early fall. *Hebe* '**Twisty**' (zone 8–10) has interesting upright branches and pointed purple leaves that spiral from the stem without stalks. The effect is reminiscent of the foliage of a purple monkey puzzle tree. (See also *Hebe* '**Red Edge**', page 76.)

Several *Hebe speciosa* cultivars (zone 9–10) have reddish purple new growth that turns dark green as it ages. *Hebe speciosa* '**La Séduisante**' is a small shrub with bottlebrush sprays of crimson flowers that accentuate the red color of the new leaves. It needs a sheltered wall or a position near the house; it is good for coastal gardens.

DECIDUOUS PURPLES

With their tough, thorny and resilient stems, **berberis** are very efficient at deterring intruders. However, their contribution is far greater than this. *Berberis thunbergii* f. *atropurpurea* '**Rose Glow**' (zone 4–8) makes a small bush with perfectly rounded, reddish purple, pink-splashed leaves. In shadier situations, they become a rich copper. The color intensifies as winter approaches. Plant it where the early sun shines through the leaves, transforming the erect stems into flaming wands. It is undemanding and thrives in any site. (See Good Companions, page 99.) The cultivar '**Harlequin**' is very similar to '**Rose Glow**', but has slightly smaller leaves and more pink mottling.

A very compact, dwarf cultivar, good for small gardens, is '**Atropurpurea Nana**' (zone 4–8). It is also useful in a rock garden and is excellent, although rarely used, as a dwarf hedge. (See Good Companions, opposite.) '**Bagatelle**' is an even more compact shrub.

The upright forms of purple berberis deserve to be more popular than they are. They are striking statement plants, excellent when planted to rise out of a mass of softer, lighter foliage. *Berberis thunbergii* f. *atropurpurea* '**Helmond Pillar**' (zone 4–8) grows to 6ft. (2m) and has rich purple foliage that turns a glowing red-orange in the fall. '**Red**

Berberis thunbergii f. *atropurpurea* '*Helmond Pillar*'

Berberis thunbergii f. atropurpurea 'Rose Glow'

Chief' is a smaller upright shrub, with bright red stems and narrow, red-purple leaves. It is not as columnlike, and its branches arch as the plant matures.

If space allows and you need a big, dramatic, purple-leaved shrub, *Berberis × ottawensis* f. *purpurea* 'Superba' ('Purpurea') (zone 5–7) is unbeatable, especially as a boundary plant. It produces vigorous, upright arching stems and superb wine purple foliage. Small yellow flowers are produced in spring, but are insignificant compared with the foliage. This is an excellent screening plant, and makes a good contrast to the solid form of the larger yellow conifers.

Cercis are normally regarded as small trees, usually growing on a single stem.

However, their stature is often more shrublike. Certainly, *Cercis canadensis* 'Forest Pansy' (zone 4–9) could not be regarded as vigorous. The pink flowers, which are produced on the dark, woody branches, are inconspicuous and secondary, while the leaves are truly glorious: heart-shaped and a rich reddish purple color, turning purple-gold in the fall. The growth habit is very attractive, with spreading branches forming a broad, funnel-shaped head. This plant has become more popular in recent years, as its ability to combine

successfully with other plants has been recognized (see Good Companions, below). It prefers a sunny position and requires good drainage.

The purple-leaf filbert, also known as hazel, *Corylus maxima* 'Purpurea' (zone 4–8) has large, rounded, heart-shaped leaves of a similarly intense color to that of the purple beech. If allowed to grow, it will make a large spreading shrub with reddish-brown catkins borne in early spring, and later carrying red-purple nuts with prominent calyces. Hard, selective pruning produces strong upright growth.

The leaves are carried at an attractive horizontal angle to the branches and, like beech, are particularly attractive

Corylus maxima 'Purpurea'

BERBERIS— NO HALF MEASURES

The larger berberis are not a pleasure to prune; good armor is required. They are, however, spoiled by half-hearted snipping, and cutting 2ft. (60cm) off the end of the branches just produces whippy shoots, way up in the air. Selective pruning of older branches, right to the base, is the only approach. If a stately specimen is too tall, it has been planted in the wrong position.

GOOD COMPANIONS

Consider *Berberis thunbergii* f. *atropurpurea* 'Atropurpurea Nana' (1) (z. 4–8) as an effective contrast to *Lavandula angustifolia* 'Hidcote' (2) (z. 5–9) in a formal scheme.

Cercis canadensis 'Forest Pansy' (3) (z. 4–9) is very striking when planted with *Cerinthe major* 'Purpurascens' (4) (z. 5–10), the blue honeywort.

when young with sunlight shining through them. It is an easy plant to grow and suits informal planting schemes with other shrubs such as buddleia, philadelphus, deutzia, and shrub roses.

The purple-leaved smoke bushes, **cotinus** (zone 4–8) are the deepest, darkest, and arguably most handsome of all shrubs. *Cotinus coggygria* **'Velvet Cloak'** is perhaps the finest. Its deep red purple leaves hold their color well into fall before they turn red. *Cotinus coggygria* **'Royal Purple'** is the best known, with deep wine purple leaves that redden toward fall (see Good Companions, page 142).

Smoke bushes are always late to break into leaf, but when they do, they steal the show. The rich mantle of leaves demands showy jewels to enhance its beauty. Burnt orange daylilies are the perfect adornment to the purple leaves (illus. pages 38–39).

Physocarpus opulifolius **'Diabolo'** (zone 2–7) associates well with herbaceous plants, evergreens, and roses. It is an ideal plant for an open, sunny position. In full sun, the foliage can be so dark that it is almost black. It is excellent as a background to shrub roses and provides structure in mixed plantings. (See Good Companions, opposite and page 113.) Hard pruning increases vigor and improves foliage. Prune early in the

Cotinus coggygria 'Royal Purple'

Sambucus nigra f. *porphyrophylla* 'Gerda'

season, while the plant is dormant, or after the flowers have faded, as with any of the deciduous flowering shrubs. Simply prune out the wood that has flowered, leaving the new, vigorous shoots to grow through.

Sambucus, or elder, responds to the same treatment. Purple-leaved elders (zone 5–7) have deservedly become very popular. *Sambucus nigra* **f. porphyrophylla 'Eva'** (formerly known as 'Black Lace'), a cultivar introduced in 2003, is less vigorous but has superb, finely cut foliage. This is an excellent plant for giving depth to herbaceous plantings: try it mixed with silver-leaved plants, herbaceous geraniums, and sweet peas. (See Good Companions, opposite.) *Sambucus nigra* **f. porphyrophylla 'Gerda'** (formerly known as 'Black Beauty'), makes a dramatic impact in any border and is fast growing if pruned hard in its first season. In subsequent years, it can be cut back hard toward the end of winter.

Viburnum sargentii **'Onondaga'** (zone 3–7), is a large, vigorous shrub similar to the guelder rose, *Viburnum opulus* (zone 3–8). New foliage is deep wine red, and the whole plant displays wonderful reddish-purple autumn color when it is grown in full sun. The flattened flower heads consist of individual fertile flowers that are red in

bud and open to reveal purple stamens. The sterile florets surrounding them stay white. Offset by the purple foliage at the end of the branches, this is a most striking combination (illus. page 147).

Viburnum sargentii **'Onondaga'** is a tall, upright shrub; poor pruning spoils this habit, and it is not a plant that responds well to control. If pruning is necessary, remove whole stems to ground level, after flowering. It grows well on any soil, including limestone, but needs an open, sunny position if it is to display good foliage color. This is a useful shrub for country gardens, where it mixes happily with native plants.

Weigela florida **'Foliis Purpureis'** (zone 5–9), is not the most intense of the red-leaved shrubs, the foliage being more brown-purple in hue. However, this color is no less useful in the garden, and there is the bonus of a mass of mauve-pink, funnel-shaped flowers in late spring and early summer. This combination of flower and foliage is most pleasing—unlike the pink and red blooms displayed by many golden-leaved shrubs. It is also more compact and slower-growing than most weigelas. To get the best from the foliage and flowers, provide a sunny aspect.

Weigela florida **'Wine and Roses'** (zone 5–9) is a recent cultivar with deep red-purple foliage that becomes bronze-green edged with purple as the season

---

COTINUS PRUNING TIPS

"Smoke bush", the common name for cotinus, comes from the purplish-gray inflorescences that, seen from a distance, resemble puffs of pink smoke. These are produced on two- to three-year-old wood, so if you want flowers, keep pruning to a minimum. Cotinus can be slow to get going, but hard pruning in the first year or two helps. Hard pruning also improves the size of the foliage. Do this in late winter, cutting stems back to two or three buds.

MORE PURPLE AND PLUM SHRUBS *Acer palmatum* 'Red Pygmy' • *Acer palmatum* 'Hessei' •
Berberis thunbergii f. *atropurpurea* 'Dart's Red Lady' • *Berberis thunbergii* f. *atropurpurea* 'Marshall Upright' •

progresses, turning deep purple in fall. The growth is dense and spreading; the flowers, borne in late spring and early summer, are reddish pink. Another attractive cultivar is *Weigela* 'Naomi Campbell' (zone 5–9), with deep chocolate foliage and bright red flowers in late spring and early summer—a striking combination that sits well in the garden with dark blue ceanothus.

Weigela florida 'Foliis Purpureis'

Cordyline australis 'Red Star'

Phormium 'Platt's Black'

Weigelas are easy shrubs to grow, and they thrive on alkaline and clay soils. Ideally, remove flowered shoots immediately after flowering to allow new, vigorous growth to come through.

SPIKY MIXERS

Phormiums with plum-colored foliage and rich red **cordylines** are dramatic creatures that make a strong statement in pots on the patio or in a courtyard, or rising from the border.

The red-leaved cordylines (zone 7–11) are less vigorous than the solid green *Cordyline australis* (see page 87), but they still make small trees in mild zones. Often seen as specimens gracing a terrace, they also suit both traditional and contemporary planting schemes. *Cordyline australis* 'Torbay Red' is a good form, with deep burgundy-red foliage and broad leaves. *Cordyline australis* 'Red Star' has bronze-red foliage. The red cordylines are not quite as hardy as the green ones, so winter protection is frequently needed.

The purple-leaved phormiums are surprisingly versatile plants, in spite of their exotic appearance. The broad, sword-shaped foliage of the larger varieties suit specimen planting in patio containers, in gravel, and as exclamation marks in the border, rising out of lower, softer planting to stunning effect.

Phormiums like good light and good drainage. The colored forms can suffer in winter, so some form of protection is advisable in areas with cold winters. They are excellent plants for coastal gardens. Plant phormiums near the front of the border, where they can rise above surrounding planting, their spiky forms bringing mixed plantings to life.

Phormium **'Platt's Black'** (zone 8–10) is one of the darkest foliage plants: it has narrow, arching, inky purple leaves of less than 3ft. (1m) long. *Phormium* **'Atropurpureum Compactum'** (zone 8–10) is larger, with broad, dark bronze-purple leaves, that point downward.

Phormium tenax **Purpureum Group** (zone 8–10) is a large plant, reaching 6ft. (2m). The bold leaves are bronze-purple and contrast superbly with both gray foliage and soft yellow grasses. This robust form reliably produces striking architectural spikes of bronze-red flowers once established.

GOOD COMPANIONS

The ebony foliage of *Physocarpus opulifolius* 'Diabolo' (1) (z. 2–7) is stunning with *Helichrysum italicum* 'Korma' (z. 8–10), against the silver of *Elaeagnus* 'Quicksilver' (2) (z. 3–9), or with the russet of the reflexed turk's caps of *Lilium henryi* (3) (z. 5–8).

For brilliant summer effect, let a shocking-pink everlasting pea, *Lathyrus latifolius* (4) (z. 4–7), clamber through. *Sambucus nigra* f. *porphyrophylla* 'Eva' (5) (z. 5–7).

55

Gold and silver variegated

Variegated plants occur only rarely in the wild; they are mostly a phenomenon of gardens. Whenever a variegated clone has arisen, its worth has been recognized by gardeners and nurserymen, who have propagated it and preserved it for ornamental use.

In the garden, shrubs with variegated leaves perform a function similar to that of flowering shrubs: they provide variety and they break up the solid green of most foliage. Whereas flowering shrubs provide limited, seasonal interest, the majority of important variegated shrubs are evergreen and therefore make a contribution all year round. They are useful to lighten shady areas, and many succeed in positions where flowering shrubs simply will not perform.

Light variegated shrubs such as *Cornus alternifolia* 'Argentea' brighten the planting.

HOW VARIEGATION OCCURS

Variegation occurs when certain areas of a leaf lack the green pigment chlorophyll. White patches are caused by a total absence of pigments; yellow variegation arises when pigments other than chlorophyll are present. Variegation is produced when there is a cell mutation; this usually happens when something goes wrong with the genetic information in the growing point of a shoot. All cells from the mutant cells then lack the green pigment chlorophyll in certain areas of the leaf. Chlorophyll is responsible for photosynthesis (food manufacture); without chlorophyll, there is a reduction in the plant's capacity to produce food and, consequently, a reduction in growth rate.

Some variegations are stable, and all resulting growth has the same variegation. In other cases, reversion occurs and the original green growth takes over (see box, page 63).

MIXING AND MATCHING

In the garden, remember that strong variegation introduces color and therefore attracts attention. Yellow variegations draw the eye; they are valuable for softening the effect of adjacent golden-leaved plants, as well as for providing a transition into green-leaved plants. Always consider what effect the color yellow has on flowering plants.

White variegations are softer and cooler than yellow variegations. They do not generally combine well with yellow variegations or with golden foliage, but are good with solid greens, which they soften and lighten. Some silver variegations work in association with gray-leaved plants.

Both yellow and white variegations provide a striking combination with purple foliage. All variegated evergreens extend the season of interest.

EVERGREEN VARIEGATED SHRUBS

The versatile qualities of the aucubas (zone 7–10) are extolled elsewhere in this book (see pages 35, 88). Excellent plants for shade and tolerant of any soil, they are among the most popular variegated evergreens in temperate zones. In some cases, the variegation is so strong that they produce a gold-leaved effect.

Aucuba japonica 'Crotonifolia' has large leaves boldly spotted and blotched with gold and has been regarded as the best golden-variegated aucuba. A female variety, it produces berries, but they are of secondary importance to the striking foliage. *Aucuba japonica* Marmorata' is an improvement on 'Crotonifolia', resistant to scorch in an open, sunny position. *Aucuba japonica* 'Golden King', a male form, is similar, but has an even more striking variegation. Plant this one in semi-shade, as it can scorch in full sun.

Buxus sempervirens 'Latifolia Maculata'

Variegated forms of common box, *Buxus sempervirens* (zone 6–9), are delightful structure plants. The tiny, variegated leaves lighten their solid shape and compact habit. *Buxus sempervirens* 'Elegantissima' is a slow-growing form that makes a dense, compact dome. Leaves are small and often misshapen,

Aucuba japonica 'Marmorata'

Buxus sempervirens 'Elegantissima'

Aucuba japonica 'Crotonifolia'

PLANTING PARTNERS

The unusual yellow marking of the variegated aucubas makes them good companions to other, more uniformly golden variegated shrubs, such as *Elaeagnus pungens* 'Maculata' (z. 6–9) and *Euonymus japonicus* 'Aureus' (z. 7–9). They also complement golden-foliage shrubs such as *Philadelphus coronarius* 'Aureus' (z. 4–8) and *Cornus alba* 'Aurea' (z. 2–8), that also enjoy semi-shade. See also page 96.

---

green with an irregular, creamy-white margin. This is considered the best "silver box," a brilliant specimen plant for making a statement, perhaps at the corner of a bed or to mark an entrance. The larger leaves of *Buxus sempervirens* 'Latifolia Maculata' are irregularly blotched dull yellow. The young growth in spring is particularly bright and attractive. Dense and compact, this shrub forms a large mound and can make an excellent hedge, clipped either formally or perhaps as an irregularly shaped "cloud hedge."

Coronilla valentina ssp. *glauca* 'Variegata' (zone 6–8) is a charming, small, variegated shrub for a sheltered spot. It is also an excellent plant for a sunroom. (Continued on page 60.)

Euonymus

Euonymus fortunei 'Emerald 'n' Gold' adds year-round color to a border.

"Euonymus" has become a household word because of the popularity of various *Euonymus fortunei* cultivars (zone 5–8), those dwarf, sprawling evergreens so widely used to bring foliage interest into seasonal planting and containers, both in gardens and in public landscaping. The evergreen euonymus have produced numerous variegated clones; in fact, in gardens it is rare to find a solid green variety. All euonymus are easy to grow and thrive on any soil.

Euonymus fortunei is a hardy trailing evergreen that grows as ground cover in sun or shade, with a habit similar to that of the English ivy. It has the ability to produce roots at intervals and has juvenile and adult stages. The various cultivars, nearly all variegated, show the characteristics of the species to varying degrees. Some have the ability to climb, if given encouragement; some are self-clinging. Most are grown as low shrubs and evergreen ground cover.

The popular *Euonymus fortunei* 'Emerald Gaiety' and *Euonymus fortunei* 'Emerald 'n' Gold' are small, compact, and bushy. 'Emerald Gaiety' is a hardy, versatile plant that mixes happily in just about any planting. It associates particularly well with hostas to provide winter structure and interest. 'Emerald 'n' Gold' is perhaps more vigorous than 'Emerald Gaiety' and climbs if supported. Its color is stronger, so it needs careful positioning but, being old gold, it does not shout as loudly as many yellow-variegated plants.

Euonymus japonicus (zone 7–9), Japanese spindle, from China and Japan, has given rise to many tough evergreen, variegated shrubs, ranging in size from small to large. Young plants are often grown in containers, for both indoor and outdoor use. These shrubs grow in any situation and tolerate pollution, shade, and coastal exposure. (See Planting Partners, page 57.)

Varieties of *Euonymus japonicus* 'Microphyllus' are small, dense, and compact shrubs, with much smaller leaves than other *Euonymus japonicus*. They serve as an alternative to box.

Some variegated euonymus have a tendency to revert (see box, page 63), including *Euonymus fortunei* 'Blondy', whose leaves, carried on slightly yellow stems, have a broad yellow blotch in the center. *Euonymus japonicus* 'Aureus' ('Aureopictus'), whose glossy leathery leaves have bright golden centers, tends on occasions to produce green and plain yellow shoots. 'Bravo' is a new cultivar, with more subtle, creamy variegation, and is less likely to revert. Cut out any reverted, plain shoots as they appear.

Euonymus fortunei 'Harlequin' is a best-seller—the name is attractive, the variegation is unusual (small, narrow, dark green leaves are heavily mottled white), and it looks good in a pot; but in the garden it is a weak plant and scorches in full sun so is not worth growing in a border.

See pages 170–71 for the deciduous euonymus, grown for the glorious color of their autumn foliage.

Euonymus fortunei
'Emerald Gaiety'
(z. 5–8) has small, dark
green leaves irregularly
edged with white and
often variegated with
paler green. They tinge
pink in winter, especially
on poor soil and in full
sun. Try it with hostas,
including a blue-leaved
variety, such as 'Blue
Wedgwood'.

Euonymus fortunei 'Silver Queen'
(z. 5–8) is a small, compact shrub, yet
has the potential to grow to 6ft. (2m)
or more against a wall. It has a glorious
variegation: the new leaves open
creamy-yellow and become dark green
with a broad, cream margin. A light,
bright, sophisticated plant, it is slow
to grow at first, but it is well worth
persevering with. In a shady spot it
associates well with *Viburnum tinus*
(z. 8–9).

Euonymus fortunei
'Emerald 'n' Gold'
(z. 5–8) has all the
attributes of 'Emerald
Gaiety' except that it
has gold-margined
leaves that turn
creamy gold, flushed
pink, in winter.

Euonymus japonicus 'Ovatus Aureus',
(z. 7–9) the most popular of the large-
leaved euonymus, has slower, more
compact growth than many. The growth
is upright, and the leaves are edged and
patterned with creamy yellow. It needs
a sunny, open position to retain its color
and variegation; in shade it can become
predominantly green.

Euonymus japonicus 'Chollipo' (z.
7–9) is an excellent large, dense shrub,
with upright growth. The leaves are
dark green and leathery, broadly edged
with yellow. *Euonymus japonicus*
'Latifolius Albomarginatus'
('Macrophyllus Albus') (z. 7–9) has
large dark green leaves with a broad
white edge.

Euonymus fortunei 'Moonshadow' (z. 5–8) is a great ground-cover plant, particularly
good on shady banks. Its long leaves are pale yellow, edged with green, making it an
excellent choice to underplant mahonia—for example, *Mahonia* × *media* 'Winter Sun'.

Elaeagnus × ebbingei 'Limelight'

Elaeagnus × ebbingei 'Gilt Edge'

The coronilla's long, arching stems are smothered in very small blue-green compound leaves, somewhat like those of *Ruta* (rue). These are so broadly margined with rich cream that the plant appears to be cream, flecked with green. The bright yellow, fragrant, vetchlike flowers appear in profusion in the first flush and then intermittently throughout the rest of the year. The harsh color of the flowers is somewhat softened by the cream of the foliage.

Unlike most of the variegated plants, *Elaeagnus × ebbingei* 'Limelight' (zone 7–11) is fast growing. It is a large shrub, with all the attributes of *Elaeagnus × ebbingei*. The new shoots are silvery brown, and the leaves are always green at first, with silvery scales. As they mature, they develop a broad central brushstroke of deep yellow and pale green. The leaves remain silver on the underside. This is one of the softer yellow-variegated evergreens, in both growth habit and color. It makes a big bold shrub, good for screening. It is able to keep pace with *Prunus laurocerasus*, *Photinia × fraseri* and other vigorous shrubs that are valuable for screening.

Elaeagnus × ebbingei 'Coastal Gold' (zone 7–11) has broad, wavy-edged leaves, silvery at first then pale yellow, edged and blotched with green.

Elaeagnus × ebbingei 'Gilt Edge' (zone 7–11) is less vigorous than 'Coastal Gold'. It is notable for its conspicuous leaves, which are attractively margined with golden yellow. It is less tolerant of exposure than other varieties, and grows best in semi-shade. In strong sunshine and on cold, exposed sites, the leaf edges can scorch.

Elaeagnus pungens 'Maculata' (zone 6–9) is one of the most popular variegated shrubs. It has a more spreading growth habit than *Elaeagnus × ebbingei*, with stiff horizontal branches that become spiny on mature plants. The dark green leaves have large, irregular splashes of bright gold—very striking. (See Good Companions, page 63.)

VARIEGATED ELAEAGNUS: A FEW TIPS

Cut out any reverted, solid green shoots as they appear; they are more vigorous than the variegated shoots, and in time will take over. Variegated elaeagnus are useful for lightening neighboring dark evergreen shrubs. All produce fragrant, small creamy flowers, which appear in fall. Beware: the strong variegation screams with pink- or red-flowering shrubs.

A large plant that is not often seen, despite its pleasing, subtle variegation, is *Elaeagnus pungens* 'Goldrim' (zone 6–9). This is a sport of 'Maculata' and has glossy, deep green leaves that are narrowly margined with bright yellow. For smaller gardens, the more compact *Elaeagnus pungens* 'Frederici' (zone 6–9) is a very good choice. Its narrow leaves of creamy yellow have an irregular green border; this is an attractive variegation, in soft, pleasing colors.

Fatsia japonica 'Variegata'

Variegated sports of the small-leaved hebes make popular impulse-buys in garden centers. Their neat, colorful foliage looks good in a container, and is strikingly different from anything else available. However, their long-term performance in the garden is yet to be proved. Some dislike high temperatures and very dry conditions, so they can be casualties in hot summers.

Hard to come by but one of the best varieties, *Hebe* 'Pink Elephant' (zone 8–10) is a compact and hardy sport of 'Red Edge'. The leaves are edged with creamy yellow and tipped pink; the color darkens to burgundy in winter. 'Sweet Kim' (zone 8–10) is similar, but perhaps not as robust. *Hebe* 'Dazzler' (zone 8–10) has slender, purplish shoots and leaves edged cream and pink. If you are lucky, you may find the new *Hebe* 'Heartbreaker' (zone 8–10), more upright and robust than *Hebe* 'Dazzler'.

The novelty variegated hebes are good plants for patio containers and can suit contemporary schemes, but they usually look out of place in a more traditional planting scheme.

Fatsia japonica 'Variegata' (zone 8–9) is one of only a few large-leaved variegated evergreens. The variegation is subtle: grayish green, handlike leaves are tipped with creamy white. It is not as large, or as vigorous, as the plain green *Fatsia japonica* (see page 36), and not quite as hardy. A good courtyard plant and a superb specimen for a pot, it suits sheltered shade. It is worth protecting in severe winter weather; this helps to prevent the growth tips from being damaged by frost.

Griselinias (zone 8–9) offer an unusual foliage form; the rounded leaves stand out well against other green or variegated shrubs. They are a useful choice where a tall, loosely upright variegated shrub is needed. They are excellent coastal plants.

Griselinia littoralis 'Variegata' has rounded, apple green leaves, boldly marked with creamy white. It combines well with the cherry laurel and is a good screening plant. *Griselinia littoralis* 'Bantry Bay' has even more striking leaves, splashed and marked creamy white over a larger area. It is a sport of 'Variegata'; similar in habit, it is much slower growing because of the amount of variegation. (See also page 33.)

Variegated hebes may not be the hardiest of small evergreen shrubs, but they are worth trying in a sheltered spot in areas such as the Pacific Northwest. *Hebe × franciscana* 'Variegata' (zone 7–11) can be used as a bedding plant instead of as a garden shrub. In Europe, they are mass-produced each year to bring foliage interest to containers. The deep mauve of the flowers contrasts well with the elliptical, white-edged leaves. A good plant in coastal gardens, elsewhere it is useful for containers and sheltered window boxes.

Ilex

The hollies boast more good variegated forms than any other type of plant. Whether you require silver or gold variegation, holly is an obvious port of call. The disadvantage of the hollies, if there is one, is their slow growth at an early age and their ungainly habit as young plants. On the other hand, they are permanent, long-lived garden residents that do not decline with age.

The foliage of variegated hollies contributes so much to the garden throughout the year that fruiting is of secondary importance. When choosing your holly, remember: if the name sounds masculine, the holly is probably female, that is, it fruits. One exception is the old, creamy-white variegated variety, *Ilex aquifolium* 'Silver Milkmaid' (zone 6–9), which is female.

Hollies are easy to grow and succeed on just about any soil. Well-prepared soil and watering during establishment will pay dividends in getting them through the slower early stages of growth.

All variegated hollies have a tendency to revert (see box, page 63), especially when young. Cut out any plain green shoots; they are more vigorous than the variegated shoots and, if left, take over.

Hollies suit both town and country gardens and can be used in formal and informal planting. It is worth planting them alongside a faster-growing partner, one that will fill the role in the early years and can be removed as the holly matures—perhaps an evergreen ceanothus or rhamnus.

Ilex × altaclerensis 'Golden King' (left) (z. 6–9) is a vigorous holly that matures to a broad, formal cone. It has broad, almost spineless leaves, with a wide gold margin. A female, it berries well in the presence of a male pollinator; the fruit is red-brown. This is regarded as the best gold-variegated holly. 'Lawsoniana' is 'Golden King' in reverse: the broad green leaves are splashed golden yellow in the center. It berries well, with red-brown fruits.

The silver hedgehog holly, *Ilex aquifolium* 'Ferox Argentea' (z. 6–9), boasts sweeping purple twigs and dark green leaves variegated creamy white. Spines edge the leaves and cover the leaf surface. More lax than many hollies, it is useful in mixed planting, where its light color and habit bring evergreen interest.

Ilex aquifolium 'Handsworth New Silver' (z. 6–9) is an upright, stately shrub, with purple stems and delightful silver-variegated foliage. The leaves are narrow, dark green, mottled gray and edged creamy white. A female clone, it produces, in a good year, masses of bright red berries. 'Silver Queen' has similar variegation but broader leaves. The young shoots are black-purple, the new leaves shrimp pink; it does not fruit.

Ilex aquifolium 'Madame Briot' (z. 6–9) is an excellent variety, with purple stems and well-spaced spiny leaves, dark green mottled yellow. A female clone, it produces plenty of scarlet fruit.

REVERSION

Most variegated plants have a tendency to produce plain green shoots. These naturally have more chlorophyll and a greater capacity to produce food, therefore they grow more vigorously. Left on the plant, they will eventually take over and smother the variegated plant. Cut out any plain green shoots as they appear, right back to the point where they emerge from the main stem. The earlier this is done in their development, the better. In the case of some variegated plants, such as *Elaeagnus pungens* 'Maculata' (right, z. 6–9), this will probably have to be done regularly throughout the life of the plant.

The variegated form of **Chinese privet** is very different from the familiar privet used for hedging. *Ligustrum lucidum* 'Excelsum Superbum' (zone 7–10) is a very large shrub or small tree with big, bright green leaves marked with paler green and edged with greenish-yellow. Unrestricted, it has a superb, broadly conical habit. Large sprays of fragrant flowers appear in fall. This is an elegant shrub, superb as a specimen, and ideal to lighten heavy laurels and conifers planted for screening.

Luma apiculata (zone 9–10), which was previously known as *Myrtus luma*, is a beautiful evergreen shrub, or small tree, from Chile. The bark is a feature of mature specimens: the cinnamon-colored outer layers peel away to reveal cream bark beneath. The leaves are dark green and pointed, and the flowers are white, in late summer and fall. The attractive variegated *Luma apiculata* 'Glanleam Gold' is more compact. The leaves are smaller and the habit denser. The leaves have a creamy white margin and are tinged red when young, especially at the end of the shoots. This evergreen mixes well with low herbaceous planting. (See Good Companions, right.) It is also good in a pot on a sunny patio.

The variegated **osmanthus** (zone 6–9) are good alternatives to holly for small gardens and are fine variegated evergreens in themselves. *Osmanthus heterophyllus* 'Variegatus' is the best. Small, dark green, hollylike leaves are edged bright creamy white. A neat, compact plant, it is easy to grow in almost any soil and site. (See Good Companions, page 65.) *Osmanthus heterophyllus* 'Aureomarginatus' is similar, but has leaf margins of deep yellow. The growth is never as good; there are better gold-variegated evergreens. Because it has the overall appearance of a soft golden shrub, the best-known osmanthus, *Osmanthus heterophyllus* 'Goshiki', is included in the golden-foliage shrubs (see page 43).

Photinia davidiana 'Palette' (zone 6–8), also called *Stranvaesia davidiana* 'Palette', is a slow-growing shrub with thin foliage. It is intensely variegated, the leaves being blotched and streaked with cream and pink when young. A novelty, it attracts attention in the garden center when presented in a pot. In the garden, however, it is a poor plant and never earns its keep. Its appeal lies in the unreal coloring of its foliage.

The variegated **pieris** (zone 5–8) are some of our most delightful variegated shrubs, but are confined to gardens on acid soil if they are to be grown in the open ground. They are, however, wonderful subjects for pots, as long as they are grown in nonalkaline, loam-based, potting mix. They enjoy a position out of full sun, so are good for a shady terrace. The pieris are described more fully in the section on acid-loving plants, page 109, but the two best cultivars for variegated foliage are *Pieris japonica* 'White Rim', also grown as 'Variegata', and *Pieris japonica* 'Little Heath'. Both are excellent silver-variegated plants but

GOOD COMPANIONS

Underplant *Elaeagnus pungens* 'Maculata' (1) (z. 6–9) with a carpet of golden creeping Jenny, *Lysimachia nummularia* 'Aurea' (2) (z. 5–7).

Luma apiculata 'Glanleam Gold' (3) (z. 9–10) goes well with *Rosmarinus officinalis* 'Severn Sea' (4) (z. 8–10) and *Thymus* 'Doone Valley' (5) (z. 5–8).

Pieris japonica 'Little Heath'

Pittosporum tenuifolium 'Irene Paterson'

Pieris japonica 'Little Heath' (zone 5–8) is unusual, having smaller, neater foliage and pinkish leaf and flower buds.

Pittosporums provide us with some lovely light-variegated shrubs, although they can be very hard to find. Good structure plants, they grow quickly, giving height without robbing much space. *Pittosporum* 'Garnettii' (*Pittosporum tenuifolium* 'Garnettii') (zone 9–10) is the easiest to grow. It quickly makes a large, broad, conical shrub, but responds to light clipping if needed (illus. page 28). Its gray-green leaves are margined creamy-white, often spotted pink in winter; they look especially pretty when the tiny chocolate flowers appear on the branches in spring. This is a must for the flower arranger's garden, and sits well in either town or country.

Pittosporum tenuifolium (zone 9–10) has such small, neat foliage that the variegated forms give the impression of having silver or lime foliage, rather than being distinctly variegated. They are some of the prettiest variegated shrubs; hence their popularity.

Pittosporum tenuifolium 'Gold Star' has yellow-green leaves edged with dark green, and there is a prominent white midrib on the older leaves. The shrub is compact and upright and is an excellent structure plant. It is a good choice when a softer variegation is required. *Pittosporum tenuifolium* 'Eila Keightley' and 'Abbotsbury Gold' share the same blotched greenish yellow foliage. The former shows the variegation more distinctly on the older foliage. The overall effect is yellow-green, so it is a useful neighbor for lightening up dark evergreens and for softening the bright variegation of plants such as *Elaeagnus pungens* 'Maculata'. *Pittosporum tenuifolium* 'Irene Paterson' is slow-growing because of the amount of variegation in its foliage. The young leaves are creamy white, becoming marbled in green and white as they mature. This is a very attractive shrub, and it always stands out in any planting scheme.

Pittosporum tenuifolium 'Silver Queen' has small, neat foliage of silver gray green, edged with white. The leaves are less crinkled than those of many varieties; the habit is neat and compact. More solid is *Pittosporum tobira* 'Variegatum' (zone 8–10), with whorls of round-ended leaves that are shiny gray-green, irregularly edged with creamy white. It is not the hardiest of plants, but is happy in a sheltered position in the milder zones. The flowers, in clusters at the end of the branches, are more conspicuous than on many pittosporums. They open white, turn yellow with age, and are deliciously fragrant. A rounded, slow-growing shrub, this pittosporum is good at the base of a warm wall.

Prunus laurocerasus 'Marbled White' (zone 6–8), originally grown as 'Variegata' and sometimes called 'Castlewellan', is an evergreen with gray-green leaves, heavily marbled white. It is slow-growing but eventually makes a large, dense bush. The habit is more open when the plant is grown in shade. It combines well with, and is an interesting alternative to, white-variegated

Pittosporum tenuifolium 'Silver Queen'

Rhamnus alaternus 'Argenteovariegata'

Rhododendron ponticum 'Variegatum' ('Silver Edge')

shrubs, such as *Pittosporum* 'Garnettii' (zone 9–10) and *Cornus alba* 'Elegantissima' (zone 2–8). It perfectly partners the latter's red winter stems.

The variegated form of Portuguese laurel, *Prunus lusitanica* 'Variegata' (zone 7–9) is not a vigorous plant, but it can be a most attractive addition to evergreen planting under the dappled shade of lighter trees. It has the attractive red leaf stalks of the species, and has horizontal branching, from which the white-margined leaves hang elegantly. It is good on all soils. (See Good Companions, below right.)

Also easy to grow on any soil and succeeding in sun or shade, *Rhamnus alaternus* 'Argenteovariegata' (zone 8–9) is fast-growing and an excellent choice where a tall but light subject is needed. It is more susceptible to cold than some evergreens and traditionally has been grown against a wall. In milder zones, it has ventured out into the open garden, but it is not good on exposed sites. Frost and cold winds may cause it to shed its leaves, but it usually recovers. To be on the safe side, a rhamnus should be firmly staked throughout its life. It can become top-heavy in maturity and is then a likely casualty in winter gales.

The growth habit is upright and sweeping. The individual leaves are margined cream and marbled with shades of gray and green, giving a pale silver-green effect overall. If a plain green shoot appears, cut it out. Mature specimens become bare at the base, so underplant with a companion, perhaps *Choisya ternata* (zone 8–10) or *Fatsia japonica* (zone 8–9).

Rhododendrons are subjects for the section that features plants for acid soils, pages 101–105. However, some of the variegated forms of hybrid rhododendron are such excellent foliage plants they deserve a mention here. Yes, they need ericaceous soil, but so long as they are grown in lime-free, loam-based mix, they are also excellent subjects for pots.

Rhododendron 'Goldflimmer' (zone 5–8) is one of the best. A variegated form of *Rhododendron ponticum*, it is a compact, slow-growing shrub. The leaves are dark green, with irregular streaks of yellow around the edge. The flowers are lilac, marked with brown spots, and appear later in the rhododendron season.

Sometimes seen for sale under the name 'Silver Edge', *Rhododendron ponticum* 'Variegatum' (zone 5–8) has leaves margined with creamy white.

GOOD COMPANIONS

A good pairing for a container is *Osmanthus heterophyllus* 'Variegatus' (1) (z. 6–9) and the silver gray and cream variegated ivy *Hedera helix* 'Glacier' (2) (z. 4–9).

The pink tinge in winter on the leaves of *Prunus lusitanica* 'Variegata' (3) (z. 7–9) makes it a wonderful partner for the dark foliage and pink buds of *Viburnum tinus* (4) (z. 8–9).

Viburnum tinus 'Variegatum'

character, it reaches 3ft. (1m) in height. *Phormium* 'Carousel' has bronze green foliage, with attractive red margins, while *Phormium tenax* 'Variegatum' has similar leaves but is a much larger-growing variety of phormium. The leaves of *Phormium* 'Sundowner' are up to 5ft. (1.5m) long, bronze-green with deep pink margins. *Phormium* 'Maori Chief' is slightly less hardy, but has striking upright leaves of scarlet, crimson, and bronze.

Viburnum tinus 'Variegatum' (zone 8–9) is much less vigorous and weather-resistant than the solid green forms. The leaves are variegated in creamy yellow, and are particularly attractive as a background for the pinkish buds and white flowers. It generally prefers a reasonably sheltered site and semi-shade. In strong sun, the leaf edges may brown, and it struggles on a cold, exposed site.

SPIKY VARIEGATIONS

The leaves of **cordyline** and **phormium** introduce a different and dramatic form to the garden, an exciting contrast to the rounded shapes of most plants. Both species like sunshine and good drainage. They are excellent subjects for planting in gravel and growing in pots, but can look out of place in a traditional scheme. (See also pages 55, 87, 124–25.)

With its creamy-white striped leaves, *Cordyline australis* 'Torbay Dazzler' (zone 7–11) is best on a warm patio. It is not as vigorous as the green form.

The **phormiums** (zone 8–10) have some of the most exotic foliage of any garden plant. They also introduce pink, red, and orange variegations—rarely seen elsewhere. As a rule, the flamboyantly colored forms are less hardy than the more subtle ones.

Phormium 'Yellow Wave' is the most reliable yellow variety. With yellow-green striped leaves of drooping

Cordyline australis 'Torbay Dazzler'

Phormium 'Yellow Wave'

VARIEGATED SEMI-EVERGREEN AND DECIDUOUS SHRUBS

The forms of *Abelia* × *grandiflora* (zone 6–9) are semi-evergreen shrubs popular for their late-summer and autumn flowers; some are variegated. *Abelia* × *grandiflora* 'Francis Mason' has small, shiny, dark green leaves with a yellow margin. However, the variegation is not distinct unless the plant is grown in full sun on dry soil. The new variety, *Abelia* × *grandiflora* 'Hopleys', has a more prominent variegation; and in the fall its leaves flush pink, picking up the pink of the flowers. The best-known of the variegated abelias, however, is *Abelia* × *grandiflora* 'Confetti'. This is a much smaller shrub than the others, with light, arching growth and leaves margined white. It is a very pretty plant, but, unfortunately, not robust.

Even at the best of times, the young foliage of the Japanese maples is at risk from scorch by strong winds and bright sunlight; and the variegated forms are especially vulnerable. The variegated forms of *Acer palmatum* (zone 6–8) are some of the most delicate of variegated plants. A few are worthy garden plants; others are only for the enthusiast. *Acer palmatum* 'Kagiri-nishiki' ('Roseo-marginatum') is one of the easiest. Reasonable vigor and a light, arching habit are in its favor. The lobed leaves are often somewhat distorted, pale green, and irregularly variegated with white and coral pink—very pretty. It tends to revert, and any plain green shoots should be cut out.

Acer palmatum 'Asahi-zuru' is also vigorous by palmatum standards. It is a spreading shrub, with white-blotched leaves, sometimes all white or pink when young. It is regarded as one of the most stable variegated Japanese maples.

The variegated forms of the box elder, *Acer negundo* 'Flamingo' (zone

2–9), have long been grown as shrubs, as well as small trees. The light, variegated foliage of *Acer negundo* 'Variegatum' (zone 2–9) was prized as a pot plant, and often grown by municipal parks departments for indoor decoration. *Acer negundo* 'Flamingo' has pretty, pale green foliage edged with soft pink, changing to white. It is a very appealing plant at the stage when it is offered for sale, but disappoints in the garden, as it stretches upward to form a leggy shrub with poor leaf color. The secret of success is hard pruning in early spring, back to one or more short stems. This annual pollarding results in vigorous growth and good leaf color.

The variegated *Buddleia davidii* 'Harlequin' (zone 5–9) is striking, even as a young shrub in a pot. The long green leaves are boldly variegated with creamy white, in strong contrast to the reddish purple flowers. The habit is low and arching. The plant is not nearly as vigorous as most buddleias. *Buddleia davidii* 'Santana' (zone 5–9) is similar, with yellow-variegated foliage and wine red flowers. Both are sports of 'Royal Red' and tend to revert. There are other variegated buddleias, but these are the best. All buddleias are valuable for their summer flowers, attractive to butterflies (see also pages 74, 148–49, 163).

Buddleias are best hard pruned in February, to promote vigorous growth and prolific flowering. The variegated forms need lighter pruning: cut back by half rather than two-thirds.

An excellent foliage plant with large heart-shaped leaves, *Clerodendrum trichotomum* 'Carnival' (zone 6–9) is at its best in late summer and fall. The leaves are blue-green, mottled gray-green, with a broad and striking cream margin. From August on, clusters of fragrant white flowers emerge from pretty pink calyxes and are carried in graceful clusters. It makes a horizontally branched shrub up to 3ft. (1m) in

Acer palmatum 'Kagiri-nishiki'

Acer negundo 'Flamingo'

Clerodendrum trichotomum 'Carnival'

Cornus alba 'Elegantissima'

height. The leaves are very slow to open in late spring; the plant needs a warm, sunny position to thrive. When touched, the foliage smells of rubber. It is resistant to rabbits and deer.

The variegated forms of *Cornus alba* (zone 2–8) are all-year-round shrubs, with colorful winter stems and interesting foliage in summer (see pages 177–78).

Cornus alba 'Elegantissima' is one of the brightest and whitest of evergreen shrubs. It is a vigorous plant and, if left unpruned, forms a large flowing mound up to 10ft. (3m) high. The leaves are green in the center, mottled and broadly margined with white. One of the best variegated plants for damp sites, it succeeds in sun or shade. For small gardens, choose *Cornus alba* 'Sibirica Variegata', smaller-growing and less vigorous than 'Elegantissima'. It is similar in foliage but often has pinkish leaf tints, particularly in the fall. (See Good Companions, pages 69, 184.)

Cornus alba 'Spaethii' offers a golden yellow variegation. 'Gouchaultii' is similar, but often has orange-red tints. *Cornus sericea* 'Silver and Gold' (zone 2–8) is similar in foliage coloring to *Cornus alba* 'Elegantissima', but has pleasing yellow stems.

Cornus mas (zone 4–8), the cornelian cherry, is a large, densely branched shrub. It is a delight in early spring when small yellow, pom-pom flowers appear all over the bare branches. Although long cultivated, this shrub is too large and has too short a

---

TRIED AND TESTED

The variegated forms of shrubs described here have all proved themselves as reliable plants. Many more are available, and gardeners may be tempted by new arrivals. Beware of novelties, however. The tried and tested variegated shrub is likely to be the more reliable choice.

---

season of interest for most gardens. However, the variegated form, *Cornus mas* 'Variegata' (zone 4–8), is a superb plant, and one of the best variegated shrubs. It is much less vigorous than the species, with an open, light branch structure and broad, pointed white-margined leaves. In the fall, as well as good leaf color, it has scarlet cherrylike fruits.

Cornus controversa 'Variegata' (zone 5–8) is really a small tree, and is certainly a plant for specimen planting. It is one of the most magnificent of variegated hardy plants, with its horizontal tiered branching and hanging silver-white variegated leaves. A mature specimen, well grown, is a splendid sight. In the early stages of growth it is worth staking and training the leader, to encourage the plant to gain height. It should never be pruned to change its shape; allow it to develop naturally.

Cornus alternifolia 'Argentea' (zone 3–7), the pagoda dogwood, is one of the most beautiful silver-variegated shrubs. Fine, light horizontal branches of dark wood carry a froth of small, creamy-white margined leaves. Seen from a distance, a mature shrub seems to sit like a white cloud in the border. If grown with a single stem, it makes a superb subject for the oriental garden; as a multistemmed shrub, it is outstanding as a specimen or for mixed planting. Growing to 10ft. (3m) tall, *Cornus alternifolia* is a hardy native plant and is tougher and easier to grow than its appearance suggests.

A low, spreading shrub, *Cotoneaster atropurpureus* 'Variegatus' (zone 6–8) (also known as *Cotoneaster horizontalis* 'Variegatus') does not have such a bold herringbone branch structure as *Cotoneaster horizontalis*. It is also less vigorous. The tiny dark green leaves are margined with cream and become tinged with red in fall, making a delightful display with the red berries. (See Good Companions, right.)

Fuchsia is associated with seasonal planting, being one of the most popular bedding plants. In milder locations, fuchsias are favorite garden shrubs, thriving in sun or shade, flowering from early summer through fall. Their graceful habit, light foliage, and pendent flowers make them versatile plants that combine well with other shrubs and herbaceous plants (see page 153).

A well-known fuchsia is *Fuchsia magellanica* (zone 6–9). It has slender, arching growth and delicate, red-and-purple hanging flowers. *Fuchsia magellanica* var. *gracilis* 'Variegata' is the

best of the variegated fuchsias. Its green leaves, edged with creamy yellow and flushed pink, make a pleasing combination with the flowers. Although it is less hardy than the green form, it is still a good shrub for a sheltered location. *Fuchsia magellanica* var. *gracilis* 'Tricolor' ('Tricolor') is more spreading and smaller. The little leaves are gray-green, tinged pink when young and becoming white-edged as they mature. The ends of the shoots retain a pink flush throughout the season. The flowers are red-and-purple, perhaps smaller than those of the species. More tender than all these cultivars, *Fuchsia magellanica* var. *molinae* 'Sharpitor' has white flowers and gray-green leaves margined white. It is a pretty plant and a good choice for mild areas.

Fuchsia 'Tom West' Meillez (zone 7–9) is a superb foliage plant. More tender than *Fuchsia magellanica*, it is often grown as a patio subject. The young leaves are bronze, edged dark pink, becoming blue-green with pink edges.

Cornus controversa 'Variegata'

MORE GOLD AND SILVER VARIEGATED SHRUBS *Acer palmatum* 'Butterfly' • *Acer campestre* 'Carnival' • *Aralia elata* 'Variegata' • *Azara microphylla* 'Variegata' • *Ceanothus* 'Diamond Heights' • *Elaeagnus pungens* 'Maculata' •

Fuchsia 'Tom West' Meillez

The shoots are reddish purple, and the flowers are red and purple. *Fuchsia* 'Sunray' (zone 7–9) is a small bushy shrub, with pale green and cream leaves, edged and flushed with red. It has red-and-mauve flowers. This is a good choice for a small garden or patio.

Hydrangea macrophylla 'Tricolor' (zone 6–9) is among the best of the variegated hydrangeas. A lacecap hydrangea, it has pale-pink flowers, turning to white. The leaves are green, variegated with gray and pale yellow.

Hypericum × moserianum 'Tricolor' (zone 5–7) has great appeal and looks good in a pot. In the garden, it often disappoints as it can be badly affected by cold and disease. It is a dwarf shrub with arching stems and classic, golden-yellow hypericum flowers of good size. The leaves are prettily mottled with pink, white, and pale green. It needs a sheltered site and can be prone to rust in a damp season. Prune back hard in early spring to promote vigorous new growth.

The variegated form of the mock orange, *Philadelphus coronarius* 'Variegatus' (zone 4–8) has leaves variegated creamy white, and the same creamy white, sweetly scented flowers as the species: single and beautiful. Although *Philadelphus coronarius* is excellent on very dry soil, the variegated form can develop brown leaf tips and margins when grown on dry soil in full sun. It is better in light shade, where the foliage will stand out against a dark background and the delicious scent can

permeate the garden. *Philadelphus* 'Innocence' (zone 5–7) is a single, free-flowering variety, with pretty arching growth and creamy white variegated leaves. This is a lovely, light shrub.

Philadelphus coronarius 'Variegatus'

Weigela florida 'Variegata' (zone 5–9) is one of the best variegated shrubs. The growth habit is compact, leaves soft green edged creamy white. The pink flowers look lovely against the pale color of the leaves. This is a very easy shrub to cultivate and it associates well with other plants in the garden—for example, roses and perennials, particularly herbaceous geraniums. (See Good Companions, below.)

Weigela 'Argenteo marginata' (zone 5–9) is similar but a little more upright. The leaves turn to shades of pink and red in the fall, adding another season of interest.

Prune both varieties lightly after flowering to remove some stems that have flowered. This encourages new growth from the base. Do not trim to shape, as this spoils the plant by taking away its natural lightness and grace.

GOOD COMPANIONS

The pink tints in the foliage of *Cornus alba* 'Sibirica Variegata' (1) (z. 2–8) complement the purple foliage of *Berberis thunbergii* f. *atropurpurea* 'Rose Glow' (2) (z. 4–8).

The salmon-red flowers of *Schizostylis coccinea* (3) (z. 6–8) work well with the autumn berries of *Cotoneaster atropurpureus* 'Variegatus' (4) (z. 5–7) grown against a wall.

Extend the flowering season of *Weigela* 'Florida Variegata' (5) (z. 5–9) by letting *Clematis* 'Purpurea Plena Elegans' (6) (z. 4–9) scramble through it.

Euonymus fortunei 'Silver Tip' • × *Fatshedera lizei* 'Annemieke' • *Lavandula* 'Goldburg' • *Leucothoe fontanesiana* 'Rainbow' • *Salvia officinalis* 'Icterina' • *Sambucus nigra* 'Madonna' •

Silver and gray

Those who garden on sand or thin, alkaline soil truly appreciate gray- and silver-leaved plants such as santolina and lavender. Hailing from Mediterranean regions, they are naturally drought-resistant and remarkably tolerant of sunny sites, where many plants just shrivel up and die. Gardeners on heavier, clay soils find that these plants do not like soggy winter weather.

Silver-leaved plants are good mixers with any color scheme.

The value of the silver- or gray-leaved shrubs is indisputable: their foliage is the perfect foil for almost any other color in the garden. They naturally associate well with plants from similar hot, dry, sunny climates, such as cistus, helianthemum, rosemary, salvia, thyme and many others (see pages 82–87). They are usually tough and thrive on poor, well-drained soil in full sun.

Silver foliage is an adaptation to environment, a means of conserving water and reducing its loss. The woolly covering of pale fibers over the foliage creates a microclimate around the leaf surface, reducing air movement and slowing evaporation of water. In some cases, this woolly coating disappears from the upper surface as the leaf matures and the leaf then reveals more of its underlying green color. This allows more light to reach the surface for photosynthesis, the means by which the plant makes its food. However, the underside stays protected, keeping its silver appearance. As an added means of reducing water loss, many silver-foliage plants have reduced the size of their leaves: a leaf that is narrow or finely cut loses less water than one with a large surface. Edges that curl under protect the underside of the leaf from excessive water loss.

Silver-leaved plants are frequently aromatic; the presence of oil in the foliage helps to prevent desiccation by strong sun and drying winds. The oil also protects the plant by repelling animals and insect pests, and its smell, combined with the felty nature of the leaves, appears to be unattractive to deer and rabbits.

Acacia baileyana 'Purpurea' (zone 9–10) is a lovely form of the Cootamundra wattle. Often considered a sunroom plant, it can be grown outside in warm zones. The finely cut, fernlike foliage is blue-gray and the new shoots a deep purple—a wonderful contrast. The bright yellow flowers in spring are of secondary importance and lack the subtlety of the soft, delicate foliage. This is a good shrub to grow against a wall. Being light and leggy in habit, it is also very useful for providing height among the low-growing mounds of other gray-leaved plants—for example, santolinas and lavenders.

CARING FOR SILVER-LEAVED PLANTS

On heavy soils, add plenty of sharp grit at the time of planting to improve drainage. Mulch with a generous layer of gravel or sharp grit to prevent rain from splashing soil onto the foliage.

Before winter, make sure you remove any leaves that have fallen from surrounding deciduous plants. These can easily lodge on the felty foliage of silver subjects, holding the wet and causing damage during the damp months.

Most silver-leaved plants are short-lived. Once they become old and fail to perform, replace them with new stock. Fortunately, they are quick to establish and grow to maturity.

Acacia baileyana 'Purpurea'

Artemisia abrotanum (zone 5–8) (southern wormwood, southernwood) has been in cultivation for centuries, the original attraction being its aromatic leaves. One of the many herbaceous and woody artemisias, it is easy to grow and quickly makes a small upright shrub with gray-green downy leaves. Grayish flower buds appear at the end of the stems in summer; these are best trimmed off to preserve the foliage and to prevent the shrub from opening up under the weight of the foliage when wet. In garden centers, it is often found with the herbs, rather than the shrubs.

Artemisia 'Powis Castle' (zone 6–9) is a well-known and widely grown artemisia. The foliage is deeply cut and feathery, the habit compact when young, becoming sprawling. It makes good ground cover, and when planted on top of a wall it cascades over the

Artemisia 'Powis Castle'

edge. This artemisia likes full sun and well-drained soil and dislikes wet, cold sites and heavy soil; on clay, add lots of grit when planting to improve drainage.

Artemisia 'Powis Castle' does not respond well to hard pruning; cut back the stems only to where new growth buds are clearly visible. Sometimes it will sprout from the base, but it rarely breaks from bare wood. Watch out for blackfly, which are particularly attracted to the new growth. Be careful which insecticide you use, as some gray-leaved plants are sensitive to certain chemicals.

MIXING AND MATCHING

Silver plant material has a wonderfully fragile quality when used en masse. It suggests sunny days and hot countries, but is also perfect in the light of cooler climes. It is ideal for softening paving, walling, and hard landscape materials, and works well in pots, tubs, and other containers.

Silver-gray foliage adds color and texture to the garden. It can be used as an addition to foliage of other colors, or as the predominant foliage. Silver reflects the light of open spaces, and its soft hue complements solid structure. Gray-foliage shrubs work well in plantings of sun-loving herbaceous perennials.

Most gray-leaved plants suit seaside situations and cope with salt winds. In the high light levels, the blueness of the gray works wonderfully with bright orange eschscholzia and the neon shades of mesembryanthemum.

Silver-leaved planting in Derek Jarman's coastal garden, in Dungeness, Kent, England.

Silver-gray is the perfect partner for blue, looks soft and pretty with pink, sparkles with lavender, and is positively regal with purple. It also has an affinity with dark red, especially the large, bold blooms of peonies and poppies. Silver foliage provides the perfect setting for gems such as amethyst alliums and sapphire brodiaea.

Be careful when juxtaposing silver with other foliage. Silver-gray shrubs with large leaves can look fine with heavy evergreens, but those with more delicate foliage can be overpowered by them and need to be combined with less solid plants.

Silver is happier in association with white variegation than it is with yellow. While gray is not a natural partner for golden foliage, it contrasts stunningly with plum-purple shades. Silver *Elaeagnus* 'Quicksilver' (z. 3–9) planted with *Physocarpus opulifolius* 'Diabolo' (z. 2–7), for example, is a striking combination that works on its own or can be built into mixed plantings (see Good Companions, page 55).

Lavenders

The lavenders are among our most popular garden plants. They are evergreen, versatile, and associate well with roses and herbaceous plants, as well as paving and stonework. The aromatic foliage is as important a feature as the flowers, which include pink-, white-, and blue-flowered cultivars, and a mass of shades in between. There are some compact growers, others of larger, looser habit. Many varieties make an excellent low hedge, and are suitable for coastal planting.

While lavenders thrive in open, sunny positions on well-drained soil, they are tolerant of some shade and will survive on heavier soils. Lavenders are short-lived, and those growing on heavy soils have a shorter life span than those on sand.

Lavandula angustifolia (zone 5–8) is the common, silver-leaved species, with strongly aromatic foliage and tall gray stems bearing pale gray-blue flower spikes. It is one of the best for hedging and is sold in vast numbers for this purpose. This lavender invariably gets larger than anticipated: if you plan to allow it to flower, make sure that you give it sufficient space. Alternatively, pinch it regularly during the season, to maintain silver new growth and a compact habit. Numerous *Lavandula angustifolia* cultivars are widely available, of which *Lavandula angustifolia* 'Hidcote' (zone 5–8) is probably the best-known. Introduced to the trade in 1920 and still a favorite, this is a superb cultivar for edging rose beds or simply to plant informally in front of shrub roses.

Lavandula × intermedia (zone 5–9) is a hybrid of *Lavandula angustifolia* with *Lavandula latifolia*. Again, there are many varieties in cultivation, generally larger, more vigorous and later-flowering than the cultivars of *Lavandula angustifolia*. *Lavandula latifolia* (zone 5–8) has large, branched flower heads, a characteristic that is often shown in the offspring.

Lavandula stoechas (zone 7–8), the French lavender, is a more dwarf, compact, aromatic, shrubby little plant

Lavandula angustifolia at Barrington Court, in Somerset, England.

with upright growth and dense, stubby flower heads of dark purple flowers. The flowers are produced over a longer period than other lavenders, appearing in succession throughout the summer. Less tolerant than other species, it needs good drainage and a warm, sunny position. Many cultivars have appeared in recent years, including some that look very attractive; however, most are not very hardy and are best grown in pots near the house, where the eaves protect the plants from damage caused by winter rain.

If you allow lavender to flower, trim the plant back immediately after flowering, to enable the new silver growth to emerge. This will keep the plant looking reasonable through the winter months. French lavenders tend to be more upright than others and need trimming to retain their bushiness. They are best lightly pruned in mid-spring, just before the flower buds appear. Do not cut back hard into bare wood, only to where growth shoots are clearly visible. Periodic trimming and deadheading during the flowering season will keep them looking good.

Lavandula angustifolia 'Hidcote' (z. 5–8) with compact growth, fine gray-green foliage, and dense spikes of violet-blue flowers, is good for hedging. The blooms are at their best in midsummer, and should be trimmed off the plants by late summer to allow for another flush of growth. The flowering time coincides with the peak of the rose season.

Lavandula angustifolia 'Imperial Gem' (z. 5–8) is very similar to 'Hidcote' but has purple flowers and more silver foliage. It is excellent for low, compact hedges and stays silver all year if cut back after flowering.

Lavandula angustifolia 'Miss Katherine' (z. 5–8) is a very fragrant, compact form with masses of deep pink flowers and gray-green foliage.

Lavandula angustifolia 'Loddon Blue' (z. 6–9) is compact and small-growing, with purple-blue flowers. It is excellent for pots and low borders.

Lavandula angustifolia 'Loddon Pink' (z. 6–9) is about the same size as 'Hidcote', but it has greener foliage and pink flower spikes.

Lavandula angustifolia 'Munstead' (z. 5–8) is similar to 'Hidcote' but it has paler, lavender-blue flowers.

Lavandula angustifolia 'Wendy Carlile' (z. 5–8), a delightful plant, has neat, upright growth, aromatic gray foliage, and silver and white flowers.

Lavandula × *intermedia* 'Arabian Night' (z. 5–9) produces long spikes of purple-blue flowers.

Lavandula × *intermedia* Dutch Group ('Dutch') (z. 5–9) is vigorous, with broad gray leaves and lavender-blue flowers; easily reaches 3ft. (1m).

Lavandula × *intermedia* 'Grosso' (z. 5–9), a shorter plant than 'Dutch', has medium-blue flowers in midsummer and very aromatic foliage.

Lavandula 'Sawyers' (z. 6–9) is a superb, compact, bushy plant with silver-gray foliage and large pointed flower spikes of deep purple.

Lavandula stoechas ssp. *pedunculata* (z. 7–8) is an excellent plant, with short flower spikes on long, wispy stems. The flowers have butterfly-like bracts at the top, hence the name 'Papillon', under which it is sometimes sold. Flowering often extends from late spring to mid-fall.

Lavandula stoechas 'Willow Vale' (z. 7–8) , a superb plant, has vigorous, gray-green foliage and long, purple, crinkly bracts.

Ballota pseudodictamnus (zone 8–9) is a beautiful dwarf shrub from the Mediterranean region, perfect for any dry, sunny garden. A grayish-white, furry covering gives a woolly look to the stems and rounded leaves, and pinkish-white flowers are borne in whorls in midsummer. This shrub forms a mound as a young plant; cut back hard each spring to preserve the shape. This is a good plant to combine with purple sage and the prostrate forms of rosemary.

Brachyglottis—see *Senecio*, page 79.

Buddleias may not seem an obvious choice when considering silver-leaved shrubs, but there are some that are well worth including. *Buddleia fallowiana* (zone 7–8) is a medium to large deciduous shrub, with white woolly stems and leaves, and fragrant, pale

Buddleia 'Lochinch'

Buddleia alternifolia 'Argentea'

WHERE CONTRAST IS NEEDED

Since many gray-leaved plants are light, with narrow, fine foliage, a silver scheme often needs the contrast of bolder forms. To find something that is both bold and silver, you may need to turn to herbaceous plants.

Few plants rival the dramatic architectural foliage of *Cynara cardunculus*, the cardoon (z. 6–9) (left). This is a truly statuesque border plant, with magnificent blue-green silver leaves that erupt from the ground in early spring and stay the course throughout much of the year. The thistlelike flower spikes are a bonus, as are the blooms of the silver, felty rosettes of verbascum (Aaron's rod or mullein). These appear reliably from random seedlings on poor sandy soil. If you do not want seedlings all over the garden, remove most of the flower spikes as the blooms fade.

Remember, too, that most silver shrubs form round mounds of fluffy, soft texture—and they need contrast. Spiky phormiums, grasses, lilies, and irises all help to relieve these soft shapes.

lavender flowers in large panicles. Unfortunately, it is not the hardiest of buddleias and needs a warm, sheltered wall to thrive.

Buddleia 'Lochinch' (z. 5–9), the hybrid between *Buddleia fallowiana* and *Buddleia davidii*, is hardier, and one of the best buddleias. It is a medium-sized shrub of bushy, compact growth. The young stems are downy gray, as are the leaves. Later, while the underside of the leaves stays white and felty, the upper surface becomes sage green in color. The flowers are pale violet-blue with an orange eye, sweetly scented and, like all buddleia flowers, attractive to butterflies. This is a lovely shrub, which is easy to grow and combine with herbaceous perennials, roses, and cottage garden flowers. Prune in late winter, cutting all stems down to about 3ft. (1m) in height.

Buddleia alternifolia 'Argentea' (z. 5–9) is the silver-leaved form of the graceful *Buddleia alternifolia*. It is a large shrub with fine, arching, spreading branches. It looks beautiful on a bank or falling over a wall. The

Convolvulus cneorum

Corokia cotoneaster

narrow, willowlike leaves flank the wispy branches, which in early summer bear scented lilac flowers. There is no need to prune this buddleia; just give it a sunny space in which to grow.

Convolvulus cneorum (z. 8–10) was introduced to Britain from south-eastern Europe around 1640. Its silver, silky leaves, compact dwarf habit, and white trumpet flowers are an appealing combination. If planted in a well-drained site in full sun, it is surprisingly hardy and needs little maintenance. The flowering period is long—from early summer into fall, which makes this convolvulus an excellent choice for patio containers. The flower buds can be trimmed off regularly if a mound of silver foliage is desired; the new shoots have a striking, almost metallic quality. *Convolvulus cneorum* 'Snow Angel' is a rare, compact form, with bold silver foliage and white to pale pink flowers.

Corokia cotoneaster (z. 8–10), the wire-netting bush, is an evergreen plant from New Zealand. The fine, twiggy branches and small silver leaves create an attractive wiry mass of a bush, studded with tiny yellow flowers in late spring. It is quite unlike any other shrub and will, if given ideal conditions, eventually make a large plant. It is not a shrub for cold, exposed sites.

Elaeagnus angustifolia (z. 2–7), the oleaster, is widely naturalized in southern

Europe and, like santolina, was cultivated in Britain from the 16th century. It is a large spiny, deciduous shrub with silvery gray willowlike leaves—similar to those of *Pyrus salicifolia* (the weeping pear). Tiny fragrant flowers in early summer are followed by oval amber fruits.

The best form to grow is *Elaeagnus* 'Quicksilver' (z. 3–9) (once sold as *Elaeagnus angustifolia* Caspica Group), a large shrub that grows quickly with vigorous, but graceful, upright then arching branches. The foliage is silver and reflective. Unlike many elaeagnus,

this plant is deciduous. The new foliage, when it appears in spring, is a delight when associated with blue ceanothus. (See also Good Companions, below.)

It is rare to find a silver-leaved plant that offers height, so this plant is very valuable. Do not underestimate its potential size: it can easily reach 10ft. (3m) in five years. It does not grow well in a pot, so container-grown plants often look weak until established in the garden. *Elaeagnus* 'Quicksilver' sways beautifully in the breeze, and in many gardens sits more happily than eucalyptus. *(Continued on page 77.)*

GOOD COMPANIONS

Underplant *Elaeagnus* 'Quicksilver' with *Brunnera macrophylla* for a pretty springtime combination.

Hebe

Hebes are grown for their evergreen foliage and attractive summer flowers. They are excellent plants for sheltered locations on well-drained soil, and tolerate relatively exposed coastal situations. However, they dislike heavy soil, shaded locations and poor drainage, and many seem happier in alkaline conditions than in acid soils. As a general rule, the larger-leaved hebes are more tender and susceptible to frost damage than those with small leaves.

The hebes provide some useful silver-foliage shrubs (for purple-leaved hebes, see page 52). All silver hebes have small leaves and are much hardier than their larger-leaved cousins. Although most hebes are native to New Zealand, the small- and gray-leaved species tend to originate from cooler, higher altitudes. They are low-growing, compact plants, excellent for containers or the front of borders, to provide solid, evergreen structure among low-growing purple and soft gray subjects. The silver hebes successfully fit into seaside gardens, associate particularly well with gravel, stone, and paving and, while they like good light, will tolerate semi-shade—although this may be at the expense of color. Some may suffer in very hot, dry conditions in summer.

Generally, silver hebes do not require any pruning. If plants become straggly, they can be cut back to wherever new shoots are visible on the branches low down in the shrub.

Hebe albicans (z. 8–10) forms a dense, rounded mound of blue-gray foliage. The closely packed tips of the new shoots form the outside of the shrub, so it is always the best part of the plant that meets the eye. Short spikes of white flowers, which give a pretty effect against the tough gray foliage, are produced in summer. This is a very hardy plant, tolerant of poor soil, pollution, and difficult situations.

Hebe 'Red Edge' (z. 8–10) (below) is the best-known hybrid of *Hebe albicans;* it is a dual-purpose plant, as its foliage turns burgundy in winter.

Hebe 'Pewter Dome' (z. 8–10) is a particularly fine hybrid, with dense foliage. It is lower-growing and more compact than *Hebe albicans*.

Hebe pimeleoides 'Quicksilver' (z. 7–8) is a dwarf shrub, prostrate in habit, with purplish-black stems. It has pale lilac flowers in summer and tiny silver-blue, well-spaced leaves, creating a lighter, prettier plant than more compact varieties. It is good in gravel, and with purple sage and rosemary. (See also Good Companions, page 79.)

Hebe pinguifoilia 'Pagei' (z. 8–10), a pretty dwarf evergreen shrub, is hardy and easy to grow. It spreads to make a broad mat of silver foliage that looks good all year. The small white flowers appear in late spring and early summer. It is a good ground-cover plant, excellent in paving.

Hebe albicans 'Sussex Carpet' (z. 8–10) makes a low mat of bluish gray foliage, excellent as evergreen ground cover. It produces plentiful white flowers, occasionally touched with pink.

Elaeagnus 'Quicksilver'

Look for *Helichrysum italicum* 'Korma', a compact form, with broader leaves of bright burnished silver. The flowers are cream in bud, opening to a softer yellow than other helichrysums.

Cut flower stems back to the base as the flowers fade, and trim plants lightly to encourage new silver growth that will persist through the winter months. It is an excellent container plant for gardeners who forget to water; it prefers full sun, but tolerates some shade.

Helichrysum italicum 'Korma'

Elaeagnus 'Quicksilver' may produce suckers; these are worth cultivating, as the plant is not long-lived and often needs to be replaced after eight or ten years. It grows on any soil, but is not at its best on shallow limestone.

Helichrysum italicum (*Helichrysum angustifolium*) (zone 8–10), the curry plant, is the most intensely aromatic and brightest of the silver stars in the garden. The growth is more open than lavender, so the plant gets less sodden in winter.

Hippophae rhamnoides (zone 3–7), the sea buckthorn, is a tall, slender, angular shrub with thorny silver-gray branches and narrow, silvery leaves. It grows almost anywhere, is wind- and salt-tolerant, and is excellent for providing height where space is limited and conditions are hostile. It is an excellent choice for banks of poor sandy soil. In winter female plants, if they have a male partner, produce orange-yellow berries that are bird-resistant; they look most attractive on the bare stems in the winter sunshine against a blue sky.

For **lavenders**, see the Plant Profile on pages 72–73.

HOW TO BUY BUCKTHORN

Hippophae rhamnoides is a plant to buy during the winter, as a bare-root hedging plant. It is inexpensive and establishes easily. Plant the stems in a group of three or five, 3ft. (1m) apart, to produce a more substantial shrub. Prune hard at an early stage if a more branched plant is required.

The gray-foliage forms of *Ozothamnus rosmarinifolius* (zone 9–10) offer a welcome upright alternative to the fluffy mounds produced by most silver-leaved subjects. Native to Tasmania and southeastern Australia, *Ozothamnus rosmarinifolius* are surprisingly hardy evergreen plants if given good, well-drained soil and a sunny spot. They are excellent plants for a dry, sheltered site, perhaps against a wall. In summer red buds appear on mature plants, later opening to white-scented flowers. Unlike the flowers of many silver-leaved shrubs, these are an attractive feature.

Ozothamnus rosmarinifolius 'Silver Jubilee' is the most widely grown cultivar, although not the hardiest. It has silvery gray foliage. *Ozothamnus* 'Threave Seedling' is becoming a more popular alternative, with slightly broader leaves of an attractive silver-gray. (See Good Companions, page 79.)

Ozothamnus require no pruning, and resent it later in life. Young plants can be encouraged to branch if the tops are nipped out at an early stage. The shrubs are best planted in late spring as a

---

EUCALYPTUS AS A SHRUB

For an evergreen silver plant with height, consider growing eucalyptus as a shrub. Eucalyptus has the ability to regenerate from the base, and readily produces growth buds at the bottom of woody stems. If you regularly cut it back hard from an early age, it produces vigorous, fast-growing, straight stems of juvenile foliage; this is normally of a more intense color than the adult foliage of trees. This technique is called stooling. *Eucalyptus gunnii* (z. 8–10) is frequently grown in this way; its round, silver-blue, juvenile leaves are particularly attractive.

FOR A SILVER EFFECT

Some white-variegated shrubs have the effect of silver foliage—in particular, *Pittosporum tenuifolium* 'Irene Paterson' (see page 64). The foliage of *Pittosporum tenuifolium* 'Irene Paterson' (z. 9–10) is a creamy white color, which results in the shrub having a gray effect when seen from a distance.

It can be used to good effect in combination with gray-leaved subjects so long as there are white flowers present.

Ozothamnus rosmarinifolius 'Silver Jubilee'

Phlomis italica

Salix elaeagnos ssp. angustifolia

young plant, rather than as a large specimen. Plants that have established naturally and have rooted well into the garden soil seem to overwinter successfully. If drainage is poor, add sharp grit when planting.

Phlomis are excellent plants for a dry, sunny position and poor soil. *Phlomis fruticosa* (zone 6–10), the Jerusalem sage, is an evergreen, gray-green felty shrub with whorls of yellow flowers throughout the summer. On a well-drained site, it is remarkably hardy. *Phlomis italica* (zone 7–10) is not as hardy, but is the most desirable variety. The leaves and stems are very hairy, with a wonderful tarnished-silver quality. The flowers are lilac, carried at the top of the stems in summer. If stems get knocked back by the frost, the plant usually shoots from the base and often suckers.

Ruta graveolens 'Jackman's Blue' (zone 5–8), or rue, is a herb long cultivated for its medicinal properties. It has pretty, divided leaves with tiny, rounded leaflets and makes a small semi-evergreen, aromatic shrub. The foliage of the variety 'Jackman's Blue' is a brilliant blue-gray. The flowers in summer are small and mustard yellow; but, although they are not unattractive, the plant is better off without them—both habit and foliage color are

superior if the flowers are removed. Easy to grow on well-drained soil, the plant has only one drawback: the foliage can cause severe skin irritation and blistering if handled in sunlight.

Salix exigua (zone 2–9), the coyote willow, is a very upright, large shrub, with reedlike stems of grayish brown and long silky, silver leaves. Fine catkins appear at the same time as the leaves. Of more delicate constitution than most willows, this shrub can be difficult to establish on some soils.

For wet sites and alongside water, *Salix elaeagnos* ssp. *angustifolia* (sometimes called *Salix rosmarinifolia*) (zone 4–7) is a better choice. This is an altogether more vigorous shrub and denser in habit. The leaves are gray and woolly, becoming green above and silver beneath as they mature; the foliage moving in the wind is a

RUE PLANTING TIPS

Plant rue (*Ruta*) (z. 5–8) in sun for best foliage color. The color is superb with lighter, fluffier gray-leaved plants. It is also good with purple: heucheras and *Festuca glauca* (z. 4–8) are natural partners. It is a superb choice for containers on a sunny patio, especially pots with blue-green glazes.

delightful sight. The stems are reddish brown and very useful for winter colour.

Santolinas, the lavender cottons, are evergreen and remarkably frost hardy—the most weather-resistant of the silver-foliage plants and more tolerant of heavy soil than most. Santolinas are mostly sold as young plants suitable for containers, for both summer and winter planting. In a well-drained soil they stay looking good throughout the winter months and make a useful contribution of lighter foliage to winter plantings. Santolinas are also tolerant of semi-shade and can be used effectively under trees to provide evergreen ground cover. If trimmed regularly, santolinas can be shaped into a dome or ball, and make a superb dwarf evergreen hedge. They are easier to manage and more consistent than lavender, but their aromatic quality is perhaps not so universally appealing.

Santolina chamaecyparissus (*Santolina incana*) (zone 6–9) is the most widely grown kind, with woolly, silver, thread-like foliage and bright lemon-yellow flowers in midsummer. It originated in the Pyrenees and was cultivated in Britain from the 16th century, when it was a useful ingredient in the knot garden. *Santolina chamaecyparissus* 'Lambrook Silver'

MORE SILVER AND GRAY SHRUBS *Atriplex canescens* • *Berberis temolaica* • *Buddleia* 'Silver Frost' • *Calluna vulgaris* 'Silver Queen' • *Cistus* × *argenteus* 'Silver Pink' • *Cytisus battandieri* • *Euryops pectinatus* •

has fine foliage and lemon yellow flowers, paler than those of the species. *Santolina chamaecyparissus* 'Lemon Queen' (zone 6–9) also produces lemon yellow flowers. *Santolina chamaecyparissus* var. *nana* (zone 6–9) is more compact, ideal for sunny areas of stonework and paving as well as pots and containers. *Santolina chamaecyparissus* 'Pretty Carol' (zone 6–9) bears soft gray foliage and pale yellow flowers. (See Good Companions, pages 49 and right.)

Cut santolinas back hard in early spring, to where the new growth is emerging near the base of the woody

Santolina chamaecyparissus

stems. You should also cut them back after flowering—or just before, if you dislike the yellow flowers—to prevent heavy growth from developing. This can weigh down the branches when the plant gets wet in the winter months.

Senecios, among the best shrubs of garden and landscape planting, have been reclassified as *Brachyglottis*. They come from New Zealand and Tasmania.

Senecio 'Sunshine' (zone 8–10), often known as *Senecio greyi*, is a safe choice where evergreen silver foliage is required on heavier soil; it is also excellent in coastal gardens. If left to grow without cutting back, it will form a broad mound up to 3ft. (1m) high and 6ft. (2m) across. The leaves are silver when young, becoming dark green on top and silver below with age. The flower buds are silver gems, opening to brash yellow daisies, which some

gardeners may prefer to remove.

This shrub does tend to open up in the center so is best pruned just before or just after flowering, cutting back to where new growth is emerging halfway down the branches. This encourages the new shoots, with their bright silver foliage, to develop. *Senecio* 'Sunshine' is an accommodating plant, so if you should leave it unpruned for a season or two, you can rejuvenate at a later date. Although this shrub prefers an open, sunny, even windswept site, it tolerates semi-shade. It is also probably the hardiest of the gray-leaved evergreens.

Senecio (*Brachyglottis*) *monroi* (zone 8–10), from South Island, New Zealand, is a smaller shrub of denser habit. It forms a broad dome and has oval

Brachyglottis (Senecio) 'Sunshine'

leaves that undulate along the edges. The underside is covered with dense white felt, while the upper surface is gray-green. This plant is not often seen and is much less widely available than *Senecio* 'Sunshine'. It is less tolerant of heavy soil and damp sites.

GOOD COMPANIONS

For contrast of shape and a good combination of colors, mix *Hebe pimeleoides* 'Quicksilver' (1) (z. 7–8) with the spiky blue grass *Festuca glauca* (2) (z. 4–8).

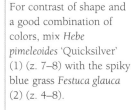

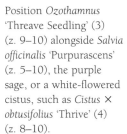

Position *Ozothamnus* 'Threave Seedling' (3) (z. 9–10) alongside *Salvia officinalis* 'Purpurascens' (z. 5–10), the purple sage, or a white-flowered cistus, such as *Cistus* × *obtusifolius* 'Thrive' (4) (z. 8–10).

Grow a santolina, such as *Santolina chamaecyparissus* 'Lambrook Silver' (z. 6–9), under the weeping pear, *Pyrus salicifolia* 'Pendula' (5) (z. 4–7), to create a beautiful silvery scene (as seen here at Apple Court, Lymington, Hampshire, in England).

Hebe albicans 'Clear Skies' • *Helianthemum* 'Rhodanthe Carneum' ('Wisley Pink') • *Perovskia* 'Blue Spire' • *Potentilla fruticosa* 'McKay's White' • *Rosa glauca* • *Salix repens* var. *argentea* • *Teucrium fruticans* •

SITUATIONS

Getting the right plant in the right place is the secret of successful design. Plants chosen only for their appearance, with no regard to the growing conditions, may disappoint the gardener. Thriving plants look good and reward with their performance; plants that are struggling for life contribute little. Shrubs are part of the permanent fabric of any garden, so deciding what to plant where is crucially important. Choosing successful planting partners— good companions that complement each other—increases the value of any individual plant.

Hot, dry, sunny sites

A hot, dry, sunny position can be a curse or a blessing, depending on what you plant. Many plants suffer severely from drought in summer, while others thrive on a good baking. Provided you choose plants that hail from very hot climates, you will not go far wrong: natives of southern Europe, north Africa, the southwestern United States, and parts of South Africa and Australia generally thrive in these conditions.

The Dry Garden, in Savill Garden, Windsor Great Park, England.

Many plants of Mediterranean origin are surprisingly tough and can withstand some cold as well as drought. However, they resent wet conditions. Damp winters are far from ideal, but give them a dry spot, poor soil, and sunshine to look forward to and they are quite happy. Most gray-foliage plants in this book (see pages 70–79) delight in these conditions. Without damp around their roots and leaves, they retain foliage color even through winter. Evergreen plants such as sedums and sempervivums are also useful additions to dry, sunny plantings, especially to fill gaps in paving and to edge dry borders.

Callistemons, or bottlebrushes, with their spectacular red flowers in summer, have established themselves as popular garden shrubs in milder zones, thriving if given a sunny, well-drained position.

Callistemon citrinus 'Splendens' (zone 9–10) is fully hardy only in the far southern states but stands up to cold and drying winter winds better than many evergreens; it suits coastal gardens and also associates well with both deck-ing and terracotta paving. *Callistemon salignus* (zone 8–10) is less often seen but is one of the hardiest bottlebrushes, with willowlike growth and pale yellow flowers. Callistemons combine particularly well with exotics and silver foliage (see Good Companions, opposite).

After flowering, callistemons must be cut back to immediately behind the seed head. None of the old seed heads should be visible. This ensures vigorous new growth and a compact habit.

Ceanothus are the best of the blue-flowering shrubs for late spring and summer (see Plant Profile, page 140).

Ceanothus arboreus 'Trewithen Blue'

All like full sun and good drainage, as the common name, California lilac, suggests. They grow on most soils but will tolerate very shallow limestone soil only if the soil is improved by digging in plenty of organic matter. Ceanothus are fast-growing and can be grown as free-standing or wall shrubs.

Evergreen varieties of ceanothus are more tender than deciduous ones, so

> ### GETTING PLANTS GOING
> Beds against sunny walls can often be problematic, particularly where overhanging eaves keep rainfall off the ground. In such areas, all new plants need special attention—even the most drought-resistant subjects. In particular, container-grown plants that have been potted in peat-based soil mix need watering until their roots are established. Without regular watering in the initial stages, roots do not venture into the surrounding soil and the plants quickly dry out.

are ideal for a warm position. Those with small leaves are more susceptible to frost than larger-leaved varieties, such as *Ceanothus arboreus* 'Trewithen Blue' (zone 8–10). In a favored spot, this gets very large and is glorious in spring, with a haze of huge panicles of deep blue flowers. For a sunny bank, choose *Ceanothus thrysiflorus* 'Skylark' (zone 8–10). It grows to an extensive low, evergreen mound of glossy, bright green foliage with masses of fluffy, medium-blue flowers in late spring (see Good Companions, page 85). *Ceanothus* 'Centennial' (zone 7–10) is also prostrate, but more compact, with neat, dark green foliage on fine stems and violet-blue flowers in late spring and early summer. Tolerant of drought, it is excellent in pots and alongside paved areas, and is good for smaller gardens.

Cistus × obtusifolius 'Thrive'

Cistus, also known as sun roses, are popular for their reliability, ease of cultivation, and attractive flowers, which are short-lived but freely produced, usually in midsummer. True Mediterranean plants, they are found in the wild from the Canary Islands to the Caucasus, and they revel in hot sunshine, poor soil, and dry conditions. Hybrids have arisen in the wild and in gardens, creating a range of sizes and growth habits; most have white or pink flowers. (See Plant Profile, page 150.)

One of the more robust and most widely planted of the sun roses, *Cistus × corbariensis* (zone 8–10) grows larger than many, producing a rounded

GOOD COMPANIONS

For an exotic touch of color, try planting *Callistemon citrinus* 'Splendens' (1) (z. 9–10) with a *Phormium* 'Yellow Wave' (2) (z. 8–10).

Coronilla valentina ssp. *glauca* (3) (z. 6–8) complements the purple sage, *Salvia officinalis* 'Purpurascens' (4) (z. 5–10), and magenta helianthemums, such as 'Ben Ledi' (z. 5–8).

Plant *Erysimum* 'Bowles' Mauve' (5) (z. 7–8) with sages and thymes. The fluffy, shrubby thymes such as *Thymus vulgaris* 'Silver Posie' (6) (z. 7–8) enjoy exactly the same conditions as erysimum.

mound about 3ft. (1m) high. The white flowers, with bright yellow stamens, emerge from green or shrimp pink buds. *Cistus × obtusifolius* 'Thrive' (zone 8–10), a neat, compact plant, is a good choice for a smaller garden. It has dark green foliage, which can be bronze-tinged in winter, and freely produces white flowers with yellow stamens from late spring on; these appear over a long period, sometimes even in late summer. (See Good Companions, pages 79, 85.)

The hardiest of the sun roses is *Cistus laurifolius* (zone 7–10), which can reach 6ft. (2m) high. The leaves are dark green and leathery, and the flowers white with yellow centers. The less hardy *Cistus ladanifer* (zone 8–10), the gum cistus, has sticky, lance-shaped leaves; the strikingly large flowers are white with dark red basal blotches. The hybrid between *Cistus ladanifer* and *Cistus laurifolius*, *Cistus × cyprius* (zone 8–10),

Cistus laurifolius

CISTUS AFTERCARE

When planting cistus, always give them plenty of space to spread sideways; drawn and leggy growth is hard to correct. Pinch back the growth of young plants in their first season to encourage a bushy habit. Many of the sun roses do not respond kindly to pruning, although *Cistus × corbariensis* and *Cistus × salvifolius* may be pruned after flowering. If you do prune, never cut back into old wood, and prune back only to where you can see vigorous young shoots emerging from the branches.

Genista aetnensis

Genista lydia

Grevillea 'Robyn Gordon'

Grevillea 'Fireworks'

has the attributes of both parents: vigorous growth, good-looking foliage, hardiness. Look for *Cistus × cyprius* var. *ellipticus* f. bicolor 'Elma' (zone 8–10), whose glorious flowers, silky and pure white with yellow stamens, look superb against the polished green leaves.

With its lax, arching growth and beautiful blue-green, ruelike foliage, *Coronilla valentina* ssp. *glauca* (zone 6–8) is an attractive small shrub for the base of a sunny wall. It bears clouds of bright yellow flowers in mid-spring, and some others through the year—even, on a very sheltered site, in winter. (See Good Companions, page 83; also 119.)

A superb, woody-based form of the perennial wallflower, *Erysimum* 'Bowles' Mauve' (zone 7–8) makes a rounded evergreen shrub with dark grayish-green leaves and spikes of soft purple, wallflower-scented flowers. It is not long-lived, so take cuttings every couple of years. A well-drained, sunny site prolongs its life. (See Good Companions, page 83.)

Genistas are related to *Cytisus*, the brooms, and need similar treatment (see page 139), though many are tougher and very suitable for hot, dry, sunny conditions. *Genista hispanica* (Spanish gorse) (zone 7–8) is one of the most reliable shrubs for a hot, dry but inhospitable site such as a dry bank. It will grow on virtually any soil and is alkaline-tolerant. Forming a dense, prickly mound (which deters rabbits and deer), it produces masses of yellow flowers in late spring. It may not be the most beautiful plant, but it is effective on a dry bank when planted with santolina, rosemary, cistus, and other maquis-type plant material. *Genista lydia* (zone 6–7) is a well-known shrub, useful for tumbling over steps and low walls, and onto paving. The fine stems curve gracefully to form a low mound of soft green, and the chrome yellow flowers are bright and smother the plants in late spring. It is very dominant in flower, so plant this only where you want to draw attention to it. *Genista aetnensis* (zone 7–9), known as the Mount Etna broom, is a useful choice when a very tall, light shrub is needed for a sunny, dry site. Its habit is elegant, open, and graceful, and the leafless shoots become a haze of yellow when the fragrant flowers appear in midsummer. The scent is delightful and may well perfume the whole garden. If it is in an exposed position, stake and support it well, as it has a habit of toppling over.

Members of the Protea family, the **grevilleas** are, for the most part, natives of Australia. Despite their hot-climate origins, some will tolerate some frost, and thrive in open sun with good drainage. *Grevillea rosmarinifolia* (zone 8–10) is a lovely light, sprawling shrub, with long, soft shoots and narrow, rosemary-like leaves. These are deep green on top but silvery on the underside, and so they look very pretty when moved by the breeze. From winter through spring into summer, curly crimson flowers bloom at the end of the shoots. *Grevillea* 'Robyn Gordon' (zone 9–11) is a beautiful shrub for a warm spot, with ferny foliage and striking bottlebrush-like flowers. Low-growing and not too vigorous, it is ideal for a small, sheltered garden. *Grevillea* 'Canberra Gem' is a hardier (zones 8–11), vigorous, rounded shrub, which is good for coastal gardens, with waxy foliage and clusters of bright pink flowers. *Grevillea* 'Fireworks' (zone 9–11) is small and compact, with neat green foliage tinged red-green at the shoot tips. The flowers are deep pinkish red, produced in clusters at the end of the shoots, from early spring into late summer. It is an excellent small shrub, particularly good for a pot on a sunny patio; plant in nonalkaline potting mix.

A hybrid between *Halimium* and *Cistus*, × *Halimiocistus* 'Ingwersenii' (zone 7–10) is a wide-spreading, low shrub with small, narrow, hairy dark green leaves and masses of pure white flowers over several weeks in late spring and early summer. It is very hardy and suitable for exposed sites. (See Good Companions, above right.) × *Halimiocistus* 'sahucii' (zone 7–10) is a better choice for a smaller space, is equally hardy, with shinier, less hairy foliage. The white flowers are produced intermittently throughout summer. Another hybrid, × *Halimiocistus*

GOOD COMPANIONS

× *Halimiocistus* 'Ingwersenii' (1) (z. 7–10) is good for low ground cover on a sunny site and combines well with *Ceanothus thyrsiflorus* var *repens* (2) (z. 8–10).

Helianthemum 'Henfield Brilliant' (3) (z. 5–8) looks lovely with the blue foliage of *Festuca glauca* (4) (z. 4–8).

The pleasingly subtle color of *Phlomis fruticosa* (5) (z. 6–10) complements yellow *Helianthemum* 'Wisley Primrose' (6) (z. 5–8) and white cistus *Cistus* × *obtusifolius* 'Thrive' (z. 8–10) (see illus. page 83).

wintonensis (zone 8–10), is beautiful, but nowhere near as tough, and needs a warm, sheltered spot. The foliage is gray, the habit dwarf and compact, the flowers pearly white and beautifully marked with maroon and yellow.

Halimiums (zone 7–9) are low, spreading shrubs related to cistus. They thrive in full sun and a well-drained soil, but can be hit by severe frost. *Halimium lasianthum* has gray-green foliage and dark-eyed yellow flowers in

late spring. *Halimium ocymoides* is similar but has smaller, gray leaves. The hybrid of these two, *Halimium* 'Susan' is compact and dwarf, with rounded leaves. The flowers, yellow blotched with brown, are freely produced in late spring. Trim all halimiums after flowering to keep them compact and bushy.

Helianthemums (known as rock roses or sun roses) (zone 5–8) are related to cistus and halimiums, and enjoy similar conditions. Usually found

× *Halimiocistus sahucii*

× *Halimiocistus wintonensis*

Halimium lasianthum

in the alpines section of garden centers, they are evergreen, very dwarf shrubs, suitable for paved areas, rock gardens, and at the base of walls. The brilliant flowers are produced all summer.

There are countless hybrids (all zone 5–8), with flowers in various shades. Particularly good are: *Helianthemum* **'The Bride'**, creamy white flowers with yellow centers, silver-gray foliage; **'Henfield Brilliant'**, orange flowers, gray-green foliage (see Good Companions, page 85); **'Fire Dragon'**, with bright orange-scarlet flowers, gray-green foliage; **'Boule de Feu'**, double, scarlet flowers, dark green foliage; **'Rhodanthe Carneum'**, pale pink flowers with orange centers, gray foliage; and **'Wisley Primrose'**, light yellow flowers with a darker center, light gray-green foliage (see Good Companions, page 85).

Dorycnium hirsutum (zone 7–10) is a

Helianthemum 'The Bride'

Phlomis 'Edward Bowles'

TRIMMING HELIANTHEMUMS

Helianthemums need regular trimming after flowering to remove old flower stems and to keep the plants compact; on mature plants, shears are best for this operation. Examine closely before you cut: some varieties keep producing flowers on the old stems, in which case a decision has to be made—compact plant with good foliage or straggly plant with flowers? The choice is up to the gardener.

---

pretty, fluffy, dwarf shrub with fairly upright growth and silver, hairy leaves, shaped like those of clover. The pale pink flowers, which are produced in summer and fall, are followed by red-tinged fruit pods. *Dorycnium hirsutum* combines well with many other soft, silvery aromatics, such as lavender and sage, and makes a pretty display when coupled with the pink *Nerine bowdenii* (zone 9–10) against a sunny wall.

Phlomis are both herbaceous and shrubby aromatic plants. The woody species are ideal for dry, sunny conditions. *Phlomis fruticosa* (Jerusalem sage) (zone 6–10) is a hardy, small, gray-green shrub, perfect for a sunny bank or border. Whorls of yellow-ocher flowers are produced in summer, reminiscent of a large dead-nettle. (See Good Companions, page 85.) *Phlomis* **'Compact Grey'** (zone 7–8) has narrower, smaller leaves, more like those of a sage. *Phlomis lanata* **'Pygmy'** (zone 8–10) is a pretty, dwarf, compact plant with yellow woolly shoots, sage-green leaves, and yellow flowers. *Phlomis longifolia* (zone 8–10) has darker green leaves carried on white woolly shoots and spikes of bright yellow flowers that appear throughout summer. *Phlomis* **'Edward Bowles'** (zone 6–10) is one of the most spectacular of these plants, somewhere between a shrub and an herbaceous perennial. Huge heart-shaped leaves form clumps and clothe the woody stems. In summer the flower stems carry whorls of yellow-

ocher flowers in candelabra fashion. It is a real statement plant, and because the habit is open, it is good for bold foreground interest. It can be knocked back by frost but usually grows again from the base. *Phlomis italica* (see page 78) (zone 7–10) offers a lilac-pink alternative to the yellow flowers of most phlomis; the cultivar 'Pink Glory' is compact, and a better choice for small gardens.

The common rosemary, *Rosmarinus officinalis* (zone 8–10), is an all-time favorite shrub. Cultivated for hundreds of years, it is still valued for its aromatic foliage and its versatility as a culinary herb. As a garden shrub it is invaluable for its soft, dark green and silver foliage and pretty growth habit. It is also said to repel some garden pests. The flowers, usually pale blue, are a delight in early and mid-spring, lasting through to summer. The species has grayish green leaves, white beneath, and a loose but upright habit, growing up to 6ft. (2m). *Rosmarinus officinalis* **'Miss Jessopp's Upright'** is probably the finest and most popular cultivar: vigorous and upright.

Rosmarinus officinalis 'Miss Jessopp's Upright'

GROWING AND USING ROSEMARY

Rosemary is the one herb that no garden should be without, however basic the skills of the resident cook. The young, woody stems of the upright forms can be used as fragrant skewers, superb to flavor meat. In addition to its culinary uses, rosemary makes excellent cut foliage, especially when it is in flower. The better the drainage and the poorer the soil, the greater will be the aromatic quality of the rosemary. Trimming for use in the house is generally enough to keep it in shape.

MORE SHRUBS FOR HOT, DRY, SUNNY SITES *Brachyglottis • Buddleia • Caryopteris • Ceratostigma • Cytisus •*

'Severn Sea', a dwarf form, has arching growth and brilliant blue flowers (illus. page 63). *Rosmarinus officinalis* **Prostratus Group** (zone 8–10) is not as hardy, but its sprawling, almost trailing form is invaluable for walls and banks. It flowers freely, producing a mass of blue flowers. There are many more blue cultivars, as well as some with white and pink flowers—a less pleasing combination.

The shrubby germander, *Teucrium fruticans* (zone 9–10), is a delightful sprawling shrub with wiry silver stems and shiny green leaves, the underside of which are white and feltlike. The pale blue flowers, produced in the leaf axils and at the end of the shoots, appear throughout the summer. Although often described as dwarf, it spreads well in a dry, sunny spot and grows upward against a wall. In a sheltered site it can even reach the upstairs windows of a house. The cultivar *Teucrium fruticans* **'Azureum'** has sapphire blue flowers.

SPIKY SUN LOVERS

The requirement for plants that will thrive in hot, dry summers has sustained our interest in palms and other hot, Mediterranean subjects. Phormiums, palms, and cordylines have an exotic appearance, and are very well suited to contemporary design, patios, and bedding schemes. Yuccas are more familiar in mixed planting and they have featured in our gardens for many years.

The toughest of the **palms**, and the most reliable for general garden planting,

Chamaerops humilis var. argentea

is *Chamaerops humilis* (zone 8–11), a dwarf palm that rarely grows to more than 5ft. (1.5m). It sometimes forms a small trunk but more usually makes a clump of long, woody-stemmed shoots. The leaves are stiff and spiky. *Chamaerops humilis* var. *argentea* is a striking, silver-blue form, which is very hardy and beautiful. Also very hardy is *Chamaerops humilis* **'Vulcano'**, a compact form with leaves silvery beneath. All are good in pots or planted in scree with dry grasses and aromatics.

Cordyline australis (cabbage palm) (zone 7–11) is used for architectural effect in more modern gardens, and can grow to tower over the house. Not strictly a shrub, but grown as one, it is related to the agaves. Architectural in quality from an early age, the dense heads of green, sword-shaped leaves provide relief from soft mounds of foliage. In summer fragrant flowers may be produced. *Cordyline australis* **'Torbay Dazzler'** is softer, prettier and smaller than most cordylines, with green leaves edged creamy white (illus. pages 66, 124; see also page 55.)

Phormiums, more spiky sun-lovers, are described on pages 55, 66, 125.

Yuccas are related to cordylines and produce rosettes of spiky, usually rigid leaves. The flowers, if they are produced, are spectacular: tall, tropical-looking spikes of white, bell-shaped blooms. Yuccas are superb architectural foliage plants, which are excellent for pots and for planting in gravel areas away from paths. *Yucca filamentosa* **'Bright Edge'** (zone 5–8) is soft-leaved and stemless. Its narrow, gold-edged leaves, which turn down at the ends, have white threads along their edges. The shape is semi-spherical, with leaves upright in the center, fanning progressively down to horizontal; the form **'Variegata'** is edged with creamy white. *Yucca flaccida* **'Golden Sword'** (zone 4–9) is similar to 'Variegata', but

Yucca gloriosa

Yucca gloriosa 'Variegata'

its leaves are broader, with a central band of creamy yellow and green edges. The attractively variegated gold and green *Yucca flaccida* **'Gold Garland'** is more free-flowering than many, producing large panicles of white, fragrant flowers. *Yucca gloriosa* (zone 6–9) is small and treelike, it has a stout stem; the leaves are straight, stiff, and spine-pointed, gathered into a dense terminal head; the flowers are creamy white, often tinged red, on upright spikes up to 6ft. (2m) high in summer. The creamy-yellow, striped foliage of *Yucca gloriosa* **'Variegata'** fades to cream on older leaves.

PROTECTING CORDYLINES

Wet weather followed by frost sometimes damages the growing tip in the center of the crown. In severe weather, it is advisable to draw the leaves gently together and wrap with burlap or horticultural fleece. Do not tie tightly, as this will cause unsightly damage to the foliage. Plants that lose the growing tip normally produce side shoots and branch.

Shady sites

Shady areas in the garden should not be seen as inferior to sunnier spots. They will never be filled with colorful flowers, but they can be places of great foliage interest. Plants take on more definition in the shade; the foliage of shade-loving plants, unbleached by the sun, is lush and luxuriant. The native plants of woodland habitats need light shade. Some plants thrive in shade; others just tolerate it.

When it comes to large evergreen shrubs for shade, both aucuba and *Viburnum tinus* prove as versatile as ever. **Aucubas** (see pages 35, 57, 95, 98) exhibit good foliage color and thrive in shade, however heavy, on almost any soil. They will withstand dry conditions, but in extreme drought may show blackening of the growth tips early in the year. *Viburnum tinus* (see pages 186–87) is one of the few shrubs that survive beneath the shade of oak trees, and is tolerant of any soil. In heavy shade, growth tends to be loose and flowers few.

On acid soils, **rhododendrons** and **camellias** are obvious options for dappled shade (see pages 101–107). Naturally woodland plants, they thrive,

Aucuba japonica 'Variegata'

and look right, under the drip-line of trees. Neither enjoys drought conditions; indeed, high temperatures and lack of water in summer can cause harm. The light, open habit of camellias suits mixed, informal planting. The denser, more upright varieties, with heavier flowers, are ideal for containers and more formal

planting schemes. Varieties of *Camellia japonica* (zone 7–10) and *Camellia* × *williamsii* (zone 6–10) all grow well in light shade, though they flower more profusely where there is a fair amount of sunlight. Dwarf rhododendrons and the larger-growing, hardy hybrids grow well with some shade. Their flowers last longer and retain their color better when they are away from strong sunlight.

Camellia × williamsii 'Saint Ewe'

Camellia japonica 'Alba Simplex'

ADDING COLOR TO A SHADY BED

Yellow foliage tends to go lime green in shade, but yellow variegations hold on to their color and shine brightly. Yellow draws the eye and so makes a feature of a shady area: *Elaeagnus pungens* 'Maculata' (z. 6–9), *Ilex aquifolium* 'Monvila' (z. 6–9), and *Euonymus fortunei* 'Emerald 'n' Gold' (z. 5–8) are excellent choices for shade.

White-variegated foliage looks cool and sophisticated. It will lighten any dark area. The silver-variegated forms of box—for example, *Buxus sempervirens* 'Elegantissima' (z. 6–9)—are delightful in shade and combine well with larger-leaved subjects, such as *Prunus lusitanica* 'Variegata' (z. 7–9).

Add color with bulbs. *Narcissus* species (z. 4–8), *Anemone blanda* (z. 5–8), *Cyclamen hederifolium* (right, z.7–9), scilla, chionodoxa, galanthus, and eranthis all bring seasonal color to shady areas.

Pulmonarias are excellent alternatives to hostas for shady situations. They grow well on damp sites, and the foliage is not as attractive to slugs and snails as that of hostas. Their mottled leaves look good throughout the season after early flowers have faded. They are particularly useful for bringing ground-cover color to solid-colored evergreens.

WHEN IS A SHADY SPOT NOT A SHADY SPOT?

Most plants tolerate some shade, so long as there is good light and, ideally, a few hours of sunshine a day.

"Deep shade" means that there is no direct sunlight: the site is overhung by trees or buildings, and light is poor.

"Semi-shade", or "partial shade," means that the position is shaded for part of the day. Perhaps there is direct sun in the morning or in the evening. The amount of shade varies according to the time of year. Most plants grow here, but those that prefer direct sun will not thrive.

In "dappled shade," direct sunlight is diffused through a light tree canopy.

Daphne pontica (zone 8–9) is a rare gem for shade. A small, spreading evergreen with bright green, glossy leaves, it has spidery yellow-green flowers in mid- to late spring. Visually these are easily missed, but their fragrance is wonderful. This is a shrub for shade under trees, excellent on heavy soil, even alkaline clay.

Daphne pontica

× *Fatshedera lizei* 'Variegata'

GOOD COMPANIONS

Try placing the large-leaved *Hedera colchica* 'Sulphur Heart' (1) (z. 6–9) under an upright gold-variegated holly, such as *Ilex* × *altaclerensis* 'Golden King' (2) (z. 6–9).

In a large container or on open ground, the pretty, white-variegated *Hedera helix* 'Glacier' (3) (z. 4–9) looks good under *Fatsia japonica* (4) (z. 8–9).

The attractive flowers and leaves of *Pulmonaria saccharata* 'Leopard' (5) (z. 3–7) bring color below *Sarcococca confusa* (6) (z. 6–8) after its flowering season.

Vinca minor f. *alba* 'Gertrude Jekyll' (7) (z. 5–8), with white flowers, is pretty under the dark leaves of *Viburnum davidii* (8) (z. 7–9).

Shady situations demand bold foliage, and *Fatsia japonica* (zone 8–9) is a natural choice (see Good Companions, above; also 35–36). In shade it stays a rich, dark green, and the growth is luxuriant. It tolerates dry conditions. × *Fatshedera lizei* (zone 8–11), a hybrid of fatsia and its relative, hedera, is a tough character. It tolerates any soil, heavy shade, coastal exposure, and pollution. Although widely grown as a houseplant, it is remarkably hardy and grows as a sprawling shrub, providing excellent ground cover. × *Fatshedera lizei* 'Variegata' has gray-green leaves with an irregular white margin.

Garrya elliptica 'James Roof' (zone 8–9) is subdued in summer and fall but is luxuriously flamboyant in winter and early spring, draped with silky silver tassels (illus. page 182). If space is limited, prune to shape as the tassels start to fade and new growth begins. It looks best grown as a tall, top-heavy wall shrub, so that the tassels dangle and sway in the breeze. In light shade, a *Rhamnus alaternus* 'Argenteovariegata' (zone 8–9) will brighten the garrya during its quiet season (see page 65). In heavier shade, the white variegated *Osmanthus heterophyllus* 'Variegatus' (zone 6–9) will set it off (see page 63). All osmanthus are

Gaultheria mucronata 'Bell's Seedling'

Hedera colchica 'Dendroides'

Mahonia aquifolium 'Apollo'

Ruscus aculeatus

good in shade, grow on any soil, and, once established, tolerate dry conditions.

A South American native, and a shrub for acid soils, *Gaultheria mucronata* (*Pernettya mucronata*) (zone 6–7) will attract attention with its marblelike berries carried on dense thickets of wiry stems. The berries are remarkable for their colors, ranging from white through shades of pink to deep burgundy red. For best effect, these shrubs should be planted in groups and with male plants (non-berrying) for pollination and fruit set. The variety 'Bell's Seedling' is both male and female, with deep green foliage on reddish stems. Large, showy dark red berries follow the white flowers.

A shrubby form of the Persian ivy, *Hedera colchica* 'Dendroides' ('Arborescens') (zone 6–9) originated as a cutting of the adult, flowering growth of the trailing ivy. It is an excellent, rounded shrub and is most attractive in winter, when it fruits. Once established, it is good in damp shade, but in the early stages it can be temperamental.

Mahonia japonica (zone 6–9) does well in light shade, as do many other mahonias (see pages 182–83). The most useful is *Mahonia aquifolium* 'Apollo' (zone 6–8). This is a very fine, vigorous form of the Oregon grape, which forms a dense, low, and spreading shrub. The leaves are deep green with red stalks and tend to flush purple in the winter. The bright yellow flowers, in large, dense clusters, appear in early spring. 'Apollo' is one of the best flowering shrubs for shade and makes a superb

combination with a number of golden-variegated evergreens such as *Euonymus fortunei* 'Emerald 'n' Gold' (zone 5–8) and *Aucuba japonica* 'Marmorata' (zone 7–10).

The tough and tolerant butcher's broom, *Ruscus aculeatus* (zone 8), is similar in leaf shape to *Mahonia japonica*, but stiffer and a duller green. What seem to be leaves are, in fact, flattened stems. In spring, tiny white flowers appear in the middle of these; on female plants, these are followed by large red berries. It forms dense upright clumps. It will grow in the driest, most inhospitable shade, so although it is not the most attractive shrub, it has its uses.

No shady garden should be without *Sarcococca confusa* (zone 6–8), Christmas box, with its shiny, evergreen leaves and stems and tiny white, deliciously fragrant flowers in winter. There are other sarcococcas; all are evergreen, and all succeed in shade. *Sarcococca confusa* is one of the glossiest, and has a pretty, arching growth habit. (See page 184; Good Companions, page 89.)

Skimmias are made for shade; in fact, their foliage discolors and goes yellow in full sun. They are especially good

plants for shady town gardens, tolerant of limestone and acid soils. Foliage, flowers, and berries are all worthwhile features. Obvious choices are *Skimmia japonica* 'Rubella' (zone 7–8), with its red buds, and the female cultivars that berry, but the white-flowering male varieties are no less worthwhile. *Skimmia* × *confusa* 'Kew Green' (zone 7–8) has clusters of fragrant, white flowers against pretty, apple green foliage. *Skimmia reevesiana* (zone 7–8) is exceptionally fragrant—the white flowers smell of lily-of-the-valley. For small spaces or pots in shade, skimmia is a particularly good choice of evergreen shrub. (See pages 184–85.)

Snowberry, *Symphoricarpos albus* (zone 3–7), tends to be disregarded in gardens because of its invasive qualities. A native species, it grows in the poorest soils and in deep shade. It suckers and spreads to form thickets of fine, arching stems with small, light green leaves. It is an airy plant, and its leaves fall to reveal the fine frame and round white berries. *Symphoricarpos albus* var. *laevigatus* grows to 6ft. (2m) and produces masses of berries. *Symphoricarpos* × *chenaultii* 'Hancock' (zone 4–7) is

MORE SHRUBS FOR SHADY SITES *Berberis* • *Chaenomeles* • *Choisya ternata* • *Cornus alba* • *Cotoneaster* •

dwarf and wide-spreading, and makes good ground cover under trees. The berries are heavily flushed pink when the light is strong. *Symphoricarpos × doorenbosii* hybrids (zone 4–7) include the well-known **'White Hedge'** and **'Mother of Pearl'** (illus. page 93)

Symphoricarpos are especially useful in country gardens where there are mature oak trees, under which they succeed. Their light, airy habit fits in well in the rural environment.

Symphoricarpos albus

ESTABLISHING PLANTS UNDER TREES

It is often overhanging trees and other surrounding vegetation that create shade in a garden. In these situations new plants have a hard job getting established, as they compete not only for light but also for water and nutrients. To achieve the best results, be especially careful to prepare the ground well before planting and to water well after planting. In dry spells you will need to water throughout the growing season, when surrounding trees and shrubs are in full leaf.

Where soil is very poor, consider using shade-loving subjects in pots. This can be very useful close to the trunk of a tree, in a key spot in the garden. Use a large container and loam-based potting mix. Remember that regular watering will be necessary.

Viburnum davidii (zone 7–9) is an extremely tolerant plant. It can make a large shrub, but it is at its best when it is still young, forming a compact mound of perfect, deep raven-green, ribbed leaves. In the presence of a male pollinator, female plants will normally produce blue-black berries in winter. (See Good Companions, page 89; see also pages 37, 123, 125.)

CLIMBERS AND GROUND COVER

Shady areas backed by a wall or fence need climbers and wall shrubs that perform without much light. The ivies are some of our most decorative and useful climbers, but they are frequently overlooked and considered the "thugs" of the garden. Use the small-leaved varieties—for example, the white-variegated *Hedera helix* **'Glacier'** (z. 4–9)—as a background for bold evergreens such as aucuba, and use the large-leaved varieties—for example, the yellow-variegated *Hedera colchica* **'Sulphur Heart'** (z. 6–9)—as a background for the neater, variegated evergreens such as osmanthus. (See Good Companions, page 89.) It is easy to forget that ivies will grow horizontally as well as vertically. In fact, ivies make wonderful ground cover, filling gaps and extending the interest and effect of evergreen foliage shrubs.

On moist, shady sites *Pachysandra terminalis* (z. 5–8) is an excellent choice for ground cover. Although pachysandra looks like an evergreen herbaceous plant, in fact it belongs to the same family as box. It is not successful in shallow, alkaline soil, but grows well under most trees and spreads by suckering. Whorls of leaves at the end of short stems create an attractive evergreen effect. The variegated form, *Pachysandra terminalis* **'Variegata'**, is particularly pleasing.

Pachysandra terminalis

Rubus tricolor

Of all the ground-cover plants suitable for shade, *Rubus tricolor* (z. 7–9) is perhaps the finest. Widely used in civic planting, it is often overlooked in garden centers, probably because its trailing growth makes it untidy in a pot. It is evergreen, with dark green, shiny leaves carried on long, trailing stems covered in chestnut bristles. White flowers, sometimes followed by edible red fruits, are produced in summer, but are of very secondary importance to the foliage. It is an incredibly efficient ground-cover plant, forming a dense carpet even on dry soil under beech trees.

The vincas, or periwinkles, are invaluable plants for ground cover in shade and on banks. The small-leaved forms of *Vinca minor* grow flatter and are less smothering than the larger-leaved forms of the greater periwinkle, *Vinca major*. *Vinca minor* **'Argenteovariegata'** (z. 5–8) has creamy-white variegated leaves and blue flowers, while *Vinca minor* f. *alba* **'Gertrude Jekyll'** (z. 5–8) has white flowers. It is pretty planted under *Osmanthus heterophyllus* **'Variegatus'** (see also Good Companions, page 89). Normally, variegated plants are less vigorous than plain green-leaved ones, but this is not true of the arching and rampant *Vinca major* **'Variegata'** (z. 8–9). Its creamy white-margined leaves and blue flowers shine light under laurels and quickly cover banks and rough ground on damp or dry sites.

Vinca major 'Variegata'

Fuchsia • Hydrangea • Itea • Kerria • Ligustrum • Lonicera • Prunus laurocerasus • Pyracantha •

Damp sites

Moist, fertile soil that has good drainage but does not dry out is the ideal growing environment. However, many soils are permanently damp and heavy, and plants may suffer from lack of oxygen around their roots. Clay soils, while very fertile, tend to have poor drainage and are therefore overly wet and heavy; poor drainage may also be the result of compaction. If you garden on a damp site, choose plants that are tolerant of such conditions.

Amelanchiers are hard-working shrubs, with pretty flowers, fine spring and autumn foliage, and fruit. *Amelanchier canadensis* (snowy mespilus) (zone 3–7) is a hardy deciduous, suckering native shrub. It is tall and erect, with upright sprays of white flowers and pretty, coppery new growth in mid-spring; in an open spot, the foliage colors well in fall. *Amelanchier lamarckii* (zone 4–8) is more spectacular, with larger, lax sprays of flowers, brighter new growth and better autumn color.

Amelanchier lamarckii

All varieties of **Cornus alba** (zone 2–8) come into their own here, growing vigorously in wet conditions on virtually any soil. These versatile and useful plants are excellent for their deciduous foliage, autumn color, and winter stems (see pages 67, 170, 177–79).

Hippophae rhamnoides (zone 3–7), the sea buckthorn, is easygoing,

Hippophae rhamnoides

ideal for sandy soil and coastal gardens, and tolerant of poor drainage and pollution. It often fruits well, retaining its yellow berries long after the silver, willowlike leaves have fallen. It is a useful plant where height is needed.

Physocarpus opulifolius (zone 2–7) is a hardy native plant that thrives in open, moist conditions. *Physocarpus opulifolius* 'Dart's Gold' has bright yellow foliage (see Good Companions, opposite); the leaves of *Physocarpus opulifolius* 'Diabolo' are dark purple,

IMPROVING DAMP SOIL

Ground preparation is all important in a wet soil. Sometimes growing conditions on heavy soils can be improved by the addition of coarse washed grit. Some low-lying gardens are just naturally wet, so it is necessary to work with the conditions rather than trying to overcome them. Either choose tolerant plants or use raised beds to lift the level of the planting areas above the wet soil.

which makes it a useful complementary shrub in almost any planting scheme.

Most **willows** (*Salix*) thrive on damp sites. Several varieties, which will grow into large trees if not contained, have attractively colored stems in winter; they can be hard pruned in the same way as *Cornus alba* (see page 176), to encourage these, and to keep them to shrub proportions. The stems of *Salix alba* ssp. *vitellina* (zone 2–9) are bright yellow, while those of *Salix alba* ssp. *vitellina* 'Britzensis' (zone 2–9) are brilliant orange-scarlet. The violet willow, *Salix daphnoides*, (zone 2–9) has purple-violet shoots, with a white bloom, and furry gray, then yellow,

Salix alba subsp. vitellina 'Britzensis'

Salix daphnoides

MORE SHRUBS FOR DAMP SITES *Calycanthus floridus* • *Cornus sericea* • *Gaultheria shallon* • *Myrica gale* •

Sambucus nigra f. *porphyrophylla* 'Gerda' ('Black Beauty')

Sorbaria tomentosa var. *angustifolia*

Symphoricarpos × *doorenbosii* 'Mother of Pearl'

catkins in spring. *Salix elaeagnos*, the hoary willow, is described on page 78.

The elders (*Sambucus*) are very accommodating plants, and grow on dry and wet soils. All are deciduous. Choose the gold-leaved *Sambucus racemosa* 'Sutherland Gold' (see page 47) for shade and the purple-leaved *Sambucus nigra* f. *porphyrophylla* 'Gerda', ('Black Beauty') (zone 5–7) for sun. The cut-leaved *Sambucus nigra* f. *laciniata* (zone 5–7), the fern-leaved elder, is a lovely plant, with finely cut foliage and heads of white flowers. (See Good Companions, right.)

Often taken for spiraeas, *Sorbarias* are big, vigorous deciduous shrubs with huge sprays of creamy white flowers, like large astilbes, in summer. *Sorbaria tomentosa* var. *angustifolia* (zone 6–7) is a very elegant form, with spreading reddish branches, fernlike foliage, and large, graceful flower stems.

Most spiraeas happily tolerate damp conditions, but *Spiraea* × *vanhouttei* (zone 3–8) excels on very damp soil. A vigorous, semi-evergreen shrub with arching branches, it is covered in white hawthornlike flowers in late spring. (See Good Companions, right.)

Symphoricarpos (zone 4–7), the snowberries, thrive in damp and dry sites, producing light, twiggy growth to about 3ft. (1m). White or pink berries add winter interest (see page 90).

Viburnum opulus (zone 3–8) and its cultivars are easy, deciduous shrubs. It is grown for its flowers as well as its autumn color (see page 172). *Viburnum*

opulus 'Roseum' ('Sterile'), snowball bush, is a vigorous deciduous shrub that can reach over 6ft. (2m). The "snowballs" of sterile florets start lime green, then progress through cream to blush pink in late spring and early summer. (See Good Companions, below.)

Wet sites, especially near water, suit naturalistic planting; all the above look good in these surroundings.

GOOD COMPANIONS

Physocarpus opulifolius 'Dart's Gold' (1) (z. 2–7) has bright yellow leaves and complements the yellow-variegated *Cornus alba* 'Spaethii' and bold-leaved *Ligularia dentata* 'Desdemona' (2) (z. 3–8).

Sambucus nigra f. *lacinata* (3) (z. 5–7) goes well with heavy, moisture-loving plants such as *Gunnera manicata* (4) (z. 7–10) and *Rheum palmatum* 'Atropurpureum' (z. 5–7).

The white flowers and fresh green foliage of *Spirea* × *vanhouttei* (5) (z. 3–8) combine prettily with the white-variegated leaves of *Cornus alba* 'Elegantissima' (6) (z. 2–8).

Viburnum opulus 'Roseum' (7) (z. 3–8) is lovely under-planted with *Alchemilla mollis* (8) (z. 4–7), whose frothy green flowers are at their best when the heavy white blooms of the viburnum are in full flower.

MOIST ACID SOILS

Plants that like moist acid soil do not tolerate drought; often, their natural, peaty habitat is moist all year.

The bog rosemary, *Andromeda polifolia* (zone 2–6), is a natural choice. This dwarf evergreen shrub is a native of Britain, with rosemary-like foliage and clusters of bell-shaped, pink flowers in late spring. *Andromeda polifolia* 'Alba' and *Andromeda polifolia* 'Compacta', bearing, respectively, white and pink flowers, are the best choices for most gardens.

The aronia species *Aronia arbutifolia* (zone 4–9) and the hybrid *Aronia × prunifolia* (zone 4–8) do not have to be grown in acid soil, but these shrubs resent shallow alkaline soils. Members of the rose family, they have hawthorn-like flowers in spring, red or purple fruits and—the main reason for growing them—exceptional autumn color.

The sweet pepper bush, *Clethra alnifolia* (zone 3–9), is an upright deciduous shrub, with spikes of scented

Aronia arbutifolia

Clethra alnifolia 'Paniculata'

Waterside planting at Le Clos du Coudray, Normandy, France.

white flowers in late summer. A hardy native related to erica, it needs lime-free soil. *Clethra alnifolia* 'Paniculata' is considered the best form.

Another very hardy North American native, *Gaultheria shallon* (zone 6–8) is a useful evergreen for damp acid sites. It produces thickets of stems up to 6ft. (2m) tall. The leaves are leathery, and the clusters of pinkish white flowers are followed by dark purple fruits.

Rhododendrons hate drought, so damp acid soil is ideal for the hardy hybrids (see page 103). They do not like to be waterlogged, but given enough moisture, they grow and color well.

SEASONAL CONTRAST

Wet sites offer wonderful possibilities when it comes to herbaceous perennials and deciduous shrubs and trees. Many moisture lovers have bold foliage, and some grow at an incredible rate. Contrast is the appeal of damp areas: in the summer they are verdant, full, lush, and leafy, while in winter a stark scene of stems and framework prevails. Evergreens are naturally adapted to resist desiccation; as a result, wet conditions are not their natural habitat, and most look uncomfortable in damp sites.

Clay soils

Aralia elata 'Variegata'

A well-known British gardener once said, "If you have free-draining acid, sandy soil, plant rhododendrons; if you have chalk [limestone], plant clematis; if you have clay, move!" What he should have said was: "If you have clay, you will have to make the best of it by choosing the right plants." Clay soil can indeed be difficult to work, but, on the plus side, it is very fertile, and you can always improve its structure (see pages 16–17).

If you chose the right shrubs, cultivation of the soil is rarely required after planting, just the removal of weeds around the plants. If you use a glyphosate-based weedkiller to do this, make sure that the herbicide does not splash the shrub's foliage. An occasional mulch of composted bark, compost, or well-rotted manure will benefit the plants and gradually improve the soil structure. The level of nutrients in the soil means that supplementary feeding is rarely required for good flowering and strong performance.

Many plants grow well on clay soils, especially such deciduous flowering shrubs as deutzias, forsythias, ribes, philadelphus, and weigelas, all of which are a natural choice for heavy clay.

For a striking architectural effect *Aralia elata* (zone 3–9), the Japanese angelica tree, is unbeatable. This is a large, suckering deciduous shrub whose upright stems grow to 10ft. (3m) or more. The vast, green fernlike leaves, all at the top of the stems, give the shrub the look of a palm, and white flowers in huge sprays appear in the fall; the foliage can color well at the same time. *Aralia elata* 'Variegata' has white-edged leaves, irregularly marked with creamy white. The flowers appear earlier and are less spectacular than on the green form. It is a choice and much sought-after plant.

All cornus do well on clay and are also valuable for wet, sticky soils. Larger-growing varieties such as *Cornus alba* 'Elegantissima' (see page 178) (zone 2–8) are ideal for filling space and covering difficult ground.

The vigorous deciduous shrub *Leycesteria formosa* (zone 7–8) grows just about anywhere and succeeds well on clay, even on damp sites. It is a Nepalese woodland species—hence its common name, Himalayan Honeysuckle. The tall, arching, hollow stems are sea green, and the flower clusters hang from the branches from early summer through fall, the claret-red bracts interspersed with small white flowers. These are followed by shiny purple fruits. When the leaves fall, remove any dead and twiggy growth, and cut out some of the old stems to ground level: this leaves the

EVERGREEN SHRUBS

When it comes to evergreens for clay soil, it is the hardy favorites that come to the fore: aucubas (see Good Companions, page 96), choisyas and *Viburnum tinus*. All of these do well in sun as well as shade, and provide that all-important structure on the heaviest of soils. Mahonias also do well on clay, and provide cheery winter and early spring color (see Good Companions, page 96).

The evergreen *Magnolia grandiflora* (z. 7–9) also grows on clay soils, but it dislikes wet conditions and resents being planted too deeply.

On slightly acid clay soils, the hardy hybrid rhododendrons grow surprisingly well. The larger-growing, later-flowering *Rhododendron catawbiense* (z. 5–7), parent of many hybrids, is ideal for screening and background planting. 'Cunningham's White' (z. 5–7) is an old cultivar, with dark green foliage and prettily marked flowers in mauve, fading to white; it is very tough and will even tolerate slightly alkaline conditions. For dark red flowers, 'Nova Zembla' (right, z. 5–7) is a winner; this is a hardy plant of upright growth with deep red, weather-resistant blooms.

attractive green stems exposed through the winter. (See Good Companions, below.)

All deciduous magnolias grow well on clay (see pages 134–35). For smaller gardens, *Magnolia stellata* (zone 4–8) is a good choice, producing a mass of starry, shiny blooms every spring. The gray, catkinlike buds are attractive in winter. Where space is not restricted, choose one of the cultivars of *Magnolia × soulangeana* (zone 4–9).

Even if the hardy hibiscus are late to break into leaf, you can depend on them for late-summer flowers. When hibiscus is flowering, **hypericums** and **potentillas** are still performing; both grow well in heavy soil conditions.

Magnolia × soulangeana

Rosa 'Rosy Cushion'

Roses (see pages 112–15) tolerate clay soils, as do many other members of the rose family. For example, **cotoneasters** and **pyracanthas** require little attention and are excellent for smothering sites where cultivation is virtually impossible (see Good Companions, below).

Purple and yellow foliage effects are easy to achieve on clay soils: **berberis**, **cotinus**, *Philadelphus coronarius* 'Aureus', **spiraea**, and *Weigela florida* 'Foliis Purpureis' all thrive under these conditions.

Clay soils are often too wet in winter to be ideal for silver-foliage plants, but *Brachyglottis* (Dunedin Group) 'Sunshine' (zone 8–10), formerly called *Senecio* 'Sunshine', copes with these conditions and, if pruned hard just before the flowers appear, remains silver throughout winter. (See page 79.)

GOOD COMPANIONS

A combination of *Leycesteria formosa* (1) (z. 7–8) with *Symphoricarpos orbiculatus* 'Foliis Variegatis' (2) (z. 2–7) and *Cornus alba* 'Gouchaultii' (3) (z. 2–8) is ideal in difficult conditions—on a heavy clay bank, for example.

The yellow flowers of *Mahonia japonica* (4) (z. 6–9) combine well with the golden variegations of *Aucuba japonica* 'Marmorata' (5) (z. 7–10).

For ground cover on tough sites, use a large shrub rose such as 'Nevada' (6) with evergreens *Cotoneaster franchetii* (7) (z. 5–7) and *Pyracantha* 'Golden Charmer' (8) (z. 6–9).

PLANTING ON CLAY SOIL

Planting on clay can be difficult. It is really important to dig as large a planting hole as you can and to mix plenty of compost with the garden soil before you replace it around the plant, to help the roots to acclimatize to their new home.

Clay soils can dry out and bake hard in the summer, so early fall is the best time to plant in order to give the shrub longer to establish. Planting in spring may be difficult if the ground is wet and heavy.

Once established, shrubs grown on clay have great stability: the weight of the soil keeps the roots firm, and the plants rarely suffer from wind damage. Provided planting is well established and good ground cover is achieved, little further maintenance or cultivation is needed.

MORE SHRUBS FOR CLAY SOILS *Abelia • Chaenomeles • Corylus • Cytisus • Deutzia • Escallonia • Garrya • Genista • Hamamelis • Leycesteria • Lonicera • Philadelphus • Potentilla • Sambucus • Skimmia • Syringa •*

Limestone soils

The depth of soils over limestone varies enormously. Where soils are deep, they can be adequately fertile and moisture retentive to support most plants; only ericaceous plants, or alkaline-intolerant plants, are taboo. Shallow soils over limestone need more consideration; these are free-draining, and can lack nutrients and be quite dry in the summer, so you need to select plants that enjoy these conditions.

Deutzia × hybrida 'Magicien'

Soil pH has a profound effect on the availability of some nutrients to certain plants. Iron, essential for the growth of rhododendrons and other ericaceous plants, becomes locked up on lime-rich, alkaline soil: as a result, the leaves turn yellow and the plant suffers. Plants that thrive on limestone soil do so because they are adapted to cope with the conditions. A vast range of plants can be grown on alkaline soil; with a little persistence, you can find as many plants for alkaline soil as you can for acid soil.

Many hardy deciduous shrubs come to the fore on lime: **deutzias** (see pages 151–52), **forsythias** (see pages 132–33), **philadelphus** (see page 160), **lilacs** (*syringa*; see page 145), **weigelas** (see page 162). All thrive and contribute color and interest throughout spring. For summer color, choose any buddleia or hibiscus. The hardy fuchsias, such as 'Mrs. Popple' (see Good Companions, page 98) grow well in sun or shade and provide color from midsummer on.

A close relative of weigela, *Dipelta floribunda* (zone 5–7) is an excellent, if

Syringa × hyacinthiflora 'Esther Staley'

Dipelta floribunda

Weigela florida 'Variegata'

Romneya coulteri

A WORD OF ENCOURAGEMENT

Alkaline soil should never be seen as a disadvantage. Ericaceous plants, if craved, can be grown in pots; in that way, the gardener gets the best of both worlds. Limestone soils can also be improved by the addition of bulky organic matter to increase the humus content of the soil; this improves texture as well as increasing the nutrient and water-holding capacity, thereby increasing the fertility.

less well known, deciduous shrub. It is lighter and more graceful in habit than many weigelas, with narrower leaves, often with a coppery tinge. The fragrant flowers are pink, flushed yellow at the throat, profusely produced in late spring all along the upright, arching branches.

The California tree poppy, *Romneya coulteri* (zone 7–8), is somewhere

Cotoneaster simonsii

between a shrub and a herbaceous perennial. It is a thicket-forming plant, spreading by underground stems. It can be difficult to establish, but on light, alkaline soils it can become positively rampant, throwing up numerous hollow gray stems that will easily reach 6ft. (2m) in height. The deeply cut, gray-blue leaves are a delightful background to the huge, tissue-paper white blooms with their yellow-stamened centers. This is a plant for a warm, sunny spot—alongside a wall, perhaps.

Spiraeas also grow well on limestone. The golden-leaved varieties of *Spiraea japonica* (see page 46) are invaluable for their colorful foliage throughout summer. *Spiraea japonica* 'Anthony Waterer' (zone 3–8), with its bright crimson, fluffy, flat flower heads, is a good shrub for the front of borders and its flowers are much loved by insects. The foliage is sometimes variegated pink and green, unlike the newer *Spiraea japonica* 'Dart's' Red' (zone 3–8), which has solid green leaves. (See Good Companions, page 99.)

EVERGREEN SHRUBS

Finding evergreens for limestone is not a problem. The ever-tolerant **aucubas** are always a good choice, as are the versatile

cotoneasters. The latter suit both town and country gardens. The white flowers attract pollinating insects and butterflies in spring. Birds appreciate their showy and appetizing fruit in fall. There is a cotoneaster for almost any situation, from ground cover to large shrubs.

Cotoneaster dammeri has long trailing shoots carrying shiny, dark green leaves and bright red berries in fall (see Good Companions, below). *Cotoneaster simonsii* is upright in habit and semi-evergreen, with neat, glossy green leaves and large scarlet fruits. It makes a fine hedge, around 5ft. (1.5m) high. (See also Plant Profile, page 175.)

Ceanothus can succeed in a sunny spot in limestone soil, given plenty of organic matter. **Cytisus** will grow on limestone and partner the early-flowering evergreen *Ceanothus* 'Concha' well (see Good Companions below and pages 140 and 146).

All euonymus grow very well on alkaline soil, and favorites such as *Euonymus fortunei* 'Blondy' (zone 5–8) and the more upright *Euonymus japonicus* forms (zone 7–9) are useful in both sun and shade (see page 58).

GOOD COMPANIONS

The sapphire clouds of *Ceanothus* 'Concha' (1) (z. 9–10) in full bloom alongside the cream wands of *Cytisus* × *praecox* 'Warminster' (2) (z. 5–7) make a breathtaking sight.

For covering limestone banks, *Cotoneaster dammeri* (3) (z. 4–7) is a natural partner for *Vinca minor* 'Argenteovariegata' (4) (z. 5–8).

To prolong the season of interest, plant the hardy fuchsia, 'Mrs. Popple' (5) (z. 7–9) or 'Riccartonii', alongside early-blooming deutzias such as *Deutzia* × *rosea* 'Carminea' (6) (z. 5–8).

MORE SHRUBS FOR LIMESTONE SOILS *Brachyglottis* • *Choisya* • *Cornus mas* • *Hypericum* • *Ligustrum* • *Lonicera* •

Hebes (see pages 52, 76, 154) are happier on alkaline soils than on acid ones—the drier conditions in winter reduce the incidence of leafspot diseases caused by damp conditions.

For shady situations on limestone, the best dwarf evergreen is **Sarcococca confusa** (see page 90; illus. page 184).

Photinia × fraseri 'Red Robin' and **Laurus nobilis** (see pages 123 and 31) are large structural evergreens that thrive on limestone. Both are excellent screening shrubs, achieving a height of 10 ft. (3m) or more if left unchecked. They also respond well to pruning. For a lower, more compact structural evergreen, consider a **Buxus sempervirens** cultivar (see page 29).

The Spanish broom, **Spartium junceum** (zone 8–9), is a member of the pea family, similar to cytisus and genista in appearance, with large, showy, fragrant yellow flowers. It looks poor as a young plant in a pot and can be leggy and awkward as an elderly shrub. The habit is loose and upright,

GOOD COMPANIONS

An ideal plant for coastal gardens, *Spartium junceum* (1) (z. 8–9) works well planted against the silver-green foliage of *Elaeagnus × ebbingei* (2) (z. 7–11).

On a sunny site *Spiraea japonica* 'Dart's' Red' (3) (z. 3–8) combines well with the silver foliage of santolina and the purple-pink branches of *Berberis thunbergii* f. *atropurpurea* 'Rose Glow' (4) (z. 4–8).

with green, sedgelike stems that appear devoid of leaves. The flowers bloom along the upper part of the stems, throughout summer and early fall. The bush will reach 10ft. (3m) or more if left unchecked, but is best pruned in spring from an early age to keep it compact. Never cut back into old wood, as new

growth is unlikely to regenerate. (See Good Companions, above.)

Many Mediterranean natives, notably **cistus** and **helianthemums**, are happy on shallow, dry, alkaline soils, while **rosemary** is more aromatic than ever in a dry, sunny spot on poor soil. (See pages 83, 150; 85–86; 86–87.)

Rosemary and lavender grace a sunny terrace at Hestercombe, Somerset, in England.

Mahonia aquifolium • *Olearia* • *Potentilla* • *Pyracantha* • *Ribes* • *Sambucus* • *Symphoricarpos* • *Tamarix* • *Viburnum* • *Yucca* •

Acid soils

The range of plants that need an acid soil includes some of the most beautiful spring-flowering shrubs, as well as some of the finest for autumn color. No wonder acid soils are the envy of many who garden on limestone. However, now that container gardening is so popular, growing acid lovers in pots, using ericaceous potting mix, is an easy option for those with alkaline soil.

Azaleas and rhododendrons at Trewithen, Cornwall, in England.

There is a complex relationship between soil pH (the measure of acidity and alkalinity) and the availability of certain nutrients to certain plants. Soil pH is measured on a scale of 1 (extremely acid) to 14 (extremely alkaline). Neutral soil has a pH value of 7.0. This, or just below, is the ideal for gardening, as it allows the cultivation of the widest range of plants.

Acid soils, whether sandy or peaty, are normally low in nutrients, and most acid-loving plants are adapted to a soil of relatively low fertility. However, there are certain micronutrients that they must have; it is these that become unavailable to them when grown on an alkaline soil. Sometimes, neutral soil can be made more acid by the addition of sulfur chips and peat moss. However, an alkaline soil is so because of the under-lying rock: add vast quantities of acidic ingredients to a limestone soil and the lime will still come through—it is not worth the battle. Instead, grow plants that are suited to the site.

Although the term "ericaceous" strictly refers to those plants that belong to the family *Ericaceae*, it is used more generally for plants that need acid soil.

All the plants in this section are acid loving, and need a pH of less than 7.0. Most can be grown in containers, so long as ericaceous potting mix is used.

GROWING ACID-LOVING PLANTS

Many acid lovers originate from open heathland or woodland conditions, and you should bear this in mind when positioning them in the garden, in the open or in pots. Some are from cool climates, and dislike drought and high temperatures: for these, a hot, sunny spot and no water can prove fatal. Most are shallow-rooting plants and have a very fibrous root system, which is dense and difficult to rewet once dry. Pay attention to watering at all times.

Acid-loving plants are not heavy feeders, so use a slow-release, lime-free fertilizer sparingly. Mulch plants with leaf mold or lime-free soil mix in spring, when the soil is moist. Keep the mulch away from the main stems, but use it generously around the drip-line of the plant (where the foliage extends onto the soil surface)—this is where root activity is at its maximum.

PLANTING IN POTS

Rhododendrons (see pages 101–105), camellias (see pages 106–107), and pieris (see page 109) make excellent subjects for pots. Choose a large pot at least 16in. (40cm) in diameter and at least 12in. (30cm) deep. Put plenty of drainage in the form of broken crocks in the bottom, and plant in ericaceous, loam-based soil mix for best results. This holds water and nutrients better than soilless mixures, prevents drying out and is less attractive to vine weevil (see box, page 103). Raise the pot slightly off the ground, using pot feet or pieces of tile to prevent waterlogging.

Plants in containers appreciate an occasional drenching in summer with a liquid fertilizer and growth stimulant containing sequestered iron. The same treatment can be used for sickly yellow specimens growing in the open ground.

Rhododendrons and azaleas

In many ways, the rhododendron offers the qualities that constitute the perfect garden plant: evergreen foliage, reliability of flowering, showy blooms, no pruning requirements, and few pests. The only drawback, for some gardeners, is that most will grow only on acid soil. The name suggests "red tree," but the rhododendron spectrum is much broader, their jewel colors lighting up our gardens through late spring and early summer.

Rhododendron 'Praecox'

The rhododendrons, a vast and diverse group, vary in stature from dwarf, compact shrubs just a few inches tall, to trees. For garden purposes, the rhododendrons fall into three principal categories: dwarf rhododendrons, compact hybrids, and hardy hybrids. The genus also includes deciduous and evergreen azaleas.

DWARF RHODODENDRONS

This group includes the small-leaved, compact species and hybrids that are frequently grown as rock garden subjects and early-flowering plants for pots. They combine well with heathers and conifers, and suit small gardens. In height they range from 1ft. (30cm) to 3ft. (1m).

Rhododendron 'Bengal' (zone 6–7) is robust and compact, with glossy dark green foliage; loose trusses of deep red flowers are reliably produced. *Rhododendron* Blue Tit Group (zone 6–8) form a dense, round bush, up to 3ft. (1m), but usually smaller; tiny, funnel-shaped flowers appear in clusters at the end of the branches in mid-spring, opening lavender-blue but darkening with age. 'Ginny Gee' (zone 5–8) is a dwarf, but spreading, compact shrub with neat foliage; the flowers are widely funnel-shaped, opening to pale pink and fading to white edged with pink (see Good Companions, right). 'Patty Bee' (zone 5–8) is strong-growing but very compact, with attractive, small, medium-green leaves and brown, felty stems and buds, opening to primrose flowers, produced in profusion in early spring and adding interest to evergreen planting; it looks good with yellow-spotted aucuba. 'Praecox' (zone 6–8) is an open shrub with small, often bronzeish leaves, which are aromatic when crushed. The pretty flowers, which are produced in twos and threes at the end of the shoots, open in early spring; they are pale rosy purple, almost translucent. Put it under light tree cover to prevent frost damage. It looks delightful when underplanted with *Primula vulgaris* (primrose) (zone 6–7).

Rhododendron 'Ramapo' (zone 4–8) is a hardy, compact, reliable shrub with blue-gray young foliage; the blue-violet flowers appear in clusters all over the bush in early spring if grown in full sun. The tough 'Scarlet Wonder' (zone 5–7) succeeds on any site with acid soil. It has attractive, dark green, rounded leaves and forms a dense mound; the bright ruby flowers are carried in loose trusses in late spring (see Good Companions, below). 'Shamrock' (zone 5–7) is a compact, spreading dwarf shrub with glossy, dark green foliage and lime-green buds that open to pale yellow flowers in early spring. 'Wee Bee' (zone 5–8) is a neat, dwarf shrub with good foliage and pinkish yellow buds that turn into pretty pink flowers with red spots.

GOOD COMPANIONS

Rhododendron 'Scarlet Wonder' (1) (z. 5–7), flowers in late spring, providing good ground cover with *Ceanothus thyrsiflorus* var. *repens* (2) (z. 8–10).

Rhododendron 'Ginny Gee' (3) (z. 5–8) is a very pretty plant, blooming after the winter-flowering heather season; it is useful for revitalizing pink and white *Erica carnea* (4) (z. 5–7).

COMPACT HYBRIDS

These are smaller-growing varieties of the typical, large-growing rhododendron hardy hybrids, and as such they have more typical rhododendron flowers and foliage than the dwarf rhododendrons. The compact habit is often the result of hybridizing vigorous varieties with *Rhododendron yakushimanum* (zone 5–8). They are hardy plants and range in size from 2ft. (60cm) to 5ft. (1.5m).

The *Rhododendron yakushimanum* hybrids are excellent plants, with a very solid habit. They are a good choice for pots, where they can stand alone. In the garden, plant them singly, with lighter plants around them—heathers in sun, ferns or pulmonarias in shade; if planted in groups, they create a solid, heavy mass. Compact hybrids with *Rhododendron yakushimanum* in the parentage include the following: **'Dreamland'** (zone 5–8) is a small, domed shrub with silvery young foliage, becoming dark green, and large, very pale pink flowers with darker edges in loose trusses. **'Fantastica'** (zone 5–8) is small, and spreading, with dark green leaves that are white and woolly beneath. The flowers, which are carried

Rhododendron 'Dreamland'

Rhododendron 'Sneezy'

Rhododendron 'Percy Wiseman'

Rhododendron 'Hotei'

in large trusses, are pale pink, shading to white, but with deep pink wavy edges. **'Golden Torch'** (zone 5–8) has neat foliage and a particularly solid growth habit. The flower buds are salmon pink, opening to bell-shaped blooms of pale yellow in tight trusses. **'Percy Wiseman'** (zone 5–8) is a lovely hybrid, with dark green foliage and

round trusses of large, funnel-shaped flowers, which open apricot, fading to cream flushed with apricot pink. **'Sneezy'** (zone 5–8) is very hardy and vigorous, with dark green leaves that are silvery when young; the flowers, which are produced in large, dense trusses in late spring, are deep pink, paler in the center with red spots.

Some other compact rhododendrons are as follows. **'Golden Gate'** (zone 5–7) is a dome-shaped shrub with reddish pink flowers with orange-yellow centers, carried in clusters of five or six. **'Hotei'** (zone 5–8) has rounded, narrow leaves and deep yellow, bell-shaped flowers; **'Kokardia'** (zone 5–8) has trusses of rich purple flowers. **'Mrs. Furnivall'** (zone 5–8) is larger but has a dense habit; its trusses of wide, funnel-shaped flowers are light rose pink, blotched with brown, with crimson centers. **'Nancy Evans'** (zone 5–8) is small, with rounded, glossy, dark green leaves that are bronze when young. Orange-red buds open to frilled, amber-yellow flowers in rounded trusses (see Good Companions, left).

GOOD COMPANIONS

Plant *Rhododendron* 'Nancy Evans' (1) (z. 5–8) with *Euphorbia griffithii* 'Fireglow' (2) (z. 5–7) for a glowing combination.

Pink rhododendrons, such as the compact hybrid 'Rocket' (3) (z. 5–7), combine well with *Hyacinthoides non-scripta* (bluebells) (4) (z. 5–8).

HARDY HYBRIDS

This group includes large, stately shrubs that produce showy flowers in big trusses. Their hardiness varies according to parentage; generally, these are plants that withstand exposed situations and are easy to grow. They range in size from 5ft. (1.5m) to 10ft. (3m).

Hybrids have been raised from *Rhododendron arboreum* (zone 5–7), as well as from *Rhododendron catawbiense* (zone 5–7) and *Rhododendron maximum* (zone 3–7), native species, and *Rhododendron ponticum* (zone 5–8), from Turkey. As new species were introduced from China and the Himalayas, other characteristics in flower shape, color, habit, and foliage emerged. The most cold hardy and heat resistant hybrids are known as "ironclads"—many are descendants of the native *Rhododendron catawbiense.*

'Albert Schweitzer' (zone 5–7) is a large, upright shrub, with conical trusses of deep pink flowers with a darker blotch. **'Gomer Waterer'** (zone 5–7), one of the best hardy hybrids, is a medium-sized shrub with healthy, thick leaves and red-brown buds; the large flowers, carried in dense, round trusses, are deeply frilled, white flushed mauve, with a mustard yellow blotch in the throat. **'Halfdan Lem'** (zone 5–7) is a

Rhododendron 'Mrs T.H. Lowinsky'

vigorous, medium-sized shrub with dark green, slightly waved foliage and red leaf stalks; the bright red flowers are carried in large trusses. **'Horizon Monarch'** (zone 5–7) is a medium-sized shrub with good foliage. The flowers, which are produced earlier in the year than on most varieties, are pinkish-orange in bud, opening to wide, lightly frilled blooms of creamy yellow, marked red in the throat. **'Lord Roberts'** (zone 5–7) is an old hybrid, but it still has the best flower color of all the reds; it has dense, round trusses of funnel-shaped flowers, deep crimson with black markings. **'Mrs. T. H. Lowinsky'** (zone 5–7) is vigorous and tall, with broad leaves.

Rhododendron 'Horizon Monarch'

The lilac flowers, paler in the center, are heavily spotted orange-brown. **'Van'** (zone 5–7) is healthy and vigorous but compact grower, with large, loose trusses of vivid deep pink flowers.

CARING FOR RHODODENDRONS

Regular watering of rhododendrons is essential. Since the roots are fibrous and compact, it is difficult for water to penetrate a dry rootball; if a plant does dry out, a dripping hose is better than a deluge. Removing fading flowers from the plant stimulates the production of the new growth next season.

Bud blast is a fungal disease that causes the buds to die on the plants before opening. The buds usually grow brown and sooty, as black fungal spore carriers appear on the buds in spring, before they develop. This fungal infection is spread the previous summer by leafhoppers. Treatment is by controlling the leafhoppers with a systemic insecticide spray, applied in mid and late summer. Spraying with a copper-based fungicide in fall and early spring also gives some control of the fungus, if present. Infected buds must be removed and destroyed, not left on the plants.

VINE WEEVIL

Vine weevil can be a problem to evergreen acid-loving plants particularly camellias and rhododendrons. To treat, apply a soil and foliar drench of a systemic insecticide recommended for this purpose. Alternatively, a biological control can be used. A solution containing a parasitic nematode is watered on in early spring or fall; the nematodes attack the vine weevil larvae that are feeding on the roots at this time.

DECIDUOUS AZALEAS

Botanically belonging to the same genus as rhododendrons, but as aesthetically and atmospherically different as frost from fire, deciduous azaleas display maturity at an early age. The deciduous quality displays a changing profile with the seasons; leaf loss reveals, and accentuates, a graceful and expressive frame, a style and deportment possessed only by the most sophisticated of shrubs. Layered branches carry elegant foliage, and graceful clusters of long-lasting, exotic blooms, which are decorative even in bud, have an oriental air. The elegant form of deciduous azaleas is an excellent contrast to the solid, heavy form of most evergreens. Autumn color is a feature of many varieties. All flower in late spring.

The range of flower colors covers almost everything conceivable, except

Rhododendron luteum

blue and purple shades. Some groups have one of the most delicious fragrances in the plant world. *Rhododendron luteum* (zone 5–6), the yellow-flowering species, has a fresh honeysuckle scent that has been imparted to many hybrids.

Rhododendron 'Fireball' (zone 5–7) is also fragrant, with copper young foliage and deep orange-red flowers. 'Cannon's Double' (zone 5–7) has

Rhododendron 'Fireball'

Rhododendron 'Irene Koster'

CARING FOR DECIDUOUS AZALEAS

After flowering, deciduous azaleas enjoy a shower of liquid fertilizer with sequestered iron. This fortifies the plant for the growing season and strengthens the foliage for the colorful days of autumn ahead. There is no need to deadhead deciduous azaleas. The open structure of the plant is part of its character. However, deciduous azaleas respond well to pruning after flowering, if a more compact plant is desired.

apricot-flushed red buds, double, creamy flowers, and long-lasting, rich bronze-purple tints in fall. 'Glowing Embers' (zone 5–7) is a vivid reddish orange with an orange blotch. 'Homebush' (zone 5–7) has small, spiky, deep pink flowers in dense round trusses, unlike any other azalea; it mixes well with other plants. 'Irene Koster' (zone 5–7) is a favorite fragrant garden hybrid, with pale rose-pink flowers with a small yellow blotch, emphasizing the beauty of the orchidlike flowers. 'Klondyke' (zone 5–7) displays bronze leaf color all growing season. 'Mount Saint Helens' (zone 7–8) is a good pink. 'Northern Hi-Lights' (zone 5–7) is hardy, creamy yellow, pretty, and fragrant. 'White Lights' (zone 5–7) is a hardy, rounded, fragrant shrub with profuse white flowers with yellow centers opening from pink buds.

WHERE TO PLANT DECIDUOUS AZALEAS

Deciduous azaleas grow well in full sun or partial shade and associate well with most schemes. Many early spring subjects team up well with them to prolong the season of interest—for example, narcissi, crocus, chionodoxa, puschkinia, and dwarf iris. Early woodland herbaceous plants, such as pulmonaria, helleborus, and primula and spring- and autumn-flowering hardy cyclamen, sit naturally beneath their elegant frames. In woodland situations, they are excellent to line a path or act as a focus in a dell or clearing, the fragrance being accentuated by still air.

Deciduous azaleas also make stately, elegant architectural features when grown in pots. Positioned close to the house, the form of the plant is light enough to give foreground interest, without blocking the view of the garden beyond. In addition, they look good near water, their oriental frame and brilliant colors reflecting hauntingly in still pools and slow streams.

EVERGREEN AZALEAS

Evergreen azaleas vary in stature from compact, upright dwarf shrubs with tiny leaves and profuse small flowers, to spreading low shrubs with bolder foliage and large, ruffled blooms. All are free-flowering; a well-grown plant will obscure all traces of foliage when in full bloom. Vast numbers of hybrids have arisen in the United States and Europe as well as Japan, home of the azalea and from where Ernest Wilson introduced the Kurume azaleas in 1920.

The garden evergreen azaleas are hardy plants that require moisture around the roots and shelter from cold winds. Winter winds can cause leaf drop in exposed positions, and heavy rain and frost can spoil the flowers of the early-blooming varieties. Partially shaded, woodland conditions are ideal; and if planted in drifts in a woodland garden, they are breathtaking in bloom, as long as attention is paid to color combinations. However, when they are struggling against the odds on the

Rhododendron 'Blue Danube'

Rhododendron 'Kermesinum'

wrong soil in a suburban back garden these azaleas have little appeal.

The hardy types are often confused with the hybrids of *Azalea indica*, widely grown as houseplants. Although these can survive outside in the mildest localities, they are not generally regarded as garden plants.

Some attractive garden evergreen azalea varieties include *Rhododendron* 'Blue Danube' (zone 6–9), which is one of the best when in full flower, with its striking blue-violet blooms. 'Geisha Orange' (zone 6–9), like all of the Geisha varieties, is mound-forming, with small, neat foliage and soft orange flowers. 'Hinomayo' (zone 6–8) is a taller shrub, reaching 5ft. (1.5m), with

graceful, shocking pink flowers; originally from the emperor's garden in Tokyo, Japan. 'Johanna' (zone 5–7) has bronze foliage through fall and winter and attractive red flowers (see Good Companions. below). 'Kermesinum' (zone 6–8) is compact and low with purplish red flowers. 'Kermesinum Rosé' (zone 6–8) is similar but has white edged, pink flowers. 'Palestrina' (zone 6–8) has plenty of pretty, white blooms tinted light green. 'Rose Greeley' (zone 6–8) has "hose-in-hose" white flowers, blotched with green; it is one of the few scented evergreen azaleas. 'Vuyk's Scarlet' has stunning, large, bright red flowers with wavy petals and a loose, flowing growth habit.

CARING FOR EVERGREEN AZALEAS

Evergreen azaleas require no pruning. Bushiness can be encouraged on straggly plants by cutting back after flowering. Follow up with a light feed and plenty of water.

Evergreen azaleas are generally pest-free. Azalea gall is occasionally a problem, resulting in individual leaves becoming severely distorted, pale green, and waxy; remove infected leaves. Old evergreen azaleas are particularly susceptible to colonization by lichen. Gray-green, mosslike lichen clothes the branches, inhibiting the plant's growth. Although lichen is not directly harmful, it is usually a sign that the plant is not growing vigorously; feeding and mulching will help.

GOOD COMPANIONS

Evergreen azaleas (1) (z. 6–8) are suitable for shaded scree areas and fit any oriental design. They associate well with dwarf pines and bamboos, such as *Pleioblastus viridistriatus* (2) (z. 7–8).

Add ground cover to evergreen *Rhododendron* 'Johanna' (3) (z. 5–7) (deep red flowers) with *Leucothoe fontanesiana* 'Scarletta' (4) (z. 4–7)— its elegant green, red-tinged foliage turns bronze in winter.

Camellias

Camellias are woodland plants by origin, widespread across Asia from India through China to Japan and Korea. When introduced into England in 1740, they were cosseted and suffocated in the stifling "stove houses" of the day, because they came from Asia. Eventually, gardeners realized that these were not delicate hothouse plants but sturdy creatures that were happiest in cold conservatories and orangeries. Today, they are specimens for the garden, but their beginnings as pot subjects underline their suitability for growing in containers—which is much appreciated by those living on alkaline soils.

Camellia 'Cornish Snow'

Camellias may flower only once a year, but they are very worthwhile plants to grow, particularly since their glorious blooms appear at a time when many shrubs are just sticks. The flowers are produced over a long period from winter into late spring. They will usually tolerate the cold as long as early sun does not damage the frozen blooms: to prevent this, choose a position that does not get morning sun. The foliage is perhaps the most handsome of the plain evergreens, and the growth habit is usually tidy and compact.

Gardens with acid soil and semi-shade welcome camellias in the open ground. They require no special treatment, just adequate watering, particularly when the plants are young.

There are numerous camellia varieties to choose from. It is a good idea to buy container-grown plants in flower, so you can see exactly what the flower looks like. Here are a few good ones:

Camellia 'Cornish Snow' (zone 7–10) is a very early- and profuse-flowering camellia, with single white flowers and small leaves. It is a strong-growing bush, loose in habit, and eventually forms a large shrub; good for a woodland setting. *Camellia* 'Inspiration' (zone 7–10) is a medium-sized shrub with attractive, neat foliage and large, semi-double, glowing rich pink flowers.

Camellia japonica cultivars (zone 7–10) are among the most popular of camellias. As a rule, they have broad, glossy dark green leaves, and most have

Camellia 'Inspiration'

Camellia japonica 'Adolphe Audusson'

strong, upright growth. *Camellia japonica* 'Adolphe Audusson' has semi-double, blood-red flowers with showy yellow stamens; it is vigorous, compact, and good for formal situations. 'Alba Plena' has an upright, bushy habit and large, double white flowers, while 'Alba Simplex' bears single white flowers with prominent yellow stamens. 'Lavinia Maggi' produces large white or pale pink double flowers, with deep pink stripes.

A mature camellia – exotic blooms in early spring.

Camellia japonica 'Masayoshi' (zone 7–10), also known as 'Donckelaeri', is a bushy, compact shrub with large, semi-double, soft red flowers, marbled white; it is a tough plant and rarely shows any frost damage even in cold weather.

For general planting *Camellia × williamsii* (zone 6–10) is regarded as the best type. The parents are *Camellia japonica* and *Camellia saluensis*. The × williamsii cultivars are free-flowering, graceful shrubs. The foliage is similar to

Camellia japonica 'Alba Simplex'

Camellia japonica 'Masayoshi'

Camellia japonica 'Lavinia Maggi'

Camellia × williamsii 'Anticipation'

that of *Camellia japonica,* but often the leaves are narrower and the growth habit is looser. In the majority of cases, the whole flower drops to the ground as it fades, instead of remaining dead on the plant; as the flowering season progresses, this proves to be a real bonus as far as the overall look of the shrub is concerned.

Good cultivars of *Camellia × williamsii* include the upright **Camellia × williamsii 'Anticipation'**, which has large, peony-like blooms of deep pink. **'Debbie'** has similar flowers, of clear pink. **'Donation'**, the best-known camellia of them all, has large, semi-double, orchid-pink blooms and is very free flowering; it has an upright, but loose, habit, especially when young. **'Les Jury'** produces double red flowers on a compact, upright plant with bronze young foliage. **'Saint Ewe'** has single, cupped blooms and open, graceful growth. This is a very pretty plant, which is not too over-powering and therefore mixes well with other shrubs.

CARING FOR CAMELLIAS

Watering is vital, ideally with rainwater; camellias will not tolerate drought. Let a camellia dry out during late summer and it will respond by dropping first its buds and then its leaves. Camellias require no pruning; if you must trim to shape, then do so immediately after the flowers have fallen.

The commonest problem with camellias is brown scale; this manifests itself as black sooty deposits on the leaves, taking away all vitality and gloss. The sooty mold is a secondary infection of the sticky excretion of scale insects, which are found lurking as tiny brown bumps along the underside of the leaf midrib. Because of their tough outer coat, and strong attachment to the leaf, they are difficult to dispose of. A modern systemic insecticide applied as a spray to the upper and lower surface of the foliage is the most effective solution. Apply at the first sign of scale.

Heathers

Although they are not great in stature, heathers contribute long-lasting flower color as well as evergreen foliage that often changes color and texture with the seasons. Versatile plants, they make excellent ground-cover shrubs and combine well with conifers for all-year-round effect.

Ericas and callunas

Daboecia cantabrica 'Bicolor'

Calluna vulgaris (zone 4–6), the European heather or ling, is a hardy evergreen plant of heathland habitat. It requires neutral or acid soil but is otherwise easy to grow, being tolerant of moist or quite dry conditions and shade, although it flowers better and retains a more compact habit in sun. There are many varieties, varying in flower color, foliage color, and height—from flat mats to low mounds (see box right, Attractive foliage and Outstanding flowers). The bud-blooming heathers (see

box right, Decorative buds) are now very popular, not only for permanent planting but also as winter color for containers. The flower buds are pointed and show color from an early age; the habit is fine and graceful.

Daboecia cantabrica (zone 6–8), Connemara heath or St. Dabeoc's heath, is often also thought of as a heather or ling. An evergreen, it is related to *Erica* but should be treated like *Calluna* (see box, Growing heathers). The large, bell-shaped, rose-purple flowers are produced from early summer to late fall. There are also a number of good cultivars, including: *Daboecia cantabrica* 'Bicolor', with white and pink-purple flowers, some striped; *Daboecia cantabrica* ssp. *scotica* 'Jack Drake', with ruby red flowers; *Daboecia cantabrica* ssp. *scotica* 'Silverwells', which has white flowers; *Daboecia cantabrica* ssp. *scotica* 'William Buchanan', a deep purple, and *Daboecia cantabrica* ssp. *scotica* 'Waley's Red', with deep magenta flowers.

For the alkaline-tolerant *Erica carnea*, *Erica × darleyensis* varieties, and the tree heaths, see pages 131–32.

GROWING HEATHERS

Groups of three or five small, pot-grown heathers produce better results than single, more mature plants. Heathers should be trimmed after flowering to promote bushy plants. Those that look good during winter because of their dried flowers, and those with colored foliage, can be left until early spring before trimming. After trimming, mulch with peat moss or leaf mold. Although heathers cope with quite dry conditions, they dislike long periods of hot, dry weather. Watering is necessary to keep plants in good condition.

CALLUNA VULGARIS CULTIVARS

Below are some of the best *Calluna vulgaris* cultivars. Although they can be hard to find, they are well worth the effort. All of them flower in summer, apart from the bud-bloomers (See 'Decorative buds' below). Foliage is medium-green unless otherwise stated.

Attractive foliage
'Joy Vanstone': Golden foliage, rich orange in winter; pink flowers.
'Kerstin': Upright with dark mauve-gray foliage tipped with pale red and yellow tips in spring; mauve flowers.
'Robert Chapman': Golden foliage in spring turning to orange, then red; soft purple flowers.
'Spring Cream': Vigorous, with dark green foliage, tipped with cream in spring; long spikes of white flowers.
'Wickwar Flame': Bright orange and yellow summer foliage turning copper-gold in winter; mauve flowers.
'Winter Chocolate': Greenish yellow foliage; lilac-pink flowers.

Outstanding flowers
'Annemarie': Double flowers opening light purple, deepening to pink-purple; compact with dark green foliage.
'Beoley Gold': Strong-growing, white-flowered variety with yellow foliage.
'County Wicklow': Dwarf and spreading, with pale pink double flowers.
'Dark Beauty': Compact, with double, deep pink flowers darkening with age; dark green foliage.
'Darkness': Deep purple-pink flowers in short, dense spikes and dense bright green foliage.
'Gold Haze': Bright golden foliage with white flowers.
'H. E. Beale': Long spikes of double bright pink flowers; good for cutting.
'Mair's Variety': Tall with white flowers, good for cutting.

Decorative buds
'Alexandra': Compact and upright with dark green foliage; red and white buds turn to deep crimson.
'Alicia': Similar in habit to 'Alexandra', with large white buds.

Pieris

Also known as lily-of-the-valley bush, or flame of the forest, pieris are desirable evergreen shrubs, mostly of neat and graceful habit. Invaluable for light shade, they offer both attractive new foliage and a showy display of buds and flowers. Reasonably hardy (zones 4–8), pieris recover well even when damaged by frost, but it is worth protecting the new growth from the cold for the stunning effect of the glowing young stems and leaves.

The flower buds appear in the fall in beaded sprays; those with red buds are particularly attractive during early winter and midwinter, the buds set against the dark green foliage. The white or pink flowers, which are similar in character to the bells of heather but are borne in sprays like lily-of-the-valley, open any time from early spring onward. Many pieris have attractive bronze, salmon, or red young growth, which is spectacular but soft and susceptible to frost damage. They are therefore best suited to a sheltered spot (zone 5–8), ideally under trees, where the branches will cast dappled shade, and where other shrubs will protect them from scorching wind.

Pieris also make excellent subjects for pots. The more compact ones lend themselves to containers for semi-shade and shelter on the patio.

Pieris formosa 'Wakehurst' is strong and vigorous, with short, broad leaves and deep, bright red new growth; it has white flowers.

PROTECTING NEW GROWTH

Do not be put off by the risk of frost damage to the new foliage of pieris; scorched foliage is easily pinched off the plant, and a new flush of growth soon follows. In very cold weather, the diligent gardener may protect the new growth from frost damage with burlap or spun polypropylene.

The cultivars of *Pieris japonica*, from Japan, eastern China, and Taiwan, are the most popular pieris in gardens of today because of their hardiness and compact habit. *Pieris japonica* 'Debutante' is a mound-forming dwarf shrub that was collected in the wild on the Japanese island of Yaku-Shima as recently as 1980; this has short, white flower panicles carried in an upright manner. *Pieris japonica* 'Katsura', compact and good for pots, is grown mainly for the new foliage, which is deep red, turning chestnut brown as it ages; the mature leaves are glossy dark green, the flowers white, the overall appearance rich and healthy. *Pieris japonica* 'Prelude' has a similar habit, with less shiny foliage that shows off white flowers to advantage.

Pieris japonica 'Variegata' is one of the oldest variegated forms, with dark green leaves with a narrow creamy margin and white flowers. It is smaller and more compact than some, so good for pots. *Pieris japonica* 'Little Heath' has dainty leaves, similarly variegated. It is

Pieris japonica 'Katsura'

Pieris japonica 'Valley Valentine'

Pieris 'Forest Flame'

not free flowering in shade, but in a sunny position produces pretty pink buds that open to white flowers.

There are also many pink-flowered varieties. *Pieris japonica* 'Valley Rose', *Pieris japonica* 'Flamingo', and *Pieris japonica* 'Valley Valentine' are all lovely in bud as well as flower, but perhaps lack the appealing simplicity of the white-flowered forms.

Pieris 'Forest Flame' is the best known of all the pieris; it is a hybrid of *Pieris japonica* and *Pieris formosa* 'Wakehurst'. It combines the hardiness of *Pieris japonica* with the brilliant red young growth that is so much a feature of its other parent. The white flowers are carried in large, heavy, drooping panicles; often branched. *Pieris* 'Flaming Silver' is a sport of *Pieris* 'Forest Flame', with the same bright red new growth, which develops a silvery white margin as it matures.

Other acid-loving plants

Gardeners on acid soils can choose from some of our most beautiful ornamental shrubs, quite apart from the obvious options of camellias, rhododendrons, heathers, and pieris. Most are woodland plants by nature, so the dappled shade of trees is the perfect setting in a garden. Conifers are natural planting partners, as they enjoy the same conditions and come into their own on acid soils.

Crinodendron hookerianum

Crinodendron hookerianum (zone 8–9), from Chile, is not the hardiest of plants and is limited to mild zones. It needs part shade, so suits an acid woodland garden or a sheltered wall facing the afternoon sun. Dark green, glossy evergreen foliage and an upright, dense frame provide the perfect backdrop for the waxy crimson, lantern-shaped flowers, which hang along the branches on long stalks in late spring.

Desfontainia spinosa (zone 8–9), a native of South America, resembles a small-leaved holly when it is not in flower. Dark, spiny evergreen leaves provide the ideal setting for the tubular, scarlet, yellow-mouthed flowers, which appear all over the bush in late summer. This is a slow-growing shrub that is not fully hardy and needs a sheltered site, ideally in dappled shade.

Originally hailing from Asia, from the Himalayas to Japan, **enkianthus** bring an oriental touch to the garden. They flower in the late spring, when their drooping, porcelain-like flowers, in the shape of Chinese lanterns, hang along the branches. This is not their only season of glory: their autumn color is some of the finest in the garden. *Enkianthus campanulatus* (zone 5–7) is an upright deciduous shrub that reaches a height of 6–10ft. (2–3m). The branches are attractively tiered and a light copper color, creating a pleasing winter frame after the leaves have fallen. The cup-shaped flowers vary from pale yellow to rich bronze and are attractively veined; they are long-lasting, as is the fall display of yellow, copper, and red. *Enkianthus cernuus* f. *rubens* (zone

Enkianthus campanulatus

6–8) is a slightly smaller shrub, with deep red, fringed flowers and rich reddish purple autumn color. Seen less commonly, *Enkianthus perulatus* (zone 5–8) is a slower-growing and more compact deciduous shrub, slowly achieving 6ft. (2m). The flowers are white and urn-shaped; the autumn color is scarlet.

The narrow form of enkianthus makes them highly suitable to underplant with acid-loving, ground-cover subjects such as gaultheria.

The **eucryphias** are magnificent evergreen and deciduous shrubs, mostly with a stately, upright habit and exquisite late-summer flowers, which are white with conspicuous stamens and resemble the blooms of a single philadelphus. Eucryphias like a sheltered position on a moist, alkaline soil but are not as alkaline-intolerant as most of the plants in this section. They prefer to have their roots shaded by nearby shrubs.

The most successful of the plants in this group is *Eucryphia glutinosa* (zone 8–10). Although deciduous, this is still one of the most desirable forms. It is upright in habit, and has pretty, divided foliage that displays beautiful autumn color; the blooms are 2½in.

Enkianthus perulatus

MORE PLANTS FOR ACID SOILS *Andromeda polifolia* 'Compacta' *(for wet soil)* • *Leucothoe fontanesiana* 'Rainbow' •

Eucryphia lucida 'Pink Cloud'

Eucryphia glutinosa

Eucryphia × nymansensis 'Nymansay'

Fothergilla major

(6cm) across and cover the plant in mid-summer and late summer. *Eucryphia × intermedia* 'Rostrevor' (zone 8–10) is fast-growing, with evergreen trifoliate leaves. It forms a dark green, broad column, so is a good structure plant. The flowers, smaller than those of *Eucryphia glutinosa* (zone 8–10), are white and fragrant and crowd the branches in late summer and early fall. *Eucryphia lucida* (zone 8–10) is a pretty native of Tasmania, with upright growth and small evergreen leaves. The fragrant flowers, which are produced earlier than most other eucryphias in early summer and midsummer, hang from the branches and are particularly pleasing on mature shrubs, where they can be viewed from below. *Eucryphia lucida* 'Pink Cloud' (zone 8–10) is a popular cultivar with pink-edged petals. *Eucryphia × nymansensis* 'Nymansay' (zone 8–10) is a popular and reliable eucryphia, growing rapidly into a dense column. Dark evergreen foliage sets off the large white flowers that cover the branches in late summer and early fall.

Fothergilla major (zone 4–8) is related to hamamelis (see page 181) but, unlike hamamelis, must have acid soil. Native to the southeastern United States, it is a deciduous, slow-growing, horizontally branched shrub. The creamy white, bottlebrush flowers appear before the leaves in spring; the brilliant autumn color is long-lasting. It is a good plant for a woodland garden. *Kalmia latifolia* (zone 4–9), the calico

bush, is a beautiful, rhododendron-like shrub, with glossy, medium green foliage and clusters of pretty, bright pink flowers in early summer. The flower buds look like piped blobs of icing, and even the open, cup-shaped flowers seem to have a confectionery sugar frosting. It does not do well in a container, so is rarely offered for sale in garden centers; it can also be a difficult shrub to get started, but it is glorious

when established. It is wise to anchor even small plants after planting with a stake; the roots take time to establish. There are many cultivars, although few have the charm and pretty disposition of the species. *Kalmia latifolia* 'Ostbo Red' (zone 4–9) is easier to grow and is more often available, but it is not such a pleasing color, and the foliage is smaller and darker.

On the whole, the finest display of autumn color is seen on plants that thrive on acid soils. **Nyssa** (zone 3–9), one of the most spectacular shrubs for fall display, grows on acid soil. All of the **hamamelis** (zone 5–8) and *Acer palmatum* (zone 6–8), both somewhat alkaline-tolerant, color better on soils with low pH. Some of the evergreens grown for late foliage color such as leucothoe (see page 173) are acid lovers. See also Fall on acid soil, page 172.

Kalmia latifolia

Lindera benzoin • Myrica gale • Nyssa sylvatica • Pseudowintera colorata • Styrax japonicus • Trochodendron aralioides •

Roses in mixed plantings

Roses are ideal for mixed plantings: they offer a spectacular range of flower form, color, and fragrance and in some cases, attractive foliage and hips, all of which complement a wide variety of other shrubs and herbaceous plants. Repeat-flowering varieties extend the season of interest, producing a good opening flush in early summer, a few blooms in midsummer and another good flush of flowers in late summer and early fall.

Le Jardin d'Angélique, Normandy, France.

Beds planted exclusively with roses have been popular at times throughout history, latterly during the great rose boom of the 1960s. At that time, large numbers of Hybrid Tea and Floribunda rose varieties were introduced, and these frequently did not combine well with other subjects, except for summer bedding. Twenty years later, the trend changed in favor of the softer shades of the old roses, which work better in borders combined with other plants. Below is a selection of the best roses to grow in mixed plantings.

OLD SHRUB ROSES

The old roses are garden classics, loved for the beauty of their flowers and for their exquisite fragrance; however, they often perform only once in the season. Old roses generally associate well with herbaceous plants and lavender.

The **Gallicas** are the oldest garden roses, descended from those grown by the Romans and Greeks. *Rosa gallica* var. *officinalis* (zone 6–8), the apothecary's rose, produces tough, disease-resistant foliage on an upright, stocky shrub reaching 3ft. (1m). It is highly fragrant, with semi-double blooms of light crimson, arranged around a bunch of golden stamens. The petals dry to ruby velvet, if gathered fresh, and retain their fragrance; they are wonderful for potpourri. *Rosa gallica* 'Versicolor' (Rosa mundi) (zone 6–8) is equally good and fragrant, but has pink flowers brushed and striped with crimson. (See Good Companions, opposite). Both these roses are now officially classified as Species roses.

The **Albas** date back to the Middle Ages. They have a large, free-branching habit, and their disease-resistant, light blue-green foliage contributes as much as the flowers. They require little care and grow on poor soil. *Rosa* × *alba* 'Alba Semiplena' (zone 7–8) has large, flat, nearly single, soft white flowers, with yellow stamens, followed by red hips; the flowers have a fabulous fragrance, and the foliage is also very attractive. (See Good Companions, opposite). *Rosa* 'Maiden's Blush' (zone 7–8) is vigorous with lovely gray-green foliage and flat, loosely double, blush pink blooms with a delicious scent. It looks good with pale blue delphiniums.

The **Moss roses** were popular in Victorian times. These are lax shrub roses that produce flower buds with a mosslike growth on the sepals, conspicuous before the flower opens and a feature of the shrub. *Rosa* 'William Lobb' (zone 4–9), old velvet moss, is richly fragrant, with dark crimson flowers fading to a softer gray violet. (See Good Companions, opposite).

The **Hybrid Musks** were considerably

Rosa gallica var. officinalis

Rosa 'Felicia'

more popular before the advent of David Austin's English roses (see page 115). Not unlike Floribunda roses, but with more grace, they are repeat flowering, have a loose, open habit, and are effective in mixed plantings. *Rosa* **'Buff Beauty'** (zone 4–9) has full blooms of soft, warm apricot with a delicious Tea-rose scent, set against dark green foliage. *Rosa* **'Cornelia'** (zone 4–10) is small, with large clusters of fragrant, double, coppery pink flowers with richer tones, dark green foliage, and vigorous growth. One of the best Hybrid Musks is the highly aromatic *Rosa* **'Felicia'** (zone 6–9). A strong-growing and profuse-flowering rose, it is very pale pink around the edge of the blooms, darkening toward the center.

There are a number of **large shrub roses** belonging to various groups that are used extensively in mixed plantings

Rosa 'Complicata'

Rosa glauca

Rosa × odorata 'Mutabilis'

because of their attractive, informal, well-branched habit (see page 144). One such example is the highly fragrant *Rosa* **'Complicata'** (zone 5–8), which forms a large, healthy, resilient shrub that can be grown as a climber into a tree and is particularly suited to a country garden. The foliage is bright green and matte, and the large, single pink flowers are paler toward the central mass of golden stamens. Although this rose is officially classified as a Gallica, owing to its parentage

(probably a hybrid between *Rosa canina*, the British native dog rose, and a Gallica), it is quite different from other Gallicas in having large flowers and a lax, arching habit. *Rosa glauca* (*Rosa rubrifolia*) (zone 2–7) is a superb foliage plant, with fine arching growth and dark mahogany stems that carry blue-mauve foliage (gray-green in shade). The single flowers are clear pink, white in the center, and followed by red hips. Officially, this is classified as a Species rose. *Rosa × odorata* **'Mutabilis'** (zone 5–10) is a vigorous, slender, shrubby China rose with fine dark foliage, copper when young, and Tea-rose-scented, long-flowering blooms. Slender buds open buff, the flowers turning to copper, through rose pink to crimson. All colors appear on the plant at the same time, like a mass of delicate butterflies or a bouquet of sweet peas. Avoid planting in cold, exposed sites.

MODERN SHRUB ROSES

In the context of this book, the term "modern shrub roses" covers a multitude of different shrubs, often hybrids between bush roses and stronger species or climbers. They are useful for their continuous flowering qualities and robust habits.

Rosa **'Ballerina'** (zone 4–9), a Polyantha rose, has a graceful habit and produces large heads of dainty, small, pretty pink flowers; it is a wonderful shrub for mixed planting, as it flowers continuously and is lightly fragrant. *Rosa* **'The Fairy'** (zone 4–9), also a Polyantha

GOOD COMPANIONS

Rosa gallica 'Versicolor' (Rosa mundi) (1) (z. 5–10), a pink rose brushed and striped with crimson, looks delightful with silver *Artemisia* 'Powis Castle' (2) (z. 6–9).

The white *Rosa × alba* 'Alba Semiplena' (3) (z. 3–8) combines beautifully with silver shrubs such as *Elaeagnus* 'Quicksilver' (4) (z. 3–9).

The tall, vigorous, dark crimson *Rosa* 'William Lobb' (5) (z. 4–9), is a good choice for the back of a border with silver- or plum-foliage shrubs, such as *Physocarpus opulifolius* 'Diabolo' (6) (z. 2–7).

rose, is a small, tough, disease-resistant shrub of spreading habit; it produces tiny pink pom-pom flowers in sprays. *Rosa* **'White Pet'** (zone 5–9) produces many small white pom-pom flowers on a vigorous, spreading mound. Attractive and delicately fragrant, this is a deservedly popular Polyantha rose.

Rosa **'Bonica'** (zone 5–9), a Shrub rose, produces sprays of double pink flowers, with a hint of salmon, and shiny green foliage; it has a spreading habit and is hardy and disease resistant.

Rosa **'Iceberg'** (zone 4–9) is the definitive white Floribunda, with an upright, bushy habit and ample clusters of pure white blooms and fresh green foliage; it is good in any context.

The **Rugosas** are the easiest roses to grow. They are very hardy, vigorous, and disease resistant, with fresh apple green foliage, and they flower through the season. Most produce excellent hips that last well into winter (see page 174). *Rosa rugosa* (zone 2–7) is a native of Japan, where it grows on sandy shores; it suits the coast and light, sandy soils, although it is tolerant of most

Rosa 'Blanc Double de Coubert'
Rosa 'Roseraie de l'Haÿ'
Rosa 'Bonica'
Rosa 'Ballerina'
Rosa 'Iceberg'

conditions. *Rosa* **'Blanc Double de Coubert'** (zone 3–7) has large fragrant, open, semi-double, tissue-paper white flowers that bloom from late spring on. *Rosa* **'Roseraie de l'Haÿ'** (zone 2–7) has huge, wine purple flowers with a delicious scent; it is almost a true old rose but requires a lot less care.

Ground-cover roses are particularly useful on sunny banks where the soil is heavy. Some of these roses, including *Rosa* **'Immensee'** (zone 4–9) and *Rosa* **'Partridge'** (zone 4–9), are very vigorous, producing long, trailing growth more like that of a climber. Others, such as the County Series roses (zone 5–10)—for example *Rosa* **'Lancashire'** and *Rosa* **'Suffolk'**—form low mounds and can be planted in groups or combined with other ground-cover shrubs. *Rosa* **'Flower Carpet White'** (zone 4–9) and *Rosa* **'Pink Flower Carpet'** (zone 4–9) are reliable and disease resistant. They produce fresh green foliage and semi-double flowers, in white or bright pink respectively, throughout summer. The colors are somewhat hard, so they are best diluted with foliage planting. Other colors are available, but they do not perform as well as these two shrubs.

GROWING ROSES

Many gardeners are put off roses, believing that they require a lot of care and are a problem when it comes to pests and diseases. Disease is best controlled at the time of purchase by buying resistant varieties. Most roses benefit from annual feeding and like a good fertile soil, although some thrive on poor soil; it is all a matter of selecting the right kind for the site.

Situation: Roses do not need full sun, but they will not thrive in shade. Do not attempt to grow them on sites that do not get a few hours of sunshine each day—there are other shrubs that will be more successful. Roses are good on heavy clay soils, because of their fertility; they are not the first choice for peaty acid soils, and need plenty of organic matter on thin, sandy soils.

Pruning: Repeat-flowering shrub roses should be cut back by between one-third and two-thirds in winter. Remember: the harder you cut, the more vigorous the growth and the later the flowers. Nonrepeat-flowering varieties should be lightly pruned in winter by no more than one-third. Tidying the shrub, by removing weak and diseased growth and old flower heads, is all that is required. In the case of mature shrub roses, whether repeat or nonrepeat flowering, you may need to cut dead or old stems to the ground periodically. When pruning David Austin's English roses, leave all the twiggy branches on the plant for more prolific flowering.

Feeding: Roses like plenty of nutrients and moisture. Apply a balanced rose feed, containing magnesium and iron, in early spring and again in midsummer, after the first flush of flowers. Mulch in spring with compost or well-rotted manure.

Pests and diseases: A healthy rose is a disease-resistant rose, so feeding is the first step in control. Where diseases such as black spot, mildew, and rust are a problem, prevention is better than cure; start spraying when the first foliage appears, and continue at two-week intervals throughout the season. If insect pests are not a problem, use only a fungicide. A combined insecticide and fungicide in the absence of pests is not only wasteful but may result in resistance to its effects at a later date. The foliage of *Rosa rugosa* (z. 2–7) can be sensitive to some sprays, so take care when spraying neighboring roses with pesticides. If deer are a problem, grow climbers or ramblers.

DAVID AUSTIN'S ENGLISH ROSES

The rose breeder David Austin brought the beauty, fragrance, and fine qualities of the old roses together with the repeat-flowering qualities and more manageable growth habits of modern varieties. It is no wonder, therefore, that his English roses are becoming increasingly popular.

Because of his dedicated and extensive breeding program, David Austin is constantly introducing new English roses with refined qualities. Many of the original favorites have been superseded by new varieties with more compact habit, superior disease resistance, longer flowering season, and better weather resistance, to name but a few improvements. Because English roses are grown in many countries with varying climates, different varieties excel in local conditions.

Rosa 'Abraham Darby' (zone 5–10) is a bushy shrub producing sumptuously huge blooms of pink, apricot, and yellow throughout the summer; it has a delicious fruity fragrance. *Rosa* 'Cottage Rose' (zone 5–10) retains the character of a true old rose and is one of the best in the group; its cupped flowers of warm pink, with a delicate fragrance, bloom freely throughout the summer.

An excellent choice for the back of the border, *Rosa* 'Leander' (zone 5–10) is a tall, arching shrub, with apricot-orange blooms that have a strong, fruity fragrance. Another tall, vigorous rose for the back of the border is *Rosa* 'Gertrude Jekyll' (zone 5–10), with large, flat, fragrant, rich pink blooms (see Good Companions, right). *Rosa* 'Golden Celebration' (zone 5–10) is one of the largest, most flamboyant English roses. It has giant, cup-shaped, rich golden yellow blooms, which are wonderfully fragrant and very reliable. *Rosa* 'Grace' (zone 5–10) produces

Rosa 'Abraham Darby'
Rosa 'Crown Princess Margareta'
Rosa 'Grace'
Rosa 'Winchester Cathedral'
Rosa 'Graham Thomas'

deliciously scented, pretty, many petaled, apricot flowers, paler at the edges, and fresh, apple green foliage; it has a tidy growth habit and is a good alternative to *Rosa* 'Buff Beauty'.

One of the most widely planted roses in this group is *Rosa* 'Graham Thomas' (zone 5–10), with upright habit and golden yellow blooms. However, a yellow rose that tolerates cold better is *Rosa* 'Molineux' (zone 5–10). Another popular and reliable shrub is *Rosa* 'Mary Rose' (zone 5–10), which has exquisite rose pink, loose-petaled, lightly fragrant blooms. For a small garden, the dark-leaved *Rosa* 'Noble Antony' (zone

5–10), with its scented magenta-crimson flowers, is a good choice. (See Good Companions, below.)

Rosa 'The Mayflower' (zone 5–10) is a small, compact, disease-resistant shrub whose deep, rose pink, old rose blooms have a strong fragrance; it is rarely without flowers throughout the summer. *Rosa* 'Winchester Cathedral'(zone 5–10) is the white form of *Rosa* 'Mary Rose'. A beautiful, reliable shrub, it has delicate, white, fragrant flowers.

The blooms of *Rosa* 'Charles Rennie Mackintosh' are an unusual, but easily accommodated, lilac or lilac pink color, with a very strong, old rose fragrance.

GOOD COMPANIONS

Plant *Rosa* 'Gertrude Jekyll' (1) (z. 5–10) with *Clematis* 'Petit Faucon'. (2) (z. 3–9); the dark purple-blue velvet clematis blooms complement the rich pink rose and extend the effect of the flowering season.

The magenta-crimson *Rosa* 'Noble Antony' (3) (z. 5–10) planted with *Nepeta* × *faassenii* (4) (z. 4–7) is a stunning sight.

Walls and fences

Walls and fences, used to mark a boundary or to divide a garden into different areas, are the ideal way to add vertical interest to the garden. They may be attractive features in their own right, but most importantly they provide a backdrop for planting, presenting the opportunity for growing a variety of shrubs and so contributing to diversity in the garden without demanding intensive maintenance.

A wall or fence, however tall, provides shelter—and the perfect opportunity to grow plants that may not survive in an open area of the garden. Wind chill, in the depths of winter, vastly reduces temperature, but the barrier of a wall or fence lessens the effect of the wind. Walls offer more protection and shelter than fences and therefore tend to support more tender subjects.

Climbers are the obvious choice for a vertical surface. However, there are also many woody shrubs that benefit from the additional support provided by a solid structure. Tall, leggy shrubs can be used to fill the higher space, while those that need shelter, and some support, can grow beneath them.

Trained pyracantha at Bourton House Garden, Gloucestershire, in England.

CHOOSING PLANTS

Before selecting plants for a wall or fence, establish the aspect. In the northern hemisphere, south (that is, south-facing) and west (west-facing) walls are warmest, the ideal spot for sun lovers. South-facing walls can get very hot in midsummer, so choose plants that will relish the heat. North (north-facing) and east (east-facing) walls are colder and shadier; high north walls get little sun. Shady walls are not necessarily a disadvantage—you just have to choose the right plants.

When selecting climbers and wall shrubs, choose plants that are suited to the height of the support. You can train most plants, but a vigorous wall shrub, such as *Parthenocissus tricuspidata* (zone 4–8) or *Fremontodendron californicum* (zone 9–11), is unsuitable for a 6ft. (2m) fence. When the plant gets too large, and you cut it back, it will just grow more vigorously above the top of the support, leaving bare branches against the fence that you wanted to cover.

If you are lucky enough to have beautiful old stone or brick walls, you should choose plants that complement rather than conceal them. Color is an important consideration: a dark red flowering shrub may be appealing, but it can be lost against a dark red brick wall. More likely, you are faced with bare fencing all around the edge of your plot. In this case, you are looking for shrubs that will cover the fence well.

ESTABLISHING PLANTS

Walls and fences are often dry at the base, partly because the height of the structure keeps off some of the rainfall. Also, many walls are constructed in such a way that rainwater drains away from them, which creates even drier conditions. Adding plenty of organic matter at the time of planting helps to retain moisture. Do not plant too close to a wall—ideally, at least 2ft. (60cm) away. This gives the shrub space to develop, and is also important in terms of support. Shrubs that have been planted too close to a wall tend to grow away from it, and eventually overbalance. Water regularly until the plants are fully established. Covering the ground with a layer of gravel will keep the roots cool and also conserve moisture.

MORE SHRUBS FOR SHADY WALLS *Azara microphylla* • *Cotoneaster franchetii* • *Cotoneaster horizontalis* •

SHADY WALLS AND FENCES OVER 10ft. (3m)

Drimys winteri (winter's bark) (zone 8–9) is a tall shrub with large shiny, leathery leaves. Clusters of fragrant white flowers are produced in late spring. Mature specimens develop very attractive bark. A native of Chile, winter's bark can grow as a freestanding shrub or small tree in a sheltered woodland garden in mild zones. It is, however, ideal for a sheltered, lightly shaded wall in a position where it can grow freely without its potential height being inhibited.

Drimys winteri

Eriobotrya japonica

Eriobotrya japonica (loquat) (zone 8–10) is the most striking evergreen that can be grown outdoors in milder zones (7–10). The large leathery, corrugated leaves, felty brown underneath and silvery green above, can easily reach 12in. (30cm) long. As the plant matures, the branches take an angular stance, giving the plant a wonderful stature. A member of the rose family, it may produce many clusters of hawthornlike flowers during winter and

spring, but normally only when grown in warmer zones; the yellow, edible fruits are rarely produced in cooler climates. Eriobotrya always creates a dramatic effect and is superb against an old stone or brick wall. It also looks stunning with modern architecture.

Garrya elliptica (zone 8–9) can easily achieve 10ft. (3m) or more on a high, shady wall. Its top-heavy habit shows off the silver gray catkins that hang from the branches in winter. *Garrya elliptica* 'James Roof' is the best variety, with exceptionally long silver tassels. At other times of the year, the garryas' dark green foliage can look somber, so plant them in front of silver-variegated ivy or with *Euonymus fortunei* 'Silver Queen' at their feet. (See also pages 89, 180, 182.)

Itea ilicifolia (zone 8–9) is a member of the escallonia family, but resembles a holly. The dark green, softly spiny leaves are carried on lax branches. In late summer the shrub is draped with soft green, catkinlike flowers, reminiscent of a garrya. It is a fairly hardy and easy shrub to grow and suits shady town gardens. Underplant it with ferns and pulmonarias.

If you have acid soil, both *Eucryphia* × *nymansensis* (zone 8–10) and *Crinodendron hookerianum* (zone

Itea ilicifolia

8–9) (see pages 110, 111) are superb shrubs for high walls out of direct sun. Both enjoy woodland conditions, so provide adequate moisture at the roots.

SHADY WALLS AND FENCES UNDER 10ft. (3m)

Camellias (see pages 106–107) are ideal for lightly shaded walls, provided they do not get the morning sun. Some of the less hardy varieties of tall, spreading habit can be trained onto the wall.

Chaenomeles

Camellia sasanqua (zone 8–9) is a beautiful plant for a sheltered wall. Very early blooming, from midwinter onward, it has smaller, more delicate flowers than most camellias, with the added attraction of a delightful scent. It may need protection when young, but mature plants withstand most winters.

Chaenomeles (see page 130) (zone 4–8) are ideal grown against a low wall or fence, either trained into wires or allowed to lean against a wall for support. The plant's spreading growth quickly makes an impact, and if the right variety is chosen to show up against the background, it will make a striking splash of color from early spring for several weeks. The glossy foliage is good throughout the summer.

For a mound-forming evergreen at the base of a shaded wall, look no further than *Choisya ternata* (zone

× *Fatshedera lizei* • *Forsythia suspensa* • *Kerria japonica* • *Mahonia japonica* • *Photinia* × *fraseri* 'Red Robin' •

8–10), the Mexican orange blossom. Although it blooms more prolifically in the sun, it will flower in shade; the foliage is always excellent (see page 33).

Most *Euonymus fortunei* varieties (zone 5–8) readily climb if grown against a wall; some reach a height of 6–10ft. (2–3m). They provide a bushier alternative to ivy for low, shady walls and thrive in difficult conditions. *Euonymus fortunei* 'Emerald 'n' Gold' is particularly happy against a wall, as is *Euonymus fortunei* 'Silver Queen'. The latter can be slow to start, but once it gets going will lighten the

Pyracantha 'Orange Glow'

darkest corner with its wonderful creamy variegated foliage. *Euonymus japonicus* (zone 7–9) varieties are excellent grown in sun or shade, in towns or by the sea.

Pyracanthas (see also page 174) (zone 6–9) are very popular wall shrubs, with shiny, evergreen foliage, white flowers in spring, and colorful red or orange berries in fall and winter. Either grow them as loose, trimmed shrubs against a wall or fence or train them as espaliers on wires. The latter can be very effective in formal situations and town gardens, particularly as an attractive backdrop for other trained evergreens. Pyracanthas cope with most soils and situations, and are useful for a drafty, shady wall where other plants fail. Trim the current season's growth back to the berry clusters in late summer to show off the ripening fruit. Pyracanthas are also suitable for walls over 10ft. (3m).

SUNNY WALLS AND FENCES OVER 10ft. (3m)

Cytisus (Argyrocytisus) battandieri, (zone 8–9) the Moroccan broom or pineapple broom, is a very tall shrub with gray-green stems and silky grey leaves, which resemble those of a large clover. The flowers appear in early summer—cones of rich yellow, tightly packed, pealike blooms, which are deliciously pineapple scented. A native of Morocco, it thrives in full sun and poor, dry soil. It will grow in the open but has a very gangly habit and often

Cytisus battandieri

grows too tall and overbalances. It is excellent against a wall, but it must be a high one as this climber can quickly reach the top of a two-story house. Seed-raised plants can take time to flower. The cultivar *Cytisus battandieri* 'Yellow Tail', with exceptionally large flower spikes, is reliable and free flowering. Never prune later than summer, as you reduce the chance of flowers the following year; hard pruning stimulates strong growth.

Fremontodendron californicum (zone 9–11) is another tall shrub, suitable only for growing against a high, sunny wall. It has gray, scaly stems and leathery leaves, which are also covered with fine, waxy scales (these protect the plant against desiccation). Spectacularly large rich-yellow flowers are produced throughout summer and fall. Fremontodendron likes full sun and good drainage and is excellent on

alkaline soils. Anchor it to the wall carefully with vine-eyes and wires; otherwise, as it matures, it can fall away. *Fremontodendron* 'California Glory' is popular for its exceptional flowers and free-flowering quality. Fremontodendrons are not plants for cold areas. Take care when cutting back or pruning, as the waxy scales can irritate the eyes and nose.

Ceanothus are natural choices for high, sunny walls. Because of their bushy habit, they are suitable for growing against a tall fence, where they are able to grow on above their support.

Fremontodendron 'California Glory'

Choose the tall evergreen varieties. They grow quickly and make an impact in the first season after planting. They cope well with hot, dry situations.

Ceanothus do not need to be trained, but if you wish to do so, choose a dense, compact grower, such as *Ceanothus* 'Blue Sapphire' (zone 9–11), and start training it in the early stages of growth. The best varieties for growing against walls and fences are the following: *Ceanothus* 'Concha' (zone 9–10), *Ceanothus griseus* var. *horizontalis* 'Yankee Point' (zone 9–10), and *Ceanothus* 'Italian Skies' (zone 8–10). (See also page 140.)

Ficus carica (zone 8–9), the fig, is a handsome, fast-growing shrub with impact. It needs plenty of space. The plant has special character from an early age, and increases greatly in size when the large, distinctive leaves unfurl in spring. Named varieties such

MORE SHRUBS FOR SUNNY WALLS *Abeliophyllum distichum* • *Callistemon citrinus* 'Splendens' •

Ficus carica 'Brown Turkey'

Abutilon megapotamicum

Clianthus puniceus

Carpenteria californica

Coronilla valentina subsp. glauca 'Variegata'

as *Ficus carica* 'Brown Turkey' reliably produce a good crop of fruit as they mature. Figs are more manageable when their roots are restricted, so plant them in a large container sunk in the ground. In colder zones, remove all embryo fruits in late winter. The fruits that are produced from then on should mature the same fall. Figs are also suitable for high walls and fences in shade.

SUNNY WALLS AND FENCES UNDER 10ft. (3m)

Abutilon megapotamicum (zone 9–11) has more lax growth than most other abutilons, so is ideally suited to growing as a wall shrub. The fine arching green stems, with narrow, maple-like leaves, need wires for support; the plant grows quickly in a sheltered situation. The flowers hang from the branches like tiny lanterns in summer and fall: orange-red calyxes with a soft yellow skirt of petals and purple anthers. *Abutilon megapotamicum* 'Variegatum' has pretty, yellow-mottled foliage, but is less vigorous than *Abutilon megapotamicum*. *Abutilon hybridum* (zone 9–11) is more upright in growth habit, with broader leaves. The flower shape varies from wide open to bell-shaped and can be white, yellow, pink or red, depending on the cultivar that is grown. Its spectacular flowers are displayed continuously in a favored location at any time of the year.

Carpenteria californica (zone 8–11), another beautiful Californian evergreen shrub, resembles a large, graceful cistus. Narrow, medium-green leaves are well spaced on upright branches. The spectacular flowers are produced in loose upright clusters in midsummer. The blooms are white with gold stamens. It does not need a wall for support, but grows best at the base of a sunny wall, where it will reach 10ft. (3m). Look for *Carpenteria californica* 'Bodnant', which has larger flowers.

Clianthus puniceus (zone 7–9), the parrot's bill or lobster's claw, is an exotic member of the pea family, a native of New Zealand. It is semi-evergreen and strong-growing but thrives outside only in mild areas. Its habit is sprawling; the vetchlike leaves have many leaflets. The spectacular flowers, red and clawlike with black eyes, are carried in clusters in early summer. *Clianthus puniceus* 'Albus' has white flowers.

Another member of the pea family, *Coronilla valentina* ssp. *glauca* (zone 6–8), also grows well at the base of a sunny wall or fence. The blue-green foliage sets off the rich yellow flowers produced year-round, but mostly in spring. *Coronilla valentina* ssp. *glauca* 'Citrina' bears pale yellow flowers; *Coronilla valentina* ssp. *glauca* 'Variegata' has pretty, cream-variegated foliage.

Any of the Mediterranean shrubs that are featured on pages 82–87 will be happy against a low wall or fence in full sun. The taller, more tender varieties of cistus, such as *Cistus* × *cyprius* var. *ellipticus* f. *bicolor* 'Elma' (zone 8–10), and the upright varieties of rosemary, are natural choices that will appreciate this type of planting.

Magnolia grandiflora at Lanhydrock, Cornwall

Grevillea rosmarinifolia • *Luma apiculata* • *Magnolia grandiflora* • *Punica granatum* • *Sophora* 'Sun King' •

Hedges and screens

Berberis thunbergii f. *atropurpurea* 'Atropurpurea Nana' at The Garden House, Devon, in England.

Hedges and screens are used for the demarcation and fortification of boundaries, the division of larger plots into smaller areas, for privacy, and for concealing unsightly views. Sadly, their decorative contribution is often of secondary importance to their physical presence. Before planting a hedge or screen, there are some important points to consider, any of which, if overlooked, can be the beginning of major problems in the future.

Hedges can serve many very useful purposes and can be highly decorative, but an important point to bear in mind is that they take up room, and when a shrub gains height it also gains width. Go out and measure the width of a hedge that you are considering planting before you decide—it is quite likely that the hedge that you thought was 12in. (30cm) wide is in fact over 3ft. (1m) wide. A large evergreen hedge, such as *Prunus laurocerasus*, can easily take 6ft. (2m) or more off your garden. In addition, hedges are greedy; they take a lot of water and nutrients from the soil, so in most cases you will not be able to plant close to them; access for maintenance is also needed. Hedges need cutting at least once a year, and a tall, broad hedge is a challenge to cut and may require power equipment; you may have to look at hiring a professional contractor. You need to ask yourself, before you get planting, if that is something you are prepared to take on .

In a small garden, if privacy is the main objective and you don't have space for a hedge, instead use a fence, trellis or wire screen, clad with climbers or wall shrubs (see pages 116–19); these are more economical on space and may give a more instant effect than a hedge.

Where space is not an issue, large evergreen shrubs can be used as screens, to block out unsightly views and to provide privacy (see page 123). Alternatively, consider providing more foreground interest to draw attention away from the object to be screened. Light deciduous trees are often more effective in hiding a building than a solid evergreen hedge.

TIPS FOR CHOOSING HEDGING PLANTS

- Any shrub that has dense, branched growth and short internodes (the lengths of stem between the leaves) should be suitable for a hedge.

- Ideally, select an evergreen or, in the case of deciduous shrubs, a plant with enough twiggy growth to maintain the structure when the leaves have fallen.

- A shrub that responds to pruning by producing new side shoots from young or old wood is usually good.

- Choose a shrub that retains good leaf cover to ground level and does not go leggy with age.

- Do not skimp on cost. A hedge is a long-term investment, and it is much better to get it right than compromise on cost.

- Plant the best stock you can find. Healthy, vigorous plants will give you the effect you are looking for more quickly.

- Bigger is not always better. Large plants may take longer to establish and grow on.

GROWING HEDGES

When planting a hedge, you need to pay as much attention to preparation and planting technique as you would with other shrubs (see pages 16–17).

Start to clip the hedge from an early age, long before it gets to the height you want it to be. The best time is just after a flush of growth. Most are clipped after the spring flush, and again in late summer, to allow time for some new growth before winter. Some hedges need more frequent clipping—for example, the shrubby honeysuckle *Lonicera nitida* (zone 7–9); others, such as beech (*Fagus sylvatica*), (zone 4–7) are cut only once a year, in late summer.

PLANTS FOR HEDGES OVER 3ft. (1m) HIGH *Griselinia littoralis* • *Hydrangea macrophylla* • *Hypericum* 'Hidcote' •

DECIDUOUS HEDGES

Some of the most popular hedging shrubs for temperate zones lose their leaves in winter. *Fagus sylvatica* (beech) (zone 4–7) and *Fagus sylvatica* Atropurpurea Group (purple beech), (zone 4–7) although deciduous, are unusual in retaining their coppery brown dry leaves through the winter, dropping them when the new leaves open in spring. Beeches make a good formal hedge up to 16ft. (5m) high, and if well maintained will enhance any garden.

Carpinus betulus (zone 4–7), the hornbeam, is similar to beech in leaf, but without the coppery twigs and

Hydrangea macrophylla

Fagus sylvatica varieties

HEDGE PLANTING DISTANCE (HPD)

For deciduous hedges in towns and evergreen hedges, plants are usually container-grown and may be planted any time. Approximate hedge planting distances (HPD) are given in the plant descriptions. The distances are taken from the center of one plant to the center of the next.

Beech, hornbeam, and deciduous hedges in rural areas are normally planted as young, bare-root plants (whips) during the dormant season. Plant in two parallel rows. The rows should be 12–18in. (30–45cm) apart, and in each row the plants should be 3ft. (1m) apart. Make a zigzag with the plants.

retention of leaves in winter. It is faster to grow and establish, and thrives on any site or soil.

Hydrangea macrophylla cultivars (zone 6–9) also make good hedges.

Hedges for rural areas

For hedges in country gardens, indigenous plants are appropriate and can give interest year-round, as well as providing a haven for wildlife.

Crataegus monogyna (hawthorn or quickthorn) (zone 4–7) is a good choice, as it is easy to establish, fast-growing, and tolerant of even severe, indiscriminate trimming. *Prunus spinosa* (blackthorn or sloe) (zone 4–8) is not the most attractive foliage plant, but it forms an impenetrable barrier and is lovely when it flowers in spring.

Hawthorns and blackthorns can be supplemented with the following plants: *Acer campestre* (field maple) (zone 4–8), *Cornus mas* (Cornelian cherry) (zone 4–8), *Corylus avellana* (hazel) (zone 4–7), *Euonymus europaeus* (spindle) (zone 3–7), *Lonicera periclymenum* (honeysuckle) (zone 5–8), *Rosa canina* (dog rose) (zone 3–8), and *Rosa rubiginosa* (sweet briar) (zone 4–9), perhaps with the evergreen *Ilex aquifolium* (holly) (zone 6–9).

Hedges for town gardens

When it blooms, *Forsythia × intermedia* sets gardens ablaze with yellow. If trimmed after flowering and

again in late summer to shorten the new wood, it can be kept as a formal hedge, solid with flowers in spring. The foliage is healthy and trouble-free; the bare stems are a pleasing tan in winter (HPD—see box, left—30in. [75cm]).

Prunus × cistena (zone 2–8) is a light, pretty hedge, up to 5ft. (1.5m) in height, with wine red leaves on dark stems and dark-eyed, white flowers in spring; it looks good with low palisade fencing (HPD 2ft. [60cm]).

Many roses make excellent informal hedges for town gardens, including *Rosa gallica* var. *officinalis* (zone 6–8), but *Rosa rugosa* (zone 2–7) is the best of them all. It is disease free, with fresh green foliage and strong, upright, spiny stems, which make an attractive and effective barrier. Its flowering period is relatively long, the blooms are fragrant and weather-resistant, and the hips that follow the flowers keep the hedge looking good into the fall. This hedging plant is particularly useful, as it tolerates poor, sandy soils (HPD 30in. [75cm]).

Rosa gallica var. *officinalis*

Prunus cerasifera 'Nigra' • *Prunus lusitanica* • *Pyracantha* 'Teton' • *Rhododendron ponticum* • *Rosa* 'Felicia' •

EVERGREEN HEDGES

Aucuba japonica (zone 7–10) is an extremely versatile plant. With its large glossy leaves and dense habit, it makes a good alternative to the cherry laurel (*Prunus laurocerasus*, see box opposite) for a hedge to 6ft. (2m). Particularly useful in shade, the light variegation is excellent to brighten a dark corner. It is very useful where traffic pollution is a problem (HPD 3ft. [1m]). For sunnier positions, and on the coast, the best

Buxus sempervirens

Escallonia rubra 'Crimson Spire'

Aucuba japonica

A "cloud" hedge

Euonymus japonicus 'Aureus'

choice for a glossy yellow-variegated hedge is *Euonymus japonicus* 'Aureus'. Although it is likely to revert, the appearance of plain green and yellow areas in the hedge is not unattractive (HPD 30in. [75cm]).

Box hedges offer the widest possible diversity in scale of any hedging plant, from *Buxus sempervirens* (zone 6–9), common box, which can easily make a broad hedge of 10ft. (3m) or more high (HPD 2ft. [60cm]), to *Buxus sempervirens* 'Suffruticosa', used to create dwarf edges in parterres and around flower beds (HPD 10in. [25cm]). Box hedges can be formal or informal;

where space permits, the "cloud" hedge, a high, wide hedge clipped in an undulating, irregular shape, is popular.

Elaeagnus × *ebbingei* (zone 7–11) tends to be more commonly used as a screening shrub than a hedge, but it is an excellent choice for either use and suits exposed coastal conditions, as well as urban sites. The silvery-green foliage is attractive throughout the year, and the inconspicuous fragrant flowers are a delight in early winter (HPD 3ft. [90cm]).

Escallonias (zone 8–10) are good hedging plants for mild coastal situations. They are drought-tolerant plants, with dark green, very glossy leaves and lovely pink or red flowers in summer. Trim in late summer to remove old flower stems; or, if heavier pruning is required, do this in early spring before the flush of new spring growth. Good varieties for hedges up to 6ft. (2m) high include *Escallonia* 'Frades', a medium to large shrub with crimson flowers; it is

wind resistant and responds well to trimming, and *Escallonia rubra* 'Crimson Spire', a strong and upright shrub with large leaves and bright crimson flowers. For taller hedges or screens, recommended shrubs include *Escallonia* 'Pink Princess', with rose-pink flowers and large aromatic leaves, and the wind-resistant *Escallonia rubra var. macrantha*, with large glossy leaves and pinkish-red flowers (all escallonia HPD 3ft. [1m]).

Ligustrum ovalifolium (zone 5–9), the oval-leaf privet, was once the most widely planted hedging shrub, but has been less so in recent years. It is very tolerant of just about any soil or aspect and is evergreen except in cold, exposed situations. Easy to cut, it regenerates even after rough treatment. Old privet hedges can be susceptible to honey fungus (*Armillaria*); this is one of the factors that have led to the demise of their popularity (HPD 2ft. [60cm]).

Lonicera nitida (zone 7–9), with its straight twigs and tiny evergreen leaves, has long been used for hedging, and offers a faster-growing alternative to box. With regular clipping, it can be kept as a very narrow hedge, so is less greedy of space than many other evergreen shrubs (HPD 2ft. [60cm]).

Olearia × *haastii* (zone 8–10) is a rounded, medium-sized shrub with small leathery, oval leaves, which are white and

PLANTS FOR HEDGES UNDER 3FT. (1M) HIGH *Berberis atropurpurea* 'Nana' • *Lavandula angustifolia* 'Hidcote' •

LOW DECORATIVE EVERGREEN HEDGES

Some hedges are used within the structure of the garden to emphasize paths, to demarcate areas, or simply as decorative divisions. Box is a natural choice (see opposite), but there are other dwarf evergreens that do the job just as well. *Ilex crenata* 'Convexa' (z. 5–7) is a superb alternative to box, and *Viburnum davidii* (z. 7–9) is an unusual bold-leaved alternative. Many of the small-leaved hebes also make excellent low decorative hedges—for example, *Hebe albicans* (z. 8–10).

In sunny, dry situations, choose the aromatics; lavenders, upright varieties of rosemary, and even sage all make excellent low hedges. The finest choice of all for a low hedge in sun is *Santolina chamaecyparissus* (lavender cotton) (z. 6–9). Its dense silver foliage will stay looking good all year round if clipped regularly and if not allowed to flower (HPD 18in. [50cm]). (See also pages 78–79.)

felty beneath, and fragrant white, daisy like flowers in summer. It makes a good, robust hedge, up to 6ft. (2m) high, for both town and coastal gardens (HPD 30in. [75cm]).

Olearia macrodonta (New Zealand holly) (z. 8–10) is a good screening and hedging plant for exposed coastal gardens. It is a strong-growing shrub, which quickly attains 6ft. (2m), eventually 10ft. (3m). The sage green, hollylike leaves, with silvery undersides, combine well with pastel colors. It produces fragrant, daisylike flowers in early summer (HPD 3ft. [90cm]).

Olearia macrodonta

Photinia × fraseri

Photinia × fraseri (z. 7–9) is unbeatable for wherever a bright, cheerful effect is needed, and where the hedge will be a feature rather than a background. It is unmissable in spring, when the new shoots of bright scarlet appear like flames all over the top and sides of the hedge. Photinia also makes an excellent large screening shrub (HPD 3ft. [1m]). (See also page 34.)

Prunus laurocerasus (the cherry laurel) (z. 6–8) is popular for hedging, and makes a good background for other shrubs. Large dark, glossy leaves and a dense habit create a fine hedge that is very useful where a tall, solid barrier is required. Its biggest disadvantage is disfigurement of the leaves when cutting. For this reason, trim the shrub early in the season. *Prunus laurocerasus* 'Marble Dragon' has leaves touched with gold and apricot.

Evergreen screening shrubs
Most of the structure shrubs mentioned in the first section of this book (pages 29–37) make excellent screening, both for privacy and for shelter. A mixed screen of large evergreens provides a low-maintenance barrier, and is very effective when it comes to absorbing noise and dust and providing shelter from wind; however, you need to allow plenty of space for them.

All screening shrubs should be thought of in conjunction with other good screening plants, such as **bamboos** and **conifers**. A combination of the different types of screening plants perhaps offers the most pleasing solution for a garden boundary and is the most natural continuation of the planting within the garden.

Berberis julianae

Some of the large-growing berberis are particularly worthy of mention here for their tough character and ability to overcome the most hostile conditions: *Berberis darwinii* (z. 7–9), with its fine dark green foliage and stunning orange flowers in spring, makes a good hedge. If left unclipped, it is also an excellent evergreen screening shrub. *Berberis julianae* (z. 5–8) is one of the best. Dense and spiny, with clusters of prickly dark green leaves, which are copper-tinted when young, it forms a large, round bush up to 10ft. (3m). Dense clusters of scented yellow flowers appear in spring. The elegant *Berberis × stenophylla* (z. 6–9), with graceful arching stems and dark leaves, is a haze of soft orange flowers in late spring.

TALL, RELATIVELY FAST-GROWING SCREENING SHRUBS

Elaeagnus × ebbingei (see opposite)
Griselinia littoralis (see page 33)
Laurus nobilis (see page 31)
Photinia × fraseri (see left)
Pittosporum tenuifolium (see page 34)
Prunus laurocerasus (see left)

Lonicera nitida 'Baggesen's Gold' • *Osmanthus × burkwoodii* • *Osmanthus heterophyllus* • *Rosa gallica* var. *officinalis* •

Pots and containers

As gardens have become smaller, patios, decks, and courtyards have become an essential element of the "outdoor room," and container planting now plays a key role in garden design. Pots allow plants to be positioned where cultivation in the ground would be difficult or even impossible: perhaps where there is no soil, or because certain plants do not grow on your soil type. They also offer ultimate flexibility, as they can be moved around at any time.

The union of plant and pot is an art form in its own right. Choose containers carefully. Appropriateness is the most important factor: a well-chosen pot looks at home in the garden all year round, so beware of bright-colored glazes in traditional settings. Think big—small pots and large plants are a poor combination, from an aesthetic and a practical point of view, as they dry out quickly and can blow over. If plants are going to need repotting, choose a container with a shape that allows this: avoid those that narrow at the neck.

Shrubs are a natural choice. Flowering time and color are secondary to foliage form, plant habit, and character.

BOLD EVERGREENS

Architectural evergreens lend themselves to pots—ideally, positioned so they make a statement. **Cordylines** and **palms** are excellent for hot, sunny situations and near the house. They suit pots in outdoor living areas but elsewhere in traditional gardens may be out of place. The light, spiky forms create foreground height and interest. (See pages 55, 66, 87.)

Fatsia japonica (zone 8–9) always makes an impact, and can be cut back hard if it grows too large; it is excellent for a shady position against a wall that gets no sun, or to add a tropical feel to a shady courtyard. (See pages 35–36.)

Cordyline 'Torbay Dazzler'

Osmanthus also make excellent plants for pots, with their compact growth and tolerance of difficult growing conditions. *Osmanthus heterophyllus* 'Goshiki', (zone 6–9) with mottled yellow-bronze and green foliage, is bright and cheerful without being brash; it looks lovely in a dark green, glazed pot. The silver-edged leaves of *Osmanthus heterophyllus* 'Variegatus' (zone 6–9) are hollylike, bright, and clean. It is a good choice for a stone container, perhaps set against gray paving. (See page 63.)

Phormiums (zone 8–9) provide spiky form and color contrast. Some of the exotically colorful ones are not the hardiest, but are good for containers in sunny, sheltered positions. *Phormium* **'Maori Chief'** bears upright leaves

---

CLIPPED SHAPES

Clipped shapes suit formal situations and can bring structure to informal schemes when used as exclamation marks. The choice of container is particularly important: the shape of the container must balance that of the plant.

Clipped box (*Buxus*) (z. 6–9) and bay (*Laurus nobilis*) (z. 8–9) are traditional choices. The privet *Ligustrum delavayanum* (z. 7–9) is a faster-growing and less expensive option, often sold as shaped balls, cones, and standards. It is dense and dark, with tiny dark green leaves and clusters of white flowers, followed by black berries. Since it dislikes cold, it is not suitable for exposed gardens, where it loses its leaves.

Buxus sempervirens 'Suffruticosa'

Lavender and rosemary offer softer alternatives for sunny, Mediterranean schemes, and both look good in terracotta. Regular clipping is the secret of success. If you are growing lavender as a shaped plant, do not allow it to flower; if it is cut back hard, patches of bare wood will be the result.

MORE SHRUBS FOR CONTAINERS *Convolvulus cneorum* • *Euonymus japonicus* 'Microphyllus Variegata' • *Hebe* 'Red Edge' • *Hebe* 'Pascal' • *Hydrangea macrophylla* 'Ami Pasquier' • *Ilex crenata* 'Convexa' •

Fatsia japonica and Pittosporum tenuifolium 'Tom Thumb'

variegated with scarlet, crimson, and bronze. For a real statement, choose the larger *Phormium tenax* Purpureum Group (zone 8–10), with large, upright, bronze-purple leaves and architectural flower stems. (See also pages 55, 66.)

Smaller pittosporums can be excellent in pots. *Pittosporum tenuifolium* 'Cream de Mint' (zone 9–10) is a good plant for containers; the growth is upright and compact and the leaves are mint green. *Pittosporum tenuifolium* 'Tom Thumb' (zone 9–10) is also a good choice, with shiny, deep purple foliage in winter and bright green spring growth. It looks good in any situation, and the unusual color suits unusual containers: lead, steel, purple glazes, and slate gray all look superb with this plant. (See pages 49.)

Viburnum davidii (zone 7–9) bears such strongly formed leaves, they look as if they could have been fired with the pot; they complement strong oriental glazes. (See page 37.)

ACID-LOVING PLANTS

Containers are the obvious solution for those who wish to grow ericaceous plants but have alkaline soil. Most acid-loving plants are suitable for growing in pots. (See pages 100–111.)

Camellias are excellent in containers. Growth habits vary according to variety, from lax to compact, and they can create a formal or informal effect, depending on the choice of plant. The glossy evergreen foliage looks good all year round, and the early spring blooms are a

delight. Site pots where early morning sun cannot damage the frozen blooms.

Some good camellia varieties with a particularly compact habit include *Camellia japonica* cultivars (zone 7–10), especially 'Junior Miss', with fragrant, semi-double, pink flowers; and 'Nuccio's Gem', which has superb, double white blooms. **Camellia × williamsii** cultivars (zone 6–10) are also good, including 'Jury's Yellow', for creamy flowers with a creamy yellow center; and 'Donation', which, though vigorous and speading, is free flowering and highly suitable.

Variegated pieris are excellent in pots, particularly *Pieris japonica* 'Little Heath' (zone 5–8); it has pretty, silver-variegated leaves, pinkish new growth and flower buds, and an airy habit.

The more compact rhododendrons are good choices for larger containers. *Rhododendron* 'Nancy Evans' (zone 7–8) is a favorite, with apricot-yellow blooms in loose clusters and dark green foliage; the habit is relatively loose.

Deciduous **azaleas** give good autumn color, interesting branch framework, and glorious flowers in late spring. One of the loveliest is rose-pink *Rhododendron* 'Irene Koster' (zone 5–7), which is fragrant and colors well in the fall. However, evergreen azaleas, with their short season of interest, are not really ideal for pots.

CULTIVATION TIPS

• Always use a properly formulated potting mix. Loam-based mixes are best for permanent plantings. Use loam-based ericaceous mix for alkaline-intolerant plants.

• Good drainage is essential. A generous layer of broken crocks in the bottom of the pot is ideal. Also, add extra grit to the potting mix for plants requiring good drainage.

• Raise pots slightly to facilitate drainage and prevent earthworms from making their home in the pot; beneficial in the open ground, they cause problems in containers.

• Pots need watering, even in winter. Dehydration can cause bud drop on early bloomers, such as camellias.

• Rather than repotting larger subjects, scrape away the top ¾in. (2cm) of potting mix and refresh with new loam-based mix and a handful of controlled-release fertilizer.

Rhododendron 'Nancy Evans'

Ligustrum japonicum 'Rotundifolium' • *Luma apiculata* 'Glanleam Gold' • *Myrtus communis* ssp. *tarentina* • *Pittosporum tenuifolium* 'Irene Paterson' • *Prunus incisa* • *Pyracantha* 'Monelf' •

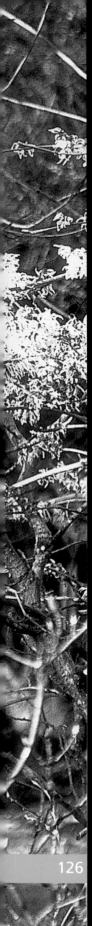

SEASONS

There is no such thing as a dead season in the garden; every season has its particular character. The fresh, cool blooms of early spring blossom into the riotous color of late spring, an exuberance that softens into the richness of summer. Fall brings the warm shades of changing leaves, illuminated with the sapphire and amber of late flowers. The hardy, fragile beauty of winter draws one year to a close, yet it also heralds the start of the next. When it comes to the interest and color provided by hardy shrubs, the

RIGHT: *Hamamelis* × *intermedia* 'Pallida'

Early spring

As the days start to lengthen, temperatures rise and some of our loveliest plants awaken, particularly the deciduous shrubs that produce their flowers on bare stems, before the leaves appear. Early spring is an unpredictable time of year, as a flower's life can be cut short by a spell of overly warm or cold weather. However, it is perhaps precisely that fragile quality, combined with the expectation of treats to come, that makes this season all the more magical.

Whichever season we may favor, all of us are moved by the awakening of spring. As we venture out for the first gardening forays of the year, it is uplifting to see how quickly the garden changes, often daily, as buds burst open and shoots and flowers emerge. The unpredictability of the weather in spring creates variability in flowering season: warm weather can entice the buds of deciduous shrubs to open overnight, while a cold snap keeps them tightly closed. When the season starts late, early- and late-spring flowers perform together in one great spring celebration.

Some winter-flowering shrubs are still blooming in early spring. *Daphne odora* (zone 7–8) goes on producing its deliciously fragrant flowers, and *Viburnum tinus* (zone 8–9) is still performing, its blooms resembling powdery elderflowers against the dark green foliage. Around now, the white candles of *Prunus laurocerasus* (cherry laurel) (zone 6–8) appear along the branches and the flesh-pink buds of

Fresh young foliage and fragile flowers herald the start of spring.

fragrant, spring-flowering evergreen **viburnums** are ready to open when warmed by the late-spring sun. **Rosemary** also delights, with its sky-blue blooms among spiky branches of soft gray green.

Spring gardens on acid soil certainly steal the variety show at this time. **Camellias** (see pages 106–107, 125) are stars of early spring—rich, gorgeous and delicate, they are great favorites. The blooms and new growth of **pieris** (see page 109), one of the most spectacular displays of this season, join the early

rhododendrons (see pages 101–105). **Magnolias** (see pages 134–35) begin a lavish but fragile display, which can last for weeks or may be extinguished overnight by severe frost.

Plants that flower early are often of woodland origin; they bloom before the leaf canopy robs them of sunlight and water. Spring hues are generally pale and fresh, but with some notable highlights; vivid yellow **forsythias**, for example, compete with the early pink **cherries** *(Prunus)* and the **flowering currants** *(Ribes)*.

USEFUL BULBS TO UNDERPLANT SHRUBS

Anemone blanda (z. 5–8)
Crocus chrysanthus 'Snow Bunting' (z. 3–9) and *C. tommasinianus* 'Whitewell Purple' (z. 3–9)
Muscari armeniacum (z. 5–8)
Ornithogalum nutans (z. 6–8)
Scilla siberica (z. 5–8)

Amelanchier lamarckii

Azara lanceolata

Amelanchiers, or snowy mespilus, are lovely light, frothy deciduous shrubs or small trees, with delicate sprays of white, starry flowers in early spring. There are a number of good species, most of which prefer acid soil and a moist site. They are accommodating plants and are frequently seen growing happily on limestone soil, although they are not generally recommended for shallow alkaline conditions.

Amelanchier canadensis (zone 3–7) is an upright suckering shrub with erect sprays of flowers; an extremely hardy, easy-to-grow plant, it is ideal on wet ground. *Amelanchier lamarckii* (zone 4–8), often incorrectly sold as *Amelanchier canadensis*, is a broad, spreading shrub or small tree, with arching sprays of white flowers produced at the same time as the delicate, coppery new leaves emerge; the leaves color brilliantly in fall on acid soil. It is an easy plant to grow. (See Good Companions, right.) *Amelanchier laevis* (zone 4–8) is similar, and is also often confused with *Amelanchier canadensis*. Look for *Amelanchier* x *grandiflora* 'Ballerina', (zone 4–7), an excellent selection, with a more vigorous habit and larger flowers.

Azaras are light, pretty evergreens from South America. All species need a sheltered spot, and are ideal grown against a wall. The yellow, mimosa-like flowers are fragrant and produced in early spring. For mild areas, *Azara lanceolata* (zone 8) is a tall, elegantly flowering shrub with attractive pointed, bright green leaves and yellow-orange flowers. *Azara microphylla* (zone 7–9) is hardier, with small leaves, which resemble shiny box foliage but are larger. The tiny yellow flowers are scented and appear on the underside of the stems. This is a lovely shrub to bring height and lightness to plantings with gold-variegated evergreens.

Berberis are extremely useful and resilient plants: they tolerate poor soil, they are resistant to wildlife damage and pests and diseases, and they do not require any pruning; with their prickly foliage, they are an excellent choice for security planting. Some berberis are deciduous, while others are evergreen. The evergreen berberis are transformed when their bright, jewel-like flowers appear against the solid background of their rigid foliage in early spring. Those with unattractive growth are ideal to plant alongside ceanothus, where the latter are useful in providing foliage bulk and continuity of flower. All the berberis described below are evergreen.

Berberis darwinii (zone 7–9) is commonly thought of as a hedging plant, but it is really one of the most wonderful evergreen flowering shrubs. It is an excellent structure plant, with its shiny, prickly, dark green foliage. In early and mid-spring, the blood orange buds appear, opening into drooping clusters of pure orange flowers. A good screening and security plant, it is glorious with springtime blues such as pulmonarias, scillas, and muscari, and will keep flowering into bluebell time. (See Good Companions, below.)

GOOD COMPANIONS

Amelanchier lamarckii (1) (z. 4–8) is pretty underplanted with *Pulmonaria* 'Roy Davidson' (2) (z. 3–7).

The orange and blue flowers of *Berberis darwinii* (3) (z. 7–9) and *Muscari armeniacum* are a striking combination (4) (z. 5–8).

129

Berberis 'Goldilocks' (zone 7–9) is a vigorous large evergreen, with spiny dark green leaves and yellow flowers in large, hanging clusters. For larger flowers and an upright form, the evergreen *Berberis linearifolia* (*Berberis trigona*) (zone 4–7) is an excellent choice. Although it has an ungainly habit, it is exquisite in flower, with gemlike blooms hanging from the branches in early spring, straight stems, and narrow, spiny leaves. *Berberis linearifolia* 'Jewel' bears scarlet buds opening to bright orange; *Berberis linearifolia* 'Orange King' has large, rich orange flowers.

Berberis × *lologensis* (zone 5–7) is a naturally occurring hybrid with variable, spiny leaves. An excellent cultivar is *Berberis* × *lologensis* 'Apricot Queen', with rich apricot flowers.

Berberis × *stenophylla* (zone 6–9) is often underrated. It has graceful, arching branches of small, dark green leaves; in early spring, it is covered with soft orange-yellow flowers. Its many cultivars include the dwarf *Berberis* × *stenophylla* 'Corallina Compacta', which rarely grows over 12in. (30cm).

Berberis × *lologensis* 'Apricot Queen'

Berberis stenophylla

Chaenomeles (zone 4–8) known as japonica or ornamental quince, and previously called *Cydonia*, is easy to grow on any soil. *Chaenomeles speciosa* and *Chaenomeles* × *superba* are delightful early-flowering deciduous shrubs that can be grown in the open or against a wall. Their angular twigs and exquisite blossoms, which open on the bare wood, bring an oriental air to the garden. All have an open, spreading habit, so they are not for tidy gardeners.

Chaenomeles speciosa 'Cameo' bears lovely, double, rich peach flowers. Another very beautiful cultivar is *Chaenomeles speciosa* 'Moerloosei' ('Apple Blossom'), with delicate pink and white blooms in abundant clusters. *Chaenomeles speciosa* 'Nivalis' is an exquisite white variant, with large flowers. However, white is not the best choice, as the flowers are spoiled in bad weather in a poor spring.

PLANTING AND PRUNING CHAENOMELES

Chaenomeles need careful siting. Plant dark colors against a light background; otherwise the flowers are lost without the backdrop of leaves to show them off. The lighter red varieties are wasted against brick walls. If pruning is required, do this straight after flowering. This is important for those trained against walls; in other situations, if a lot of pruning and control are required, perhaps this is the wrong shrub.

Chaenomeles × *superba* 'Crimson and Gold', one of the most popular of the ornamental quinces, has crimson blooms with wonderful gold anthers. Where pink is preferred, *Chaenomeles* × *superba* 'Pink Lady' produces beautiful deep pink buds opening to clear pink flowers. The blooms of *Chaenomeles* × *superba* 'Rowallane' are a glorious dark red color.

Chaenomeles × *superba* 'Pink Lady'

Chaenomeles speciosa 'Moerloosei'

Corylopsis pauciflora

Corylopsis (zone 6–8) are delightful deciduous shrubs, closely related to witch hazel (*Hamamelis*) (see page 181).

Corylopsis pauciflora is a small, spreading shrub that can eventually reach 6ft. (2m), although such large ones are rare. The tiny, hazel-like leaves, which are pink when young, normally appear after the flowers. The blooms are extremely pale, primrose yellow, and borne in hanging, translucent clusters; they are cowslip-scented. Normally a low shrub in gardens, this should be underplanted with evergreen ground cover, such as a small dark-leaved ivy, to show off the flowers to best effect. *Corylopsis pauciflora* needs neutral to acid soil to succeed.

The considerably larger *Corylopsis sinensis* var. *sinensis* 'Spring Purple' is upright in habit, with larger hanging clusters of pale lemon yellow flowers. The new foliage is plum purple before it turns to green in summer. The leaves emerge at the same time as the flowers, creating a pleasing effect. *Corylopsis sinensis* var. *sinensis* 'Spring Purple' tends to prefer neutral to acid soil, although it will also grow successfully on good alkaline soil.

Winter-flowering heathers (*Erica*) are evergreen and a valuable source of very early color. Most varieties, such as *Erica carnea* and *Erica × darleyensis*, are in full flower in late winter and early spring. They suit alpine planting and gravel areas and are a good choice for early containers. On a larger scale, the tree heaths come into their own from early spring onward (see page 132). The cultivars of *Erica carnea*, *Erica × darleyensis,* and *Erica erigena* are all alkaline-tolerant, but none truly thrive on shallow limestone.

Erica carnea (zone 5–7) originates in the Alps of central Europe, so it is extremely hardy. As a very widely planted small shrub, it has many cultivars; most grow into dense hummocks, about 6in. (15cm) high, smothered in flowers. In early winter, the swelling buds are cheery and full of promise; the flowers start to open in early spring. The bristling mats of pink, white, and deep purple red are at their best with the early spring bulbs, such as crocus, scillas, and dwarf irises. Some cultivars have bright gold foliage.

Some of the best *Erica carnea* cultivars include the following: the slow-growing **'Ann Sparkes'**, with golden foliage, bronze-tinged in winter, and purple flowers; **'Foxhollow'**, which has yellow-green foliage, tinged red in winter, and pale pink flowers; **'Golden Starlet'**, with lime-yellow foliage and white flowers; **'Myretoun Ruby'**, which produces dark green foliage and deep pink flowers; the popular **'Pink Spangles'**, with its profusion of pink

Erica carnea 'Myretoun Ruby'

Erica carnea 'Foxhollow'

Erica × darleyensis 'Arthur Johnson'

Erica × darleyensis 'White Perfection'

flowers; **'Rosalie'**, with bronze-green foliage and pink flowers; the strong, trailing **'Springwood White'**, the best white-flowering heath, with bright green foliage (see Good Companions, page 133); **'Vivellii'**, with bronze-red winter foliage and vivid carmine flowers.

Erica × darleyensis (zone 4–7), a hybrid of *Erica carnea* and *Erica erigena*, is a taller-growing shrub than *Erica carnea*. The garden cultivars of *Erica × darleyensis* have inherited this taller character, growing to about 10–12in. (25–30cm) high, and producing a bigger, looser-growing plant—one that is useful to bring color at a greater height to mixed plantings of heathers, conifers, and dwarf evergreens.

Some of the best *Erica × darleyensis* cultivars include: **'Arthur Johnson'**, with tall stems bearing long sprays of magenta flowers, excellent for cutting; **'J. W. Porter'**, with pink flowers, dark green foliage, and reddish new shoots in spring; **'Kramer's Rote'**, with bronze-green foliage and magenta flowers; **'Silberschmelze'**, with dark green leaves tinged red in winter and sweetly scented white flowers over a long period; **'White Perfection'**, with bright green foliage and white flowers.

Erica erigena (zone 8–9) is another alkaline-tolerant winter-flowering heath

that forms a dense, small to medium-sized shrub. **'Golden Lady'** has golden-yellow foliage and white flowers, and is a good, compact alternative to a dwarf yellow conifer, growing to some 12in. (30cm) high; **'Irish Dusk'** is one of the best known and loveliest of the winter-flowering heathers, growing to about 50cm (18in) high with healthy dark foliage and salmon pink flowers, an unusual shade for a heather; **'W. T. Rackliff'** is extremely dense and compact, and makes an excellent low hedge up to 30in. (75cm) in height; it produces dark green foliage and white flowers with brown anthers.

PLANTING AND CARING FOR WINTER HEATHERS

Winter-flowering heathers are offered for sale in several sizes. Where space permits, buy smaller plants and plant one variety in groups of three or five—this will produce a better overall effect. Follow the general advice on planting on pages 16–19.

Ericas should be trimmed after flowering to remove faded blooms and promote bushy growth; use large pruning shears for this.

Mulch after trimming with organic, alkaline-free soil mix and slow-release, alkaline-free fertilizer.

Erica arborea var. 'Alpina'

Forsythia × intermedia

The **tree heaths (*Erica*)** are lovely large evergreen shrubs with fragrant, pollen-laden flowers, which are a delight in early spring. All those described here are recommended for neutral to acid soils; however, they will grow on clay soils and are not totally intolerant of alkalinity. Tree heaths associate well with rocks and stone and tolerate dry conditions. They can be hard-pruned back to the old wood after they have finished flowering, in order to promote long, straight, floriferous growth.

Erica arborea (zone 7–8) is an attractive, soft evergreen that offers foliage contrast in mixed plantings; it is also good to cut for floral decoration. It can grow to 16ft. (5m), but is normally seen at half this height in gardens. A mountain plant, it produces extremely hard root nodules, which are fire-resistant and used to make briar pipes. The medium-sized **Erica arborea var. alpina** is more commonly grown and is hardier and more upright. Foliage is bright green, and flowers are white with brown anthers. (See also page 41.)

Another very hardy, medium-sized tree heath is **Erica australis** (zone 5–9), the Spanish heath, which is later-flowering and has rosy purple flowers.

Erica lusitanica (zone 7–9), the Portuguese heath, is earlier-flowering than *Erica arborea* and continues over a long period from winter into spring. The fine, plumelike green stems are crowded with white tubular flowers.

Erica × veitchii (zone 7–9) is a hybrid between *Erica arborea* and *Erica lusitanica*. The cultivar **Erica × veitchii 'Exeter'** is a superb shrub, growing to around 6ft. (2m). The foliage is bright green and the flowers white and fragrant, produced profusely in early spring. Although not good on cold, exposed sites, it is easy to grow. *Erica × veitchii* **'Gold Tips'** has bright yellow young foliage, becoming dark green.

Like them or loathe them, there is no denying the impact of **forsythias** in our gardens in early spring—the eruption of bright yellow seems to be everywhere. Members of the olive family, forsythias arrived in our gardens in the mid-19th

century. Since then, they have been widely planted as freestanding shrubs, wall shrubs, and hedges. They are very easy to grow, and are a good choice on difficult sites and poor soil.

Forsythias look good planted as a screen or structure plant at the back of a border, where the medium-green leaves will provide a good summer backdrop. To extend the season of interest, plant *Clematis viticella* or perennial sweet peas to grow through the forsythia's branches. Forsythias should be pruned after flowering, cutting out some of the flowered wood, allowing vigorous new shoots to develop. Most of the commonly grown varieties root easily from cuttings.

Forsythia suspensa (zone 5–8) was the earliest forsythia to be introduced. A rambling, deciduous shrub, it is a lovely plant to grow over a wall, where it will grow to 10ft. (3m) or more. The yellow flowers are well spaced, dainty and graceful in appearance. Hybridized with *Forsythia viridissima* (zone 5–8), a late-flowering variety with an upright

Forsythia × intermedia WEEKEND ('Courtalyn')

Kerria japonica 'Golden Guinea'

Kerria japonica 'Pleniflora'

habit, *Forsythia suspensa* has given rise to *Forsythia × intermedia* (zone 5–9), a vigorous, medium to large, upright deciduous shrub, our familiar garden forsythia. There are numerous cultivars: *Forsythia × intermedia* 'Lynwood Variety', the best and most widely planted, has broader petals and profuse flowers; *Forsythia × intermedia* 'Spectabilis', one of the original selections, is very free-flowering—the whole shrub is a mass of yellow when in flower (see Good Companions, right); *Forsythia × intermedia* 'Week-End' is a mutation of *Forsythia × intermedia* 'Lynwood Variety', it retains its excellent qualities but has a smaller, more compact habit and so is better for small gardens or where space is restricted.

Other colorful deciduous shrubs that dominate the garden in early spring are **kerrias**, which have been resident in Western gardens since Victorian times. Their upright green stems form a clump, arching when mature. They look good in winter, and the medium-green, well-spaced foliage has a light, airy quality. Kerrias are excellent flowering shrubs for shade and thrive on any soil. They are lovely when used to lighten dark evergreens, and to plant against green ivy if grown against a wall. Prune by cutting out selected older stems after the flowers have faded, in order to keep the plant open and graceful and to prevent unattractive, bushy growth. *Kerria japonica* (zone 4–9), which is not often seen, has single, pale orange buttercup flowers all along the branches in spring. *Kerria japonica* 'Golden Guinea' is the widely grown cultivar, with large, single flowers. However, it is *Kerria japonica* 'Pleniflora' ('Flore Pleno') that is the favorite: the double, pale orange flowers are scattered, like loose pom-poms, over the plant from early spring; it is more upright than the single-flowered form.

Osmanthus delavayi (zone 7–10) is a beautiful, small evergreen shrub of rigid but graceful growth. The arching stems are tan brown with small, dark green leaves. It is slow-growing, but from an early age produces exquisite, tiny white tubular flowers, which are very fragrant. For those gardeners who look forward to the scent of jasmine, this is an early fillip. This shrub is easy to grow, and tolerant of most soils and some shade. Plant near a path, where the fragrance can be enjoyed. (See Good Companions, below.)

GOOD COMPANIONS

The white flowers of *Erica carnea* 'Springwood White' (1) (z. 5–7) complement the white bark of *Betula utilis* var. *jacquemontii* 'Silver Shadow' (2) (z. 4–7).

Let a *Clematis* 'Kermesina' (3) (z. 6–9) scramble through *Forsythia × intermedia* 'Spectabilis' (4) (z. 5–9) to extend its season of interest.

Osmanthus delavayi (5) (z. 7–10) is delightful with the pure white, *Pulmonaria* 'Sissinghurst White' (6) (z. 3–7) and a silver-variegated ivy such as *Hedera helix* 'Glacier' (z. 4–9).

133

PLANT PROFILE

Magnolias

Perhaps the most magnificent of all hardy trees and shrubs, magnolias are a stunning sight in full bloom in early spring. Their flowers, almost otherworldly in appearance, seem all the more miraculous when they burst from bare branches, before the leaves appear.

Magnolias are mostly deciduous, although there are also evergreen varieties (all the magnolias described and illustrated on these pages are deciduous). They are easy to grow and are tolerant of heavy clay, and although they prefer acid to neutral soils, most are reasonably tolerant of lime. Many magnolias are too large for the average garden, and some tree magnolias can take several years to flower, so you need to select the species carefully. When planting, consider the ultimate size and shape of the shrub; most magnolias are beautiful specimen shrubs that need space around them and are not seen at their best overcrowded by surrounding planting. The early-flowering magnolias are susceptible to frost and wind damage to the flowers, so choose a sheltered site to avoid damage.

Magnolias need no pruning. If you prune to control size, take care not to ruin the shape. When pruned, the larger magnolias, such as *Magnolia × soulangeana*, produce unwanted vigorous, upright growth; remove whole branches rather than cutting halfway.

Magnolia liliiflora 'Nigra' (zone 5–8) is a good choice for a small garden. It forms a wide, spreading, large shrub, usually about 6ft. (2m) high, but can grow to 13ft. (4m). The flowers are carried upright on the branches, like waxy, deep purple candles, retaining their slender tulip form as they open to reveal a creamy white interior. They are produced from early spring to summer, never with the same profusion as some magnolias but always with supreme sophistication.

Magnolia × loebneri (zone 4–8) is a hybrid of *Magnolia stellata* with *Magnolia kobus* (zone 4–8). It is usually grown as a large shrub and flowers freely from

A *Magnolia stellata*'s starry white flowers sing in the spring sunshine.

an early age. The flowers are fragrant, with long, straplike petals, and a more open and starry bloom than *Magnolia stellata*. *Magnolia × loebneri* is the best choice for alkaline soil.

Among the best known of all magnolias is the wide-spreading *Magnolia × soulangeana* (zone 4–9), known as the tulip tree. A heart-stopper in bloom, this glorious shrub produces a profusion of large, pointed buds that open to goblet-shaped, creamy white blooms, flushed pink at the base. The flowers start to appear before the leaves, but continue until the young lime green leaves start to unfurl. This magnolia copes with atmospheric pollution and so is often seen in urban situations. There are many cultivars, all of which flower at an early age.

Unless you have plenty of space, the best magnolia is undoubtedly *Magnolia stellata* (zone 4–8). A slow-growing shrub from Japan, it forms a compact, broad shrub, eventually reaching 10ft. (3m) high. The winter buds on the bare branches resemble large pussy willows, and are an attractive feature in their own right. The fragrant white flowers, which are borne profusely in early spring, have narrow petals, rounded at the tips, and are sweetly scented; they are much more weather-resistant than most magnolias. There are many cultivars.

Magnolia 'Heaven Scent' (z. 6–9) is a large shrub or small tree, with highly fragrant, narrow, cup-shaped flowers with pink petals flushed darker at the base, and a darker stripe on the back of the petals.

Magnolia × *loebneri* 'Leonard Messel' (left) (z. 5–8) is the best-known × *loebneri* cultivar, with pale lilac-pink flowers. Upright in growth and open in habit, it suits mixed plantings and combines well with other shrubs in a large border. The cultivar 'Merrill' has white flowers.

Magnolia stellata 'Centennial' (z. 4–9) is superb, vigorous and free-flowering, with many-petaled flowers that are incurved at the petal tips.

OTHER GOOD MAGNOLIAS

Magnolia × *soulangeana* 'Lennei' (z. 4–9) has large leaves and flowers, rose purple outside and creamy-white stained pink purple inside.

Magnolia × *soulangeana* 'Alba' (z. 4–9) has scented, pure white flowers, without the pinkish flush of other soulangeanas.

Magnolia × *soulangeana* 'Brozzonii' (z. 4–9) bears large white flowers, shaded purple at the base. It blooms later than other soulangeanas.

Magnolia × *soulangeana* 'Rustica Rubra' (z. 4–9) is vigorous, with cup-shaped, rich rosy red flowers.

Magnolia stellata 'Rosea' (z. 4–9) bears white, pink-flushed flowers.

Magnolia stellata 'Waterlily' (left) (z. 4–9) has large white, waterlily-like flowers.

Magnolia × *soulangeana* (z. 4–9) is the most popular magnolia of them all.

Magnolia 'Susan' (z. 4–7) is an upright, medium-sized shrub, ideal for the smaller garden. The elegant, candle-like flowers are dark red purple in bud, opening to soft reddish purple. It is lovely planted with silver dollar (*Lunaria annua*) (z. 7–9).

Prunus incisa 'Kojo-no-mai'

The **bush cherries (*Prunus*)** offer a spectacular display when in flower in early spring, although the season is generally short-lived. They are plants for large gardens, where they need not occupy key positions. All of the bush cherries described here are deciduous.

Prunus cerasifera 'Newport' (zone 3–8) and *Prunus cerasifera* 'Krauter's Vesuvius' (zone 3–8) are often seen as trees, but both can be grown as large shrubs. Delightful in early spring, when they explode in a cloud of tiny, single blossoms of pale pink or white, they are useful for their deep plum foliage, which follows later on dark twigs. However, they are rarely perfect, due to shot-hole virus and fungal disease, so should not be viewed at close quarters.

As a shrub, the purple-leaf sand cherry, *Prunus* × *cistena* (zone 2–8), is a better choice. Light and dainty in growth, it is upright in habit, slowly reaching 6ft. (2m). Red-purple leaves on burgundy stems follow the shower of white flowers in spring. It is an excellent, if rarely used, hedging plant.

Prunus incisa 'Kojo-no-mai' (zone 5–7) is an exquisite variety of the Fuji cherry and flowers for longer than the other bush cherries. It is a small, slow-growing shrub, with wonderful zigzag twigs and a bonsai-like habit. In early spring, the branches are loaded with pretty, delicate pale pink, paper-thin blossoms (the Japanese name means "flight of butterflies," an apt description). The leaves color beautifully in fall. This is a delightful plant to grow in a gravel garden with scree and rocks, or is perfect for a pot on the terrace. It grows on any soil, in sun or semi-shade.

The other bush cherries are certainly not as popular as they were. All have their problems in terms of disease, often suffering from dieback caused by

Prunus glandulosa 'Alba Plena'

bacterial canker. Warm, wet winters do not help these conditions, and their decline in popularity may be partially due to climate change. Although the early spring flowers are delightful, the shrubs are not attractive for the rest of the year and do need some attention.

Prunus glandulosa (zone 4–8) is a small shrub, with slender, erect stems carrying flowers before the leaves in early spring. It needs a warm, sunny position and is lovely for cutting for the house; it has long been cultivated in Japan for just this purpose. *Prunus glandulosa* 'Alba Plena' has large, double white flowers; those of *Prunus glandulosa* 'Sinensis' are also double, but bright pink. Both can be forced into flower early, and may be grown in a pot to be brought into a cool conservatory in midwinter for a flush of early flowers.

Prunus triloba 'Multiplex' (zone 3–8) is a larger version of *Prunus glandulosa*, with double, sugar pink flowers, like crumpled balls of tissue paper, in early spring. The dark twigs are the ideal setting for the perfectly spaced blooms, and a plant in flower is a real delight. The flowering shoots should be carefully pruned once the flowers have faded, to encourage strong, straight stems to flower profusely in the following year.

Prunus triloba 'Multiplex'

Ribes sanguineum 'Koja'

Sophora microphylla SUN KING ('Hilsop')

Another good, reliable deciduous spring favorite is the flowering currant *Ribes sanguineum* (zone 6–7). It is extremely useful in the garden as it is medium-sized, up to 6ft. (2m), easy to grow and is tolerant of any conditions. Perhaps cast aside because of its ubiquitous planting in the middle of the last century, it has a certain nostalgic charm as a reminder of 1960s gardens. Poor positioning often spoils this plant: it should not be teamed up with forsythia, as the two do not make a pleasant combination. The currant fragrance of the foliage and wood is a feature of the plant; if you do not appreciate it, avoid planting this shrub close to a path.

The flowering currant should be pruned after flowering. Some of the old flowered stems can be cut back hard to ground level as soon as the flowers have faded; later pruning can result in poor, weak growth.

Ribes sanguineum 'King Edward VII' is a compact bush with crimson flowers; *Ribes sanguineum* 'Koja' is a newer, red-flowering variety with large flower clusters and healthy foliage. A softer alternative to the red-flowered cultivars is *Ribes sanguineum* 'Poky's Pink', with pink flowers flushed white; the strong, upright *Ribes sanguineum* 'Pulborough Scarlet' has flowers of a deep pink-red; *Ribes* 'White Icicle' produces large, drooping clusters of pure white flowers, which open early in the flowering season.

A relative newcomer to our gardens is the hardy *Sophora microphylla* 'Sun King' (zone 8–11). A Chilean plant, it arose as a chance seedling in a batch of nothofagus seedlings. The original plant grew on in the Sir Harold Hillier Gardens, in England, for several years, surviving hard winters and performing reliably, before it was introduced as a garden plant. It is a vigorous shrub of rather angular growth with dark green, usually evergreen, pinnate leaves. Severe cold can cause leaf-fall but the foliage is soon replaced in spring. The hanging, bright yellow flowers are produced over a long period in late winter and early spring. This sophora can be grown as a freestanding shrub or trained on a wall. It flowers reliably even as a young plant. (See Good Companions, below.)

Stachyurus praecox (zone 6–8) is an extremely beautiful shrub with reddish brown stems growing upright, then arching. For most of the year it is an ordinary green deciduous shrub, not unlike *Leycesteria* (pheasant berry) in habit (see page 95). Once the leaves have fallen, dark reddish brown buds appear at the nodes. These remain over winter and start to open in very early spring, gradually developing into stiff, pendent flower clusters of palest yellow, hanging like drop earrings all along the branches. Stachyurus will grow in any fertile soil, in sun or part shade, although it does not thrive on shallow limestone. It needs a dark background to display the flowers, and is perfect in oriental garden settings, with bamboos and ferns, or sited over water. (See Good Companions, below.)

GOOD COMPANIONS

For a pretty, sunny spring combination, underplant *Sophora microphylla* 'Sun King' (z. 8–11) with blue muscari (z. 5–8), which flower at the same time (1).

Stachyurus praecox (2) (z. 6–8), *Phyllostachys nigra* (3) (z. 7–10) and *Polystichum setiferum* (4) (z. 7–8) make an attractive grouping of contrasting shapes and foliage.

Late spring

As the garden heads toward summer, flowers abound, and wave after wave of color rolls through the borders. Bare earth disappears as the borders fill out, fresh green foliage unfurls, and the colors become stronger and the production bolder. Cherries are at their most floriferous, the apple trees draw the bees, and the irises, euphorbias, and primulas are in bloom.

Some of the most beautiful **abutilons** start to flower in late spring and continue into summer. Members of the mallow family, they are fast-growing deciduous shrubs, ideal for a warm, sunny, sheltered site, such as against a wall (see p.119), on well-drained soil. They grow well on limestone, and tolerate soil of low fertility, but dislike heavy wet soil. Abutilons are useful shrubs where height is required quickly, growing 3ft. (1m) or more a year.

Abutilon vitifolium (zone 9–11), which bears downy leaves like a vine, grows quickly to 12ft. (4m). The

Abutilon × suntense 'Jermyns'

Azara serrata

Abutilon vitifolium 'Tennant's White'

ABUTILON AFTERCARE

Abutilons become leggy and woody as they age. From the first year after planting, they should be pruned in midsummer, straight after flowering, cutting back by one-third. Abutilons are not long-lived plants and should be replaced after five years or so in most situations; sometimes whole branches die out at the end of winter, particularly in wet conditions. They are best staked, except in very sheltered sites, as they can quickly become top-heavy.

growth is upright and spreading, the shoots pale green. The pale mauve, saucer-shaped flowers are paper-thin. A lovely cultivar is *Abutilon vitifolium* **'Veronica Tennant'**, which bears large mauve flowers in a deeper shade than the species. *Abutilon vitifolium* **'Tennant's White'** is slightly more upright and pure, shimmering white.

Abutilon × suntense (zone 9–11), a hybrid of *Abutilon vitifolium*, is a

beautiful, large, and fast-growing shrub, with less downy foliage and clusters of smaller, saucer-shaped flowers, which open in succession, ranging from white in some cultivars to violet blue in others. *Abutilon × suntense* **'Jermyns'** is the original Hillier form, with clear mauve-blue flowers. It starts to flower from mid-spring onward and puts on an amazing show for many weeks. It is a superb plant and can be surprisingly hardy.

Azara serrata (zone 8–9) is one of the more robust azaras. It is a large, narrow shrub, ideal for growing against a wall in a sheltered position. The oval, bright evergreen leaves shelter the orange-yellow flowers, which explode from buds formed the previous season. Often likened to an orange ceanothus, a plant in flower has a wonderful mimosalike quality. The fine stems and glossy foliage make this shrub an attractive evergreen throughout the year. Plant it with other dark evergreens to show off the attractive flowers.

Choisya 'Aztec Pearl'

praecox 'Allgold' bears long-lasting, strong yellow flowers; *Cytisus* × *praecox* 'Lilac Lady' is a new cultivar, with pale green stems and small, dainty lilac flowers; *Cytisus* × *praecox* 'Warminster' is the original form, and still the best. Usually growing to 5ft. (1.5m) and no more, in flower it is a rich, beautiful cream cascade. (See Good Companions, page 143.)

There are many hybrid brooms, all deciduous, some with exceptionally showy, large flowers. *Cytisus* 'Boskoop Ruby' (zone 5–8) is small and rounded

Cytisus 'Boskoop Ruby'

Choisya 'Aztec Pearl' (zone 8–10) is a reliable, easy, compact shrub, reaching 6ft. (2m). The evergreen palmate leaves have very narrow leaflets, giving a delightful light foliage effect offered by few other evergreens. The fragrant flowers appear from knobbly buds in late spring and again in fall. They are pink-flushed in bud, opening to white, and are produced in such profusion that the foliage can be totally obscured when the shrub is in full flower As with other choisyas, growth can be slow for the first two years. Shelter from cold winds to prevent leaf drop.

Choisya ternata (the Mexican orange blossom) (zone 8–10) is one of the evergreen mainstays of the temperate garden (see page 33). Neatly rounded and medium-sized, it can start to produce its fragrant white flowers any time from midwinter, but the main flush comes with the warmer weather.

Cytisus × praecox (zone 5–7) is a popular broom, a small shrub, with fine, arching, leafless green shoots that have a light, grasslike quality and offer a useful contrast to other broad-leaved shrubs. It can begin to bloom anytime from mid-spring onward: tiny buds appear all the way along the stems, each one opening into a very fragrant, pealike flower. *Cytisus* × *praecox* 'Albus' has white flowers; *Cytisus* ×

HEALTHY BROOMS

Brooms prefer a neutral soil, not too acid and not too alkaline. They can be pruned to encourage bushiness by trimming immediately after flowering and from an early age; hard pruning later in life is often fatal. Never cut back into bare wood, as they do not regenerate. Crowded among other shrubs, brooms can become leggy and woody at the base. There is no way of reversing this, and replacement is the only solution. Brooms are short-lived plants, particularly on shallow limestone soils, and normally need replacing after a few years. Never try to move an established broom; instead, replace it with new stock.

---

in habit with deep crimson flowers, *Cytisus* 'Burkwoodii' (zone 5–8) is larger-growing and more vigorous, and has cerise flowers with deep crimson "wings" edged with yellow; *Cytisus* 'Hollandia' (zone 5–7) produces pale cream and cerise flowers on arching branches, *Cytisus* 'Lena' (zone 5–8) is a compact, spreading shrub with showy deep red and yellow flowers; *Cytisus* 'Luna' (zone 5–8) has large flowers and is available in shades of yellow, tinged with red; *Cytisus* 'Minstead' (zone 5–8) has small flowers in white, flushed with lilac and gives a frothy pink effect in mixed plantings; *Cytisus* 'Zeelandia' (zone 5–8) is a neat bush with flowers of lilac, pink, and cream; and is lovely when combined with blue ceanothus.

There are also two good dwarf deciduous brooms. They are useful for areas alongside walls and paving in a sunny position. *Cytisus* × *beanii* (zone 5–7) grows to only 12in. (30cm) high; neat and compact, it is smothered with golden yellow flowers in late spring and makes a good alternative to *Genista lydia*; *Cytisus* × *kewensis* (zone 6–7), of similar height, has horizontal growth, creating a sheet of pretty cream flowers in late spring. (See Good Companions, page 142.)

Cytisus 'Minstead'

Ceanothus

The California lilacs, or *Ceanothus*, are extremely distinctive shrubs. When they burst into bloom, the color of summer skies erupts from our gardens, lifting our spirits with the promise of sunny days ahead.

Late spring is just the beginning of the season for these lovely plants. Some ceanothus bloom in summer, others in fall (see pages 82–83, 118, 150). They are very versatile plants and offer just about everything a gardener could wish for in a shrub: they are free-flowering, have attractive foliage, are easy to cultivate, and are fast-growing—a young ceanothus can, depending on the variety, put on up to 3ft. (1m) of growth in a year. In addition, many are evergreen.

Ceanothus are excellent in seaside gardens, and the upright varieties are ideal for growing against a wall. They like full sun and good drainage; most are alkaline-tolerant. They may be pruned lightly after flowering, but never cut back into old wood, as they rarely regrow. This does depend on the variety, but if new shoots are emerging from the wood it is usually safe to cut back to this point.

Most ceanothus are not long-lived plants. Ten years is an average lifespan, so be prepared to replace them after that time. There are white-flowered varieties, but why bother with these when there are so many beautiful blue ones available?

Ceanothus 'Blue Mound' (z. 8–10) is a superb hardy ceanothus that forms a mound of stiff, arching branches smothered with small, fluffy heads of bright blue flowers in late spring, and often again in early fall. It is an excellent structure shrub, but needs a lot of space—it can reach 6ft. (2m) across, by nearly the same height.

Ceanothus 'Concha' (z. 9–10) is a glorious, reliable shrub. It is fairly upright in habit, but with strong, arching stems and rich dark green foliage. The red-brown flower buds explode like an exotic firework into a cloud of sapphire blue in spring. (See Good Companions, pages 98, 146.)

Ceanothus 'Puget Blue' (z. 7–10), a beautiful shrub, was once the most popular of the dark sapphire ceanothus, being hardy and flowering over a long period. The growth habit is stiff and upright, with rather rigid branches and small, tight foliage.

OTHER GOOD CEANOTHUS

Ceanothus arboreus 'Trewithen Blue' (z. 8–10) is large and vigorous, with deep blue arching flower sprays.

Ceanothus 'Blue Sapphire' (z. 9–11) has sapphire blue flowers on cascading green stems.

Ceanothus 'Dark Star', (z. 7–10) an arching shrub, has tiny dark green leaves and small clusters of deep purple-blue flowers.

Ceanothus griseus var. *horizontalis* 'Yankee Point' (z. 9–10) has a sprawling habit and purple-blue flowers.

Ceanothus 'Italian Skies' (z. 8–10) is vigorous and spreading, with deep blue flowers.

Flowering dogwoods (Cornus)

The flowering dogwoods are the real heart-stoppers of late spring. They are hardy, deciduous plants. Although not totally intolerant of alkalinity, they prefer a neutral or slightly acid soil, with plenty of depth and organic matter. A sheltered open woodland situation is the ideal, although they can also thrive in town gardens, and fine specimens are to be seen on reasonable soil over limestone.

Cornus florida (zone 5–9), the North American dogwood, is a large shrub or bushy small tree of elegant stature, normally upright. The flowers consist of four slightly wavy, petal-like bracts, with a round boss in the center that is a tight cluster of the true flowers. The branches arch gracefully when the shrub is in full bloom in late spring. In addition to the spring display, the leaves color beautifully in fall.

Cornus kousa (zone 5–8) comes from Japan and Korea and its oriental origins are a distinct characteristic. It is a large shrub, with attractive pointed mid-green leaves that color richly on neutral or acid soils in autumn. In spring, the horizontal, arching branches are covered with delicate white, four-bracted flowers that sit daintily above the leaves like white butterflies. Strawberrylike fruits follow in autumn. *Cornus kousa* needs to be well established before it flowers freely.

Cornus 'Norman Hadden' (zone 5–8) and *Cornus* 'Porlock' (zone 5–8) are two very similar hybrids, equally beautiful, originating from the same garden in Devon, England. They are semi-evergreen, large shrubs of graceful, spreading habit, and can bring height to mixed plantings in smaller gardens. Both grow well in a tub of lime-free, loam-based compost.

Cornus florida 'Cherokee Chief' (z. 5–9) has beautiful, deep rose pink bracts. The round buds appear on the branches during winter, opening in late spring.

Cornus 'Norman Hadden' (left) (z. 5–8) has four-bracted flower heads, creamy with a dark eye, held on short stalks above the leaves. The flowers grow larger as they mature and blush pink in early summer. In fall some of the foliage turns soft red and hanging, strawberry-like fruits are produced.
Cornus 'Porlock' (z. 5–8) is very similar. (See Good Companions, page 142.)

Cornus kousa 'Satomi' (z. 5–8) is a Japanese variety, with deep salmon pink bracts and an open, arching habit as it matures. The leaves turn rich purple red in autumn.

OTHER GOOD FLOWERING DOGWOODS

Cornus kousa 'Gold Star' (z. 5–8) has large white bracts and yellow-blotched variegated foliage.

Cornus florida 'White Cloud' (z. 5–9) has bronze-green foliage and large white bracts.

Cornus kousa var. *chinensis* (z. 5–8) has an open, graceful habit with creamy bracts turning pink. 'China Girl' is a vigorous form with a mass of large flower heads.

Exochorda × macrantha 'The Bride'

Olearia × scilloniensis

Aptly called the pearlbush, *Exochorda × macrantha* **'The Bride'** (zone 5–7) is one of the gems of the spring garden. A loose, spreading bush, with arching branches and pale green leaves, it is transformed in late spring when round white buds break into open, pure white, apple-blossom flowers. At its peak, a mature plant is a large mound of shimmering white. It is easy to grow, but needs feeding on shallow alkaline soil. It also requires plenty of space, and is not best placed immediately alongside a path or packed in among other shrubs. Ideally, plant it at the end of a border or to cascade over the edge of a terrace. (See Good Companions, opposite.)

The Tasmanian daisy bush, *Olearia phlogopappa* (zone 8–10), is a pretty, tender shrub for a sunny, warm, sheltered spot. It has upright branches and narrow aromatic leaves, clustered densely on the stems. The Splendens Group consists of colored cultivars, including *Olearia phlogopappa* **'Comber's Blue'** and *Olearia phlogopappa* **'Comber's Pink'**, both with Michaelmas daisylike flowers in late spring. Growing to 5ft. (1.5m), they are ideal to plant at the base of a wall with lavenders and gray foliage plants.

Olearia × scilloniensis (zone 8–10), a hybrid of *Olearia phlogopappa*, is an outstanding tall but compact shrub, also with upright growth and neat gray foliage. The white daisylike flowers, with silver-white centers, are so freely produced that they smother the plant completely when it is in full bloom. (See Good Companions, page 146.)

Peonies are thought of mostly as herbaceous perennials. However, the woody species—the tree peonies—are among the most spectacular deciduous shrubs in both flower and foliage. Native to China and Tibet, the tree peonies are hardy, although the new growth of some may be susceptible to frost damage, so a sheltered spot is preferred. They like full sun and good drainage; most are good on lime, especially *Paeonia delavayi*. All are tall and upright, with few stems.

Paeonia delavayi (zone 6–9) is a suckering shrub, with upright brown stems with peeling bark up to 6ft. (2m) high. Even a small plant is an impressive sight when the large, deeply cut architectural leaves unfurl. They are as much a feature of the plant as the single ruby flowers with golden anthers;

GOOD COMPANIONS

Cornus 'Norman Hadden' (1) (z. 5–8) sits well with *Cotinus coggygria* 'Royal Purple' (2) (z. 4–8) and *Rosa* 'Geranium' (3) (z. 5–7).

The cream-colored blooms of *Cytisus × kewensis* (4) (z. 6–7) make it a good partner for the blue-flowered *Ceanothus* 'Centennial' (5) (z. 7–10) .

Paeonia delavayi var. lutea

Paeonia suffruticosa 'Double Deep Pink'

Paeonia suffruticosa 'Rock's Variety'

these are followed by large black-seeded fruits shaped like a jester's hat. *Paeonia delavayi* var. *lutea* (zone 6–9) produces similar foliage, but the flowers, which are produced at the ends of the branches, are yellow, resembling large kingcups.

Paeonia × *lemoinei* (zone 5–9) is a hybrid of *Paeonia delavayi* var. *lutea* and *Paeonia suffruticosa*. The cultivars have very large yellow or bicolored flowers. *Paeonia* × *lemoinei* 'Souvenir de Maxime Cornu' has bright yellow blooms edged with carmine.

Paeonia ludlowii (zone 6–9) is similar to *Paeonia delavayi*, with larger, saucer-shaped flowers.

Paeonia suffruticosa (zone 7–9), the Moutan peony, is the most spectacular of all tree peonies, growing

---

PLANTING TREE PEONIES AND AFTERCARE

Tree peonies are not attractive in winter, when the leaves fall, exposing a few rough, upright stems; for this reason, plant them against an evergreen background that will take over to provide winter interest. They require no pruning—if you cut them back when the leaves fall, you will remove the flower buds. Protect new growth and flower buds with a floating row cover in early spring.

---

to 6ft. (2m) high. The flowers are very large, usually over 6in. (15cm) across. In the wild, the flowers are white, but the cultivars include the most gorgeously colored, extravagant blossoms.

Prostanthera (the mint bush) is a genus of very aromatic, fast-growing evergreen shrubs suitable for a warm, sunny position. They have become increasingly popular in recent years. *Prostanthera cuneata* (zone 9–10) is one of the cultivated species. A native of Australia, it is surprisingly hardy. It has small leaves, which are crowded on the stems of a low, spreading bush and are sweetly aromatic when brushed

against. The tiny flowers, which are produced in profusion in late spring, are lilac white. It looks very pretty planted with silver foliage and purple sage. (See also Good Companions, page 146.)

Although fairly rare, **rhaphiolepis** are worthy of a mention. These members of the rose family have attractive leathery evergreen foliage and pretty clusters of apple-blossom flowers in late spring. They are not the hardiest of plants, but in a sheltered position, they remain unscathed through all but the coldest winters. Rhaphiolepis like well-drained, fertile, acid or alkaline soil, and a position in full sun. The cultivars of *Rhaphiolepis*

GOOD COMPANIONS

Cytisus × *praecox* (1) (z. 5–7) is lovely with purple silver dollar and deep burgundy tulips such as *Tulipa* 'Queen of Night' (2) (z. 4–9).

The arching branches of *Exochorda* × *macrantha* 'The Bride' (3) (z. 5–7) are perfect for showing off the flowers of *Clematis* 'Alba Luxurians' (4) (z. 4–9) in late summer.

× *delacourii* (zone 8–11) are lovely shrubs for a warm, sheltered garden: *Rhaphiolepis* × *delacourii* 'Coates' Crimson' has rose-crimson blooms, and *Rhaphiolepis* × *delacourii* 'Spring Song' bears pale pink flowers over a relatively long period. *Rhaphiolepis umbellata* (zone 8–10) is a tougher species; it is a low evergreen, growing only to 3ft. (1m) or so in height; the flowers are white pink and produced at the tips of the branches in late spring.

On acid soils, it is undoubtedly the **rhododendrons** and **azaleas** that steal the late-spring show, as the dense evergreen mounds are transformed

Ceanothus 'Blue Mound' and Rosa 'Nevada'

Rhaphiolepis 'Spring Song'

Rosa xanthina 'Canary Bird'

with blooms of translucent pastels and rich silk shades. See pages 101–105.

As spring finally heads toward summer the early **roses** start to bloom (see also pages 112–115). Some of the large shrub roses, such as *Rosa* 'Frühlingsgold', (zone 5–10) display their large open blooms on upright stems. With its big, single or semi-double creamy-yellow flowers, this is a lovely screening plant combined with gold-variegated shrubs.

Rosa 'Nevada' (zone 5–9) is a tall shrub with a mass of large creamy flowers, with golden stamens, in late spring and early summer. It is easy to grow where space needs filling. Prune out older shoots after flowering, right to the base. It may flower again later.

Several cultivars of the Scotch rose or Burnet rose, *Rosa pimpinellifolia* (*Rosa spinosissima*) (zone 4–8), deserve much

wider planting in the garden. The prickly stems are covered with small, neat leaves, and maroon-black fruits often follow the pretty, early flowers that stud the compact bush. *Rosa pimpinellifolia* 'Andrewsii' produces pink and cream, semi-double flowers with yellow stamens, and sometimes repeats in fall; *Rosa pimpinellifolia* 'Glory of Edzell' has clear pink, lemon-centered flowers; *Rosa pimpinellifolia* 'William III' is short and dense, with red-purple flowers and black fruits.

The **rugosa** hybrids (zone 3–7) will already be clothed in their apple green pleated foliage by late spring, and in warm situations, they are also in flower at this time. They repeat-flower throughout the season and are perhaps the best choice for gardeners who prefer steady flowering to an ephemeral

seasonal display. Their hips are an autumn highlight (see page 174).

Rosa xanthina 'Canary Bird' (zone 5–7) is a delightful shrub rose. In late spring, it opens large buttercup-yellow blooms along the arching wands of emerging fernlike foliage; the display of flowers is not long, but it is a prominent signal that summer is on its way. The single, creamy-yellow blooms of *Rosa xanthina* f. *hugonis* (zone 5–7) clothe the arching stems of this graceful shrub while the first ceanothus are in flower.

As gardens have become smaller and shrubs have to work harder to earn their place, some of the larger shrub roses that bloom only once have become less popular. However, they are easy to grow and reliably produce a superb display, becoming the most outstanding plants in the garden, if only for a few days.

Lilacs (Syringa)

Late spring is lilac time. Members of the olive family, lilacs (or syringas) are some of our most popular deciduous garden shrubs. The fragrance of lilac is one of the definitive floral perfumes.

Syringa vulgaris (zone 3–7), the species from which our garden, or common, lilacs are descended, is a native of the mountains of eastern Europe. The garden lilacs (hybrids and cultivars of *Syringa vulgaris*) are large shrubs and need space. This, combined with the fact that their flowering season is relatively short and they are not the most attractive of plants for the rest of the year, means that there are better flowering shrubs for small gardens. So familiar are the garden lilacs that other syringas are often forgotten; but some of these, including *Syringa × prestoniae* hybrids (zone 3–7), and *Syringa pubescens* subspecies (zone 4–8), are more useful shrubs, with a longer season of interest and a more attractive growth habit.

Lilacs are generally easy to grow, thriving on most well-drained soils, especially limestone; they prefer full sun. Although lilacs flower from an early age, the flower size is usually small for the first few years.

Prune lilacs immediately after flowering, cutting back the wood that has flowered. Some gardeners cut the whole plant back to about 3ft. (1m) each year, to stimulate the production of straight flowering shoots and for an even distribution of flowers. Old lilacs can be rejuvenated by sawing old branches to ground level.

Syringa vulgaris 'Andenken an Ludwig Späth' ('Souvenir de Louis Spaeth') (z. 3–7), one of the most popular garden lilacs, has single, wine red flowers and is a reliable and excellent cultivar.

Syringa vulgaris 'Madame Lemoine' (z. 3–7), a garden lilac, has creamy white, double flowers. The Lemoine family from Nancy, France, were responsible for the introduction of many cultivars in the 19th and 20th centuries.

Syringa × prestoniae hybrids are vigorous, quickly attaining 6ft. (2m). *Syringa × prestoniae* 'Elinor' (z. 3–7) is a superb choice, with dark purple-red buds opening to strong, upright, pinkish lavender flower sprays.

Syringa pubescens ssp. *patula* 'Miss Kim' (z. 4–8) is a delightful selection of the Korean lilac, with purple buds opening to palest lilac. The flowers are very fragrant. Plant in a sheltered site—late frosts can damage the buds.

OTHER GOOD LILACS

Syringa × josiflexa 'Bellicent' (z. 5–6), very robust, with huge loose plumes of scented, dusty pink flowers.

Syringa meyeri 'Palibin' (z. 3–8), lilac pink; slowly reaches 3ft. (1m) or so—ideal for a small garden or container.

Syringa pubescens ssp. *microphylla* 'Superba' (z. 4–8), tiny leaves and dainty mauve-pink, fragrant flowers mainly in late spring but can continue until fall.

Syringa vulgaris 'Charles Joly' (z. 3–7), gorgeous double, dark purple-red flowers.

Syringa vulgaris 'Firmament' (z. 3–7), single, lilac-colored flowers.

Syringa vulgaris 'Katherine Havemeyer' (z. 3–7), double purple flowers, fading to lilac-pink.

Syringa vulgaris 'Vestale' (z. 3–7), single, pure white flowers.

Spiraea 'Arguta'

Viburnum × burkwoodii 'Anne Russell'

Viburnum 'Eskimo'

Spiraea 'Arguta', known as the Garland Spiraea (zone 5–8), is one of the most free flowering of all deciduous shrubs. In mid- to late spring, the fine, arching stems are smothered with pure white flowers in flat clusters all along the top of the slender branches. After the flowers have finished, the narrow, oval, soft green leaves create a pleasing mound of summer foliage. This medium-sized plant does not have a long flowering season, but it is an unmissable harbinger of summer.

Spiraea nipponica **'Snowmound'** (zone 3–8) flowers after *Spiraea* 'Arguta', at the end of spring or in early summer. This is a small, dense mound of a shrub, not as graceful as *Spiraea* 'Arguta' but every bit as free flowering. The white flowers totally smother the plant, making it worthy of its name.

These two spiraeas are easy to grow on any soil. Neither requires pruning, but if cutting back is essential to control size, it must be carried out immediately after flowering. Avoid trimming *Spiraea*

'Arguta', if possible, as it will rob the plant of its graceful arching habit.

Viburnums are such important plants in all seasons, they feature throughout this book. In late spring, they excel both in flower spectacle and fragrance. *Viburnum × burkwoodii* (zone 4–8) is a broad evergreen shrub of open stature. The shiny leaves are well spaced on straight, light brown branches; waxy pink buds in rounded clusters open into white, pink-tinged flowers with the most delicious fragrance; *Viburnum × burkwoodii* **'Anne Russell'** is a superb cultivar, with large flower clusters; *Viburnum × burkwoodii* **'Park Farm Hybrid'** is vigorous and more spreading, with larger flowers than *Viburnum × burkwoodii*.

Viburnum × carlcephalum (zone 6–9) is a more compact deciduous shrub, growing to approximately 6ft. (2m) high. The pretty, rounded flower heads are pink in bud, opening white, and have a delicious fragrance. If sited in an open position, the leaves color beautifully in the fall.

Viburnum carlesii (zone 4–7) is also deciduous. Compact and rigid in habit, with straight shoots and pale brown, downy shoots, it produces rounded heads of pink buds that open to white, richly fragrant flowers. The leaves are felty and grayish green and can display good autumn color. *Viburnum carlesii* can suffer from aphid infestation, in which young leaves become distorted and crinkly. *Viburnum carlesii* **'Aurora'**

GOOD COMPANIONS

For an attractive grouping, plant *Olearia × scilloniensis* (1) (z. 8–10), *Elaeagnus* 'Quicksilver' (2) (z. 3–9) and *Ceanothus* 'Concha' (3) (z. 9–10).

Plant *Salvia officinalis* 'Purpurascens' (4) (z. 5–10) and *Helichrysum* 'Korma' (5) (z. 8–10) with *Prostanthera cuneata* (6) (z. 9–10) for an attractive, aromatic combination.

is a favorite variety, with salmon red buds that open to flesh pink, richly fragrant flowers *Viburnum carlesii* 'Diana' is similar, but the young foliage is tinged purple. *Viburnum carlesii* cultivars are normally grafted, so watch out for suckers: strong, upright-growing shoots, usually of the much more vigorous *Viburnum lantana*, which will take over if not removed.

Viburnum 'Eskimo' (zone 6–8) is a compact hybrid, semi-evergreen with glossy, leathery leaves and exceptionally large, snowball-like flower clusters. The blooms are magnificent and scented, but not as fragrant as *Viburnum carlesii*.

Viburnum × hillieri 'Winton' (zone 5–8) is a spreading, semi-evergreen shrub with oval leaves, which are copper when young and turn bronze red in winter. The flowers, which resemble large flowering currant blossoms, are creamy white and are followed by red fruits, which turn black.

Viburnum × juddii (zone 4–7), a hybrid of *Viburnum carlesii*, is a small, bushy, deciduous shrub with felty leaves and scented, pink-tinged flowers. It is less susceptible to aphids, but is not as popular as *Viburnum carlesii*.

The snowball bush, ***Viburnum opulus* 'Roseum' ('Sterile')** (zone 3–8), is a familiar and spectacular deciduous

Viburnum plicatum f. *tomentosum* 'Mariesii'

Viburnum opulus 'Roseum' ('Sterile')

Viburnum sargentii 'Onondaga'

GOOD COMPANIONS

Viburnum plicatum f. *tomentosum* 'Mariesii' (1) (z. 5–8) is lovely with silver-variegated plants such as *Cornus alternifolia* 'Argentea' (2) (z. 3–7).

flowering shrub. Green flower clusters appear all along the branches in spring, gradually enlarging, turning to cream, then white and flushing pink. When mature they hang like snowballs from the upright yet arching branches.

Another glorious spring-flowering deciduous shrub is *Viburnum plicatum* f. *tomentosum* 'Mariesii' (zone 5–8), which is superb for specimen planting. It grows to 6ft. (2m) or more, but the spreading horizontal branches create a shrub that is wider than it is high. The deeply veined leaves hang from the branches, and the lacecap hydrangea-like flowers are borne all along the top of the branches in late spring. More flowers sometimes appear in the fall, before the leaves change color. (See

Good Companions, left.) *Viburnum plicatum* f. *tomentosum* 'Pink Beauty' (zone 5–8) has smaller blooms that turn pink as they mature, and the less spreading *Viburnum plicatum* f. *tomentosum* 'Summer Snowflake' (zone 5–8) flowers intermittently throughout the summer; although it produces a less spectacular display than the other cultivars, it is very useful for its long flowering period. *Viburnum plicatum* f. *tomentosum* cultivars should be given space and not pruned to control the size, as this spoils the shape.

Viburnum sargentii 'Onondaga' (zone 3–7) is an upright deciduous shrub, much prized for its striking purple foliage and pretty lacecap flower heads (see page 54).

Summer

Summer is a season of richness in the garden: lush foliage, plentiful flowers, and delicious scents. Summer bloomers compete for the attention of pollinating insects with the color and fragrance of their flowers. The deciduous shrubs take center stage: against a backdrop of foliage at its most flamboyant, the performance of the flowers has to be strong.

The Red Border, Hadspen, Somerset, England.

In early summer, philadelphus, deutzia, weigela, and cistus vie with roses, lilies and delphiniums for the leading role. Once the first flush of roses comes to an end, the competition is less intense; in this quieter season of late summer flowering shrubs prove their worth. Old garden favorites such as buddleia and hydrangea provide warm summer hues, whatever the weather, while caryopteris and perovskia supply that essential blue, regardless of the color of the sky.

Most buddleias are very hardy, easy-to-grow shrubs. The butterfly bush,

Buddleia davidii (zone 5–9), is the best known and is widely naturalized. In summer its arching branches and long heads of lilac flowers are a familiar sight on wasteland and railroad embankments. It thrives on poor soil in sunny, well-drained conditions. Frequently seen growing in crevices on old buildings, it can survive anywhere.

The cultivars of *Buddleia davidii* are popular, not only for the scent and color of their flowers, but also for their unfailing ability to attract butterflies. They grow quickly to 6–10ft. (2–3m), with an

elegant, arching habit. They give height and structure to herbaceous plantings, mix well with roses, and extend the season of deciduous shrubs that flower early in the season.

Buddleia davidii **'Nanho Blue'** is comparatively compact, suitable where space is limited. It has narrow panicles of violet-blue flowers with orange eyes. The other *Buddleia davidii* 'Nanho' varieties **'Nanho Alba'**, **'Nanho Indigo'**, and **'Nanho Plum'** are also small, growing to about 5ft. (1.5m). Other cultivars of *Buddleia davidii* include: **'Black Knight'**,

Buddleia davidii 'Dartmoor'

Buddleia davidii 'Royal Red'

Caryopteris × clandonensis 'First Choice'

Caryopteris × clandonensis 'Summer Sorbet'

with long flower heads of deep violet; **'Border Beauty'**, a compact variety with crimson flowers; **'Dartmoor'**, with large-branched panicles of magenta flowers; **'Empire Blue'**, a beautiful plant with violet-blue, orange-eyed flowers; **'Royal Red'**, with massive red-purple flower heads; **'White Profusion'**, with large, yellow-eyed flowers of pure white.

Buddleia globosa

The best buddleia of all is the lovely **Buddleia 'Lochinch'** (zone 5–9), described in the 'Silver and gray' section. **Buddleia alternifolia** (zone 5–9) has a different habit, with arching branches and narrow leaves. (See page 74.)

Buddleia globosa (zone 8–10), the Chilean orange ball tree, is vigorous, with a more upright habit and broader

foliage than *Buddleia davidii*. Stiff clusters of orange, spherical flowers—quite unlike any other buddleia—appear in early summer.

Buddleias need no special attention, except pruning. Hard prune *Buddleia davidii* varieties in early spring, cutting back to 3ft. (1m) or so in height. This may seem drastic but it keeps the plants young and vigorous. Deadheading as the flowers fade helps to keep the plant looking good through late summer.

Buddleias work well when planted with screening shrubs; the latter provide the evergreen structure, the buddleia provides the summer color (see Good Companions, below).

Caryopteris (zone 7–8) are valuable for color in late summer and early fall. Their aromatic foliage and shrubby habit suggest a Mediterranean origin, but they hail from eastern Asia. They need well-drained soil and full sun. The caryopteris grown in gardens are generally varieties of **Caryopteris × clandonensis.** Many are similar, leading to confusion over the identity of a plant offered for sale (see box). All are small and compact, reaching

GOOD COMPANIONS

Buddleia 'Black Knight' (1) (z. 5–9) provides summer color for evergreen shrubs such as *Elaeagnus × ebbingei* (2) (z. 7–11).

no more than 2–3ft. (60cm–1m). Cut them back hard in late winter. By then new shoots are visible on the lower third of the plant, and the top two thirds of the stems can be removed.

Probably the best-known cultivar of *Caryopteris × clandonensis* is **'Heavenly Blue'**, with clusters of sapphire blue

A TIP ON BUYING CARYOPTERIS

Because of the confusion between so many similar varieties, it is best to buy caryopteris while it is in flower, so you can see what you are getting.

flowers in the axils of the gray-green, willowlike leaves in late summer (see Good Companions, page 151). **'Arthur Simmonds'** is similar to, and often confused with, 'Heavenly Blue', but the flowers are a lighter color. It is one of the most reliable. **'First Choice'** has large, deep blue flowers—a stunning color—and excellent foliage. Full sun and good drainage are essential; it fails on damp sites in cold winter weather.

Other *Caryopteris × clandonensis* cultivars include: **'Kew Blue'**, a seedling of 'Arthur Simmonds', with slightly darker flowers; **'Summer Sorbet'**, with blue flowers and sage green foliage edged soft yellow (this is an acquired taste); and **'Worcester Gold'**, with soft gold foliage and bright blue flowers (see page 44).

149

Cistus

Cistus (zone 8–10), the sun rose, is a plant that enjoys full sun, good drainage, and poor soil—classic Mediterranean conditions (zone 8). Many are surprisingly hardy, although some of the larger-leaved varieties need a sheltered site to thrive. They do well near the coast, like alkaline soils and require little attention: no deadheading and no pruning. They are also remarkably free from pest and disease problems.

Most cistus have large flowers, either white or shades of pink and red. The flowers are short-lived but are produced in rapid succession—as one flush fades, the next opens. Most flower in early to midsummer and deliver an outstanding performance, even if their season is not very long. Cistus are excellent plants to combine with silver foliage shrubs, lavenders, and roses (see 'Hot, dry, sunny sites', pages 82–87; see Good Companions, page 151).

Some varieties of cistus take exception to pruning, while others will withstand light trimming after they flower, so long as this is done regularly from an early age. Ideally, young plants should be pinched back after flowering to encourage bushy growth. Never cut back into bare wood.

Container-grown cistus can suffer from instability and wind damage after planting. A low stake is a good idea on windy sites, until the plants become established. Do not make the mistake of planting too deeply in an effort to overcome the problem.

Cistus × *dansereaui* '**Decumbens**' (z. 8–10) is low and spreading, 2ft. (60cm) high. It has sticky, dark green leaves and large white flowers with crimson-blotched centers. *Cistus* '**Snow Fire**' (left) (z. 8–10) is similar but makes a more rounded bush—a very good, reliable variety.

Cistus × *purpureus* (z. 8–10) is a small shrub with narrow wavy leaves and large rosy crimson flowers with deep maroon central blotches and yellow stamens.

Cistus × *pulverulentus* '**Sunset**' (z. 8–10) has cerise flowers with yellow stamens. Its habit is open and upright; it looks very good planted with silver foliage.

GOOD CISTUS

Large-flowered white cistus

Cistus × *aguilarii* '**Maculatus**' (z. 8–10), with bright green, wavy-edged foliage and very large white flowers with a central ring of crimson blotches.

Cistus × *dansereaui* '**Decumbens**'.

Cistus '**Snow Fire**' (see left)

Cistus populifolius ssp. *major* (z. 8–10), with wavy-edged leaves, red buds, and white flowers; one of the hardiest.

Large-flowered pink cistus

Cistus × *argenteus* '**Peggy Sammons**' (z. 8–10), a vigorous, medium-sized shrub; gray-green foliage, purple-pink flowers with paler centers.

Cistus × *argenteus* '**Silver Pink**' (right) (z. 8–10), a very hardy cultivar, with long clusters of satin, peach-pink flowers and gray-green foliage.

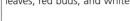

Cistus × *pulverulentus* '**Sunset**' (see left).

Cistus × *purpureus* (see left and Good Companions, right).

Cistus × *rodiaei* '**Jessabel**' (z. 8–10) has dark green leaves and large, almost red flowers with maroon centers.

Ceanothus thyrsiflorus 'Skylark'

Ceanothus thyrsiflorus 'Gloire de Versailles'

Deutzia setchuenensis var. corymbiflora

Ceanothus span the seasons. If you select the right varieties, it is possible to have a ceanothus in flower from mid-spring to the onset of winter. (See pages 82–83, 118; Plant Profile page 140.

Ceanothus thyrsiflorus 'Skylark' (zone 8–10) blooms after the spring-flowering evergreen ceanothus. Upright and bushy in habit, it grows quickly to 6ft. (2m) or more. Its habit suits planting as a freestanding shrub for the center of a border. The evergreen foliage is bright green and glossy, the perfect foil for the brilliant blue flowers that appear over several weeks in early summer.

The deciduous ceanothus are open, airy shrubs, producing their light, fluffy flower heads through summer and into fall. Most *Ceanothus* × *delileanus* varieties (zone 7–10) grow to about 5ft. (1.5m). 'Gloire de Versailles' is a popular variety, with powder blue flowers. 'Henri Desfossé' is similar in habit and size, and has deep violet-blue flowers. 'Topaze' has light indigo-blue flowers.

Pink ceanothus are not to everyone's taste. However, think of them simply as pretty pink-flowering shrubs and they become useful additions to mixed planting. *Ceanothus* × *pallidus* 'Marie Simon' (zone 7–9) has light pink flowers. *Ceanothus* × *pallidus* 'Roseus' (zone 7–9) has bright rose-carmine smoky blooms.

Deciduous ceanothus flower on new growth, so they should be lightly pruned and tidied after the coldest weather. They like an open, sunny position and usually perform better than evergreen varieties in alkaline soil.

Deutzias are rarely a first choice when it comes to selecting flowering shrubs. However, they are problem-free and easy to grow on any soil. *Deutzia scabra* (zone 5–8) has masses of white flowers in early summer on a large, upright woody bush that can reach 10ft. (3m). Other deutzias have pretty flowers and are refined, deciduous garden shrubs, growing to 4–6ft. (1.2–2m). They flower best in early summer, in full sun. Many lovely hybrids originated in the Lemoine nursery, as did many forms of philadelphus and lilac (*syringa*).

Some of the best are: *Deutzia* × *elegantissima* 'Rosealind' (zone 5–8), with loose sprays of deep pink, fragrant flowers; *Deutzia* × *hybrida* 'Strawberry Fields' (× *magnifica* 'Rubra') (zone 5–8), a free-flowering

GOOD COMPANIONS

For a colorful late-summer pairing, plant *Caryopteris* × *clandonensis* 'Heavenly Blue' (1) (z. 7–8) with the purple-red *Echinacea purpurea* (2) (z. 4–8).

Cistus × *purpureus* (3) (z. 8–10) is lovely with the gray foliage of *Lavandula stoechas* ssp. *pedunculata* ('Papillon') (4) (z. 7–8) and *Artemisia* 'Powis Castle' (5) (z. 6–9).

variety with large mauve-pink flowers, edged white and tinged purple on the reverse; *Deutzia* × *hybrida* 'Mont Rose' (zone 5–8), abundant rose pink flowers with darker markings; *Deutzia longifolia* 'Veitchii' (zone 5–8), long, narrow leaves and large clusters of rich lilac-pink flowers—the loveliest of the deutzias; *Deutzia* × *ningpoensis* (zone 5–8), a very different flower form— reflexed petals with yellow stamens and long sprays of flowers, pink or white all over the bush; *Deutzia setchuenensis* var. *corymbiflora* (zone 6–8), small starry white flowers later than most deutzias (illus. page 151).

Prune deutzias immediately after flowering, cutting out some of the stems that have flowered. This results in graceful, arching growth that rises above other planting. Avoid snipping later in the season—this will ruin the effect.

Escallonia (zone 8–10) is much more than an excellent evergreen hedging shrub. Its glossy foliage and resistance to drought and wind make the plant an excellent garden structure subject, with the added bonus of plentiful, pretty blossoms over a long period in summer.

Natives of South America, escallonias are not the hardiest evergreens so are only suitable for warmer zones. As with most flowering evergreens, those that have small leaves are hardier than those with larger leaves. Escallonias are not plants for cold sites, but they can withstand coastal winds. Inland they are best planted with the protection of a wall or fence, or among other shrubs to provide shelter. They grow on any well-drained soil. Like many evergreens, they can be slow to grow in the first season after planting.

Escallonias are useful medium or tall shrubs to bring evergreen interest to plantings of roses and herbaceous plants; they prolong the interest, and the color and character of the flowers sit well in mixed planting.

Escallonia 'Apple Blossom'

Escallonia 'Apple Blossom' is the best-known hybrid, and the most widely planted. It is slow growing and relatively compact compared to other escallonias, slowly reaching 5ft. (1.5m). The dark green foliage is the perfect background to the pink-and-white flowers. (See also pages 41, 122.)

Prune escallonias immediately after flowering or the following spring. Cutting out the old flowered growth keeps the plant tidy and compact. Old, straggly specimens can be hard pruned at the same time. Escallonia regenerates well, even from older wood.

OTHER RECOMMENDED ESCALLONIA CULTIVARS

Escallonia 'C. F. Ball' (z. 8–10), vigorous, growing to 10ft. (3m) or more, with aromatic leaves and crimson flowers.

Escallonia 'Iveyi' (z. 8–10), slightly more tender than some, with larger, very dark green leaves and large sprays of pure white flowers; a vigorous shrub, quickly reaching 6ft. (2m) or more.

Escallonia 'Donard Radiance' (z. 8–10), highly recommended, strong-growing, medium-sized shrub with large shiny dark green leaves and large bright, rose-red flowers.

Escallonia 'Langleyensis' (z. 8–10), with smaller leaves, growing to 8ft. (2.5m), with profuse rose-pink flowers on arching branches; a good choice for colder gardens.

Escallonia 'Peach Blossom' (z. 8–10), similar to 'Apple Blossom' but with flowers of clear peach-pink.

Escallonia 'Pride of Donard' (z. 8–10), large, bright pink bell-shaped flowers throughout the summer and large glossy leaves.

Fuchsia is a favorite bedding plant, so it is not surprising that the hardier varieties are widely planted as flowering shrubs. Fuchsias originate from Central and South America, Tahiti, and New Zealand. Some are hardier than others; as a rule, those with smaller leaves and flowers are hardier than those with larger leaves and flowers.

In colder zones fuchsias often die right back in winter, performing like a herbaceous plant. In mild zones they keep on growing, and the more vigorous varieties, such as *Fuchsia* 'Riccartonii' (zone 6–9) and *Fuchsia magellanica* (see right and page 68), can grow up to 10ft. (3m) in height.

Fuchsias are versatile plants and mix well with other shrubs and herbaceous perennials; they grow and flower in sun or shade. They can be grown as hedges and are a delight in summer when their arching branches hang with dainty red and purple flowers.

Because fuchsias are so popular there has been extensive hybridization and selection. There are numerous varieties. (See also pages 45, 68–69; illus. 42.)

Fuchsias should be pruned in early spring. Either cut them back hard to ground level or, if you want to preserve height, just give them a light trim.

FUCHSIA PESTS AND DISEASES

Pests and diseases can be a problem, especially where bedding fuchsias are grown in close proximity. Look out for rust, a fungal infection causing red-brown powdery spots on the leaves in late summer. Treat with a fungicide, and repeat the following spring when new leaves appear.

Vine weevil may attack fuchsias grown in pots in a peat-based mixture. Watch for notching on the edge of the leaves. Treat with a systemic pesticide, or use biological controls.

A SMALL SELECTION OF FUCHSIA VARIETIES

Fuchsia 'Alice Hoffman' (z. 7–9), a compact variety, to 18in. (45cm), with small purple-tinged leaves and flowers with a scarlet calyx and white petals.

Fuchsia 'Army Nurse' (z. 7–9), a vigorous, upright grower with carmine calyx and blue-violet petals.

Fuchsia 'Hawkshead' (z. 7–9), a lovely small variety, with deep green foliage and slender white flowers.

Fuchsia 'Lady Thumb' (z. 7–9), dwarf and bushy, with light red and white flowers.

Fuchsia 'Lena'(right) (z. 7–9) semi-double with pale pink calyx and purple petals flushed pink. Good for training.

Fuchsia magellanica var. *gracilis*, (z. 6–9) a graceful, pretty shrub, with slender, arching stems and many small, delicate flowers of scarlet and purple.

Fuchsia 'Mrs. Popple' (below) (z. 7–9), an excellent small plant, with large flowers and a compact habit; scarlet calyx and violet petals.

Fuchsia 'Riccartonii' (z. 6–9), the best fuchsia for general planting where a tall shrub can be accommodated.

Fuchsia 'Snowcap' (z. 7–9), dwarf and compact but with large flowers; red calyx and white petals veined red.

Fuchsia 'Tom Thumb' (z. 7–9), a dwarf shrub, with masses of small freely produced flowers with scarlet calyx and violet petals.

153

Hebe 'Spender's Seedling'

Hebe **'Emerald Gem'** ('Emerald Green' or 'Green Globe') (z. 8–10), a rounded bun-shaped bush, very dwarf and compact, with tiny green leaves packed on tight branches; white flowers in summer; a superb plant for a pot or for planting in gravel.

Hebe rakaiensis (z. 6–8), dwarf, compact and very hardy, forming dense mounds of bright green foliage; the leaves are tiny and crowd the stems, the white flowers frost the bush in early summer; a superb plant for fresh green foliage in full sun.

Hebe salicifolia (z. 7–9), a medium-sized shrub reaching 6ft. (2m); its willowlike foliage withstands most winters, the flowers are white or lilac in long, narrow, drooping spikes throughout the summer; an excellent choice in coastal or urban areas.

Hebe **'Spender's Seedling'** (above left), (z. 7–9) a small, hardy shrub with narrow foliage and fragrant, white, lilac-tinged flowers over a long period.

Hebes, often referred to as veronicas, are attractive, evergreen shrubs. The genus includes a number of our most popular variegated, silver-leaved and red-leaved shrubs. The dwarf green forms offer an alternative to box as compact, structural shrubs, while the larger hardy species are frequently used for structure and mass planting. Nearly all flower in summer; and the more flamboyant, larger-leaved varieties, with big, showy bottlebrush flowers, are attractive to bees and butterflies. (See Plant Profile, page 76.)

Many hebes have a long flowering season. They like well-drained soil and suit coastal situations. Those with lusher foliage do not suit cold exposed sites.

Pruning is not essential but may be necessary if growth becomes leggy or the bush falls open with age or if it is severely damaged by winter weather. If

GOOD COMPANIONS

The yellow flowers of *Hypericum* 'Hidcote' (1) (z. 6–7) are perfectly complemented by yellow-variegated *Euonymus* 'Emerald 'n' Gold' (2) (z. 5–8).

Indigofera potaninii (3) (z. 7–9) works well with *Nepeta* × *faassenii* (z. 4–7) or *Salvia* × *sylvestris* 'Mainacht' (4) (z. 5–10).

Hebe **'White Gem'** (above) (z. 8–10): dwarf and compact, with a profusion of white flowers in early summer.

HEBES TO GROW FOR SUMMER FLOWERS (WITH THE BONUS OF GOOD FOLIAGE)

Hebe 'Autumn Glory' (z. 8–10), a small, open shrub with glossy green leaves tinged purple and intense violet-blue flowers in short, dense spikes through summer and fall.

Hebe 'Blue Clouds' (above) (z. 8–10), a small shrub with dark, glossy green leaves, purplish in winter; long spikes of blue flowers during summer and fall.

Hebe × *franciscana* 'Blue Gem' (z. 7–11), a small, compact, dome-shaped shrub with dense spikes of bright blue flowers; one of the hardiest hebes, very resistant to salt spray; good for a low coastal hedge.

Hebe 'Great Orme' (above) (z. 8–10): a reasonably hardy, compact shrub growing to 3ft. (1m); long, narrow leaves and bright pink flowers in long, tapering flower heads; good with purple foliage plants such as *Physocarpus opulifolius* 'Diabolo'.

Hebe 'Marjorie' (above) (z. 8–10) neat and compact, growing to 3ft. (1m) in height; spikes of light violet and white flowers through the summer.

Hebe 'Midsummer Beauty' (z. 8–10), a fairly hardy form with handsome foliage, and reddish undersides to the leaves; long spikes of lavender flowers throughout the summer.

Hebe 'Pink Paradise' (z. 8–10) compact, with profuse pink flowers throughout the summer.

Hebe 'Simon Délaux' (z. 8–10), a small, rounded shrub with rich crimson flowers in large bottlebrush spikes.

Hebe 'Youngii' ('Carl Teschner') (below) (z. 8–10), a dwarf shrub of spreading habit with small neat foliage and pretty violet flowers in summer; a good ground-cover plant.

you do prune, do so in spring, after the coldest weather has passed. Cut back to where new green shoots are appearing on the lower part of the stem; never cut back into old wood if there are no signs of growth shoots.

The more tender large-leaved hebe varieties can be prone to leaf-spot diseases after a damp winter. Treat with a fungicide. In severe cases, cut back in spring and regrow.

Hoheria sexstylosa 'Stardust'

Hoherias originated in New Zealand and are not plants for cold, exposed gardens. The most widely grown species is *Hoheria sexstylosa* (zone 8–9), a tall evergreen shrub of light and airy habit. The narrow leaves are often serrated and toothed and are shiny medium-green. When it flowers the plant unexpectedly produces welcome showers of starry white blooms like spring blossom. *Hoheria sexstylosa* 'Stardust' is a very compact, upright form, with glossy foliage and clouds of flowers. The hybrid *Hoheria* 'Glory of Amlwch' (zone 8–9) keeps its leaves in mild winters. The flowers are much larger than those of *Hoheria sexstylosa*, 1in. (3cm) across, crowded on the branches in midsummer.

Hydrangea arborescens 'Annabelle'

Hydrangea aspera Kawakamii Group

Hydrangea involucrata 'Hortensis'

Hydrangea conjures images of large mounds of foliage and heavy rounded flower heads of pink, blue, and white; a familiar sight in suburban gardens. In fact, these "mopheads" are only one part of this wonderful group of plants.

Two types of floret make up the flower heads of hydrangeas: tiny, insignificant fertile florets, and showy sterile florets with conspicuous, colored sepals (which look like petals). In some cases, as with the mopheads, the flower head is almost entirely made up of sterile florets; in others, as with the lacecaps, it consists of both types.

Hydrangeas are excellent shrubs for light shade. They also benefit from overhead shelter from trees. Although they are hardy, the new growth is often damaged by late frosts. All hydrangeas like a reasonably fertile soil and some moisture. Mulching and feeding in spring, with a slow-release fertilizer and some organic soil mix, improves the plants' performance.

Leave the dead flower heads on the plants over winter. Remove them in early spring, cutting back to the first pair of fat buds behind the flower head. No other pruning is required, but older plants can be rejuvenated by removing some old branches to ground level.

See right for the **Lacecap** and Hortensia (mopheads) groups.

See pages 167–68 for *Hydrangea paniculata*, 'Preziosa' and *quercifolia.*

Hydrangea arborescens cultivars (zone 3–9) are small, loose bushes with upright stems, pale green, serrated leaves, and dense, domed flower heads up to 6in. (15cm) across. The blooms of *Hydrangea arborescens* 'Annabelle' start lime green and develop into clusters of small, cream, sterile florets. This is not a good plant for a windy site because of the weight of the flowers. It looks lovely in semi-shade with ferns and hostas. Prune in spring.

Hydrangea aspera (zone 7–8) is a very different animal—a medium-sized species, with velvety leaves and an open, branched habit. Semi-shade is preferred, and fertile soil that does not dry out. The *Hydrangea aspera* **Kawakamii Group** is a very late-flowering form with deep violet flower heads with white sterile florets, looking attractive against the exotic, luxuriant foliage. Prune selectively only to control size and shape. *Hydrangea aspera* 'Mauvette' has large flower heads of sterile and fertile florets that start out mauve then gradually turn to gray pink. *Hydrangea aspera* **Villosa Group** is one of the loveliest of the late summer-flowering hydrangeas, medium-sized, with a spreading habit and velvety stems and leaves. The huge flower heads are lilac blue with dainty serrated, sterile florets. *Hydrangea aspera* 'Velvet and Lace' is a particularly fine form, with superb foliage and flower heads of purple blue and mauve pink.

A superb choice for a large tub in a shady spot is *Hydrangea involucrata* 'Hortensis' (zone 5–9). This glorious hydrangea is an upright suckering shrub with fresh green foliage and loose, creamy flower heads of double, sterile florets in summer. The flowers open lime cream and blush pink with age.

Hydrangea serrata (zone 5–7) is a dwarf shrub, rarely growing to more than 3ft. (1m), with smaller foliage than most hydrangeas and pretty lacecap flowers. 'Bluebird' is the best known cultivar. Its blue fertile florets are surrounded by large ray florets, red purple on alkaline soils and sea blue on acid.

Hydrangea macrophylla

The *Hydrangea macrophylla* group (zone 6–9), familiar as garden shrubs and as pot plants, consists of the Hortensia group (mopheads) and the Lacecap group. Most grow to around 5ft. (1.5m), but can get much larger in favored locations. On shallow alkaline soils, the foliage becomes yellow and chlorotic; remedy this by mulching and feeding. Some pink varieties are blue on acid soils. On alkaline soils, aluminum sulfate can be used to attempt to change the color to blue, but it is not worth the effort in the open ground. White varieties cannot be changed but will often blush pink as the flowers age in full sun. The Lacecap group, with their distinctive flower heads of fertile florets surrounded by a ring of sterile florets, are lighter and prettier than the mopheads, more satisfactory in mixed planting.

The flowers of mophead hydrangeas can be dried for winter decoration. Cut them when fully mature and hang them upside down to dry.

Hydrangea macrophylla **'Ayesha'**, Hortensia group: a mophead but totally different from others in the group, with grayish lilac flowers like those of a large syringa (lilac).

'Ami Pasquier' Hortensia group: a mophead with a dwarf habit; deep pink-red flowers.

Hydrangea macrophylla **'Mariesii Grandiflora'** ('White Wave'), Lacecap group: a small shrub good for an open position, with blue to pink flower heads surrounded by white ray florets.

'Mariesii Perfecta' ('Blue Wave'), Lacecap group: a strong-growing shrub best in light shade; large heads varying from pink to deep gentian blue.

OTHER GOOD MOPHEAD HYDRANGEAS

'Altona' (left), rose-colored large florets, blues well; best in shade.

Japanese Lady group: white-edged flowers; several forms and colors.

'Madame Emile Mouillère', large serrated florets with blue or pink eyes; the best white.

'Maréchal Foch' (left), rich rosy pink or purple to deep blue, free flowering.

'Nigra', distinctive black stems and rose florets.

OTHER GOOD LACECAP HYDRANGEAS

'Lanarth White' (right), compact habit; flat heads of pink or blue surrounded by large white ray florets.

'Lilacina' (below), broad heads of pink or blue flowers.

'Veitchii', medium-sized shrub with dark green foliage, white florets aging to pink; best in semi-shade; alkaline tolerant.

Hydrangea serrata 'Bluebird'

Hydrangea serrata 'Tiara'

Autumn color is good. Other cultivars of *Hydrangea serrata* that are recommended include **'Grayswood'** (its white ray florets turn pink and then finally crimson) and **'Woodlander'** (with blue florets turning mauve pink and foliage that gives a colorful display in the fall).

Hypericum **'Hidcote'** (zone 6–7) has all the qualities we look for in a shrub: it is easy to grow and free flowering, and has a long flowering period throughout summer and fall. It is semi-evergreen and, left unpruned, will reach 6ft. (2m) or so. The large saucer-shaped flowers are a clear golden yellow, just like huge buttercups—pure summer sunshine. Their weight makes the branches arch gracefully. This wonderful shrub is thought to have come originally from the gardens at Hidcote Manor, Gloucestershire, in England.

Hypericum 'Hidcote' can be pruned in early spring, before it makes the new growth that will flower next summer. Light trimming or harder pruning is possible. It is a wonderful planting partner for golden-variegated evergreens and for spiraeas with golden foliage (see Good Companions, page 154).

Hypericum **'Rowallane'** (zone 7–8) is rarely seen but worth seeking out. It is a more tender form than 'Hidcote' and needs a warm, sheltered garden. The impressive flowers are the largest of any hypericum: glorious golden saucers up to 3in. (7cm) across, weighing down the branches. Good against a sheltered wall, it can reach 6ft. (2m) and is a spectacular sight when in flower.

Indigofera heterantha (zone 6–10) is not an attractive shrub in the winter and is usually very late to break into leaf; when it does, it is a reliable performer. A medium-sized shrub, spreading and spiky in habit when not in leaf, it can be knocked back by cold winter weather. The new growth quickly emerges, fine, soft-green pinnate leaves

Indigofera heterantha

on arching branches and a flower cluster in every leaf axil. The pealike, bright purple-pink blooms are carried in sprays.

Indigofera potaninii (zone 7–9) has clear pink flowers throughout the summer and early fall. It is large enough to support a summer-blooming clematis, such as the pale blue **'Prince Charles'**, a delight with the indigofera's horizontal sprays of pink, vetchlike blooms.

Indigofera likes good drainage and full sun; it is an ideal partner for salvia or nepeta (see Good Companions, page 154). In spring, cut dead wood back to the new shoots. Untidy plants can be cut back hard at the same time.

Kolkwitzia amabilis (beauty bush) (zone 4–8) is a lovely, medium-sized shrub from western China. Graceful and arching, it forms a dense, well-branched mound of soft green foliage. The branches are smothered with pink, bell-shaped flowers in early summer. *Kolkwitzia amabilis* **'Pink Cloud'** is the best form, an aptly named plant.

Kolkwitzia is an easy shrub to grow in sun, or light shade, on any soil. Treat

Kolwitzia amabilis

as any other deciduous summer-flowering shrub: cut out some of the older stems when the flowers fade.

Lavandula, the lavenders, are such a feature of summer gardens that it would be wrong not to mention them here. The best varieties are described in detail with the gray-foliage plants, on pages 72–73. New cultivars are being introduced all the time, particularly of *Lavandula stoechas*. Many are very decorative—for example, *Lavandula stoechas* ssp. *sampaioana* (zone 7–8), a selection of which is sold as **'Purple Emperor'**. With its soft purple-brown flower heads and upright growth, it is an appealing creature, but suits only a well-drained, sunny site in a mild zone. However, lavenders of this type are useful container plants for sunny patios.

Until the 1990s the shrubby mallow, **Lavatera,** was generally offered for sale as a herbaceous plant, and only a few small, soft specimens were sold each year. Since then its qualities have been recognized, and it has now become a garden staple. It grows quickly, flowers for a long period, and mixes well with herbaceous plants and other shrubs. Lavateras are good in hot, sunny sites, grow well in alkaline soil and are excellent for seaside gardens.

The best lavateras to grow in gardens are cultivars of *Lavatera* × *clementii* (zone 6–9). Once listed as either *Lavatera olbia* or *Lavatera thuringiaca*, they are, in fact, hybrids of the two. All

---

LAVATERA TIPS

Lavateras are not long-lived plants. Expect to replace them after five or six years, and sooner on heavy clay soils.

They can be wobbly when first planted; a short stake to anchor unstable plants aids their establishment.

Tidy them in fall; hard prune, back to 1ft. (30cm) or so, in early spring.

Lavatera × *clemntii* 'Rosea'

Lavatera × *clementii* 'Blushing Bride'

are vigorous, medium-to-tall plants. The first cultivar to be grown was *Lavatera* × *clementii* 'Rosea' (*Lavatera olbia* 'Rosea'). This has large pink flowers from early summer until late autumn. It resembles a hollyhock and combines superbly with nepeta and blue salvias.

Lavatera × *clementii* 'Barnsley' is now the best-known cultivar, a sport of 'Rosea', named after Rosemary Verey's garden in Gloucestershire, England. The flowers are palest pink with a red eye. It does tend to revert, and shoots bearing clear pink flowers must be removed or they will quickly take over. **'Blushing Bride'** is very similar to 'Barnsley' but is more compact and less likely to revert. A more reliable plant, it is rapidly becoming the more popular choice. **'Burgundy Wine'** has deep purplish pink flowers. It can look drab in the wrong setting, but is lovely with silver foliage and purple heucheras. Other × *clementii* cultivars include **'Bredon Springs'**, with wide-open funnel-shaped blooms of deep dusky pink (a better choice than 'Rosea'); **'Candy Floss'**, a pale pink option; and the less commonly found **'Memories'**, whose pale pink buds open to white flowers with a pink eye.

Lavatera maritima **'Princesse de Lignes'** (zone 7–9) is more tender than the × *clementii* cultivars, suitable only for a sunny sheltered spot. It is smaller-growing with grayish, downy leaves. The large flowers are saucer shaped with elegantly turned-back petals, a pale lilac, with a dark eye and veins.

Lavatera maritima 'Princesse de Ligres'

Leptospermum scoparium 'Red Damask'

Leptospermum scoparium (zone 8–10), the New Zealand tea tree, is related to myrtle and is a native of New Zealand and Australia. A compact evergreen with wiry, arching stems and tiny leaves, it is an interesting contrast to broad-leaved shrubs. It is ideal against a sunny wall and looks good in pots. It suits Mediterranean-style planting and mixes well with silver-leaved plants. It is a plant for warm coastal gardens. It needs full sun, good drainage, and acid-to-neutral soil. It resents total desiccation, particularly in pots. Allowed to dry out, it sheds leaves and flowers.

There are numerous forms, with white, pink, or deep red flowers. A good one to look for is *Leptospermum scoparium* 'Nanum Ruru', a medium-sized shrub with pink flowers and dark summer leaves. Another variety, **'Ruby Glow'** also has dark summer foliage but double, deep red flowers. Similar in size, **var. *incanum* 'Keatleyi'** has large waxy-petaled, pink flowers; the young shoots are crimson and silky. **'Kiwi'** is dwarf, with pink flowers and bronze foliage.

Philadelphus

Philadelphus, the mock oranges, are often incorrectly known as syringas (lilacs), perhaps because they too are much-loved, easy-to-grow shrubs with heavily fragrant flowers. Most of the best-known hybrids were raised by the French nursery Lemoine in the early 1900s. This may also have led to the confusion over the name, as many of our most popular hybrid lilacs came from the same grower, at the same time.

When selecting a philadelphus, make sure that it is a fragrant one. The scent is one of the great delights of the summer garden. A philadelphus that has no perfume is nothing more than an inferior deutzia. These are deciduous shrubs, ranging in height from dwarf to tall, with elegantly arching branches, heavy with white, four-petaled single, semi-double, or double flowers often with prominent yellow stamens.

Philadelphus grow on any soil and are particularly happy over limestone. Prune immediately after flowering, cutting out some of the older stems that have flowered, and allowing the new vigorous shoots to develop. Whatever its size, a philadelphus should be a graceful arching shrub, not a trimmed ball or mound.

Philadelphus coronarius (z. 4–8) is a commonly cultivated species. A medium-sized, vigorous, easy-to-grow shrub, very tolerant of dry conditions. The flowers are smaller than many of the hybrids, more bell-like, creamy white, and wonderfully fragrant. The golden and variegated forms are seen more often (see pages 45, 69).

Philadelphus 'Belle Etoile' (z. 5–7) is one of the most beautiful philadelphus, with large, wonderfully fragrant, single creamy white flowers, flushed maroon at the center, on a fairly compact and upright, medium-sized shrub. Looks stunning planted with a purple-leaved cotinus or physocarpus.

Philadelphus 'Manteau d'Hermine' (z. 5–7) is the best choice for a small garden. A dwarf, compact plant, it grows to 3ft. (1m), with graceful, arching stems. The flowers are creamy white, double, and fragrant. It is a lovely shrub to plant with silver foliage in a sunny position.

OTHER GOOD PHILADELPHUS

Philadelphus 'Beauclerk', (z. 5–7) a graceful, arching, medium-sized shrub, bears large open flowers, rounded white petals flushed pink toward the mass of stamens.

Philadelphus lewisii (z. 5–10), is a tall, upright native species. 'Snow Velvet' has huge fragrant, semi-double flowers.

Philadelphus microphyllus (z. 6–9), a dwarf with tiny sage green leaves and starry, single, richly fragrant flowers.

Philadelpus 'Minnesota Snowflake' (z. 4–7) has arching branches that are weighed down with fragrant double flowers; medium and dwarf forms.

Philadelphus 'Virginal' (z. 5–7) is probably the best-known and most widely planted philadelphus. The large, double flowers are richly fragrant. Old plants left unpruned can grow to at least 10ft. (3m), ideal to support a late-flowering *Clematis viticella*.

Perovskia 'Blue Spire'

Perovskia (zone 5–8) is a graceful, upright shrub, reaching up to 3ft. (1m) in height. The silvery white stems carry soft, fernlike foliage and spikes of lavender-blue flowers in late summer. It is a plant for well-drained soil and full sun, where it associates well with silver-foliage plants and lavenders. **'Blue Spire'** is the best variety to grow and has the largest flower spikes. **'Filigran'** has even more finely cut foliage; in isolation this looks pretty but, as perovskia is a plant to mix with others, it is of secondary importance.

Perovskia has attractive white stems. Leave these in the border for winter interest and then cut back to 8in. (20cm) before the warmer weather begins. The tops of the stems die back naturally and if left on the plant will become untidy and unsightly.

Potentillas belong to the rose family and include both herbaceous and woody plants. The shrubby ones are hardy (zones 2–7) and easy to grow and provide reliable summer color. They grow in sun or semi-shade and perform on any soil. A potentilla in winter is not a particularly pretty sight, with its tangled brown stems and remains of last season's leaves and flowers. But, after a light trim in early spring, it soon bursts into life and begins its long succession of small, bright, single roselike flowers.

The display starts in early summer and can easily extend into late fall.

The white and yellow varieties are the best choice for full sun. Red, orange and pink varieties prefer semi-shade and more moisture; their colors bleach in strong sunlight.

Recommended cultivars of *Potentilla fruticosa* (zone 2–7) are described below. Most reach less than 3ft. (1m) and are rounded or spreading in habit.

Tamarix, or tamarisk, is a large, light, feathery shrub. It is often planted near the sea, as its supple branches withstand exposed conditions. The pale green, plumelike foliage is transformed when the fine, fluffy flowers appear, turning the whole shrub from green to pink for several weeks. Note that in some zones, it may become invasive. For more information, see the APWG website at www. nps.gov/plants/alien.

RECOMMENDED *POTENTILLA FRUTICOSA* CULTIVARS

'Abbotswood', a favorite white-flowered variety with spreading growth and dark green leaves; the flowers are freely produced over a long period; good with silver-foliage and white-variegated shrubs.

'Elizabeth', an excellent plant raised by Hillier Nurseries, in Britain; dome-shaped, over 3ft. (1m) in height, with large canary yellow flowers from spring to fall.

'Hopley's Orange', dwarf and spreading, with bright green, fine foliage; flowers orange with a narrow yellow margin to the petals.

'Katherine Dykes' has lemon yellow flowers set against attractive silver-green foliage.

'Pink Beauty' ('Lovely Pink'), dwarf, with bright green foliage, single and semi-double soft pink flowers.

'Snowbird', abundant large, double, white flowers make a pleasing contrast with the dark green leaves.

'Marian Red Robin', low, compact, and spreading with red flowers; a stronger color than 'Red Ace' and less likely to fade over time.

'Medicine Wheel Mountain', compact, low, and spreading, with red-flushed shoots and large yellow flowers.

'Primrose Beauty', this is one of the best; small, spreading, and free flowering,

with gray-green foliage and primrose-yellow flowers—a soft color combination that mixes well in any planting scheme.

'Sunset', a small, bushy shrub with light orange to brick red flowers; looks pretty planted with *Spiraea* 'Firelight'.

'Vilmoriniana', a large one; upright growth to 6ft. (2m), with silvery foliage and cream flowers.

Tamarix tetrandra

Weigela 'Bristol Ruby' with ceanothus

Weigela 'Majestueux'

Tamarix ramosissima (*Tamarix pentandra*) (zone 2–8) has reddish brown branches and flowers in late summer on shoots produced earlier the same season. The whole shrub becomes a feathery mass of rose pink—which looks delightful in association with a purple-leaved sambucus (see page 54) or *Elaeagnus* 'Quicksilver' (see page 75). *Tamarix ramosissima* 'Rubra' is a very good form, with darker flowers.

Prune *Tamarix ramosissima* in early spring. Usually light pruning to tidy and control the shrub is all that is necessary. Maintain the light, open habit.

Tamarix tetrandra (zone 6–8) has dark branches and greener foliage. It flowers in late spring and early summer. These flowers are light pink, transforming the branches into long, waving plumes. Because this tamarisk flowers on the previous season's wood, it must be pruned straight after flowering, and never in spring.

Weigela (zone 6–8) is a flowering shrub that produces a splendid display of tubular flowers for a few weeks in early summer and, occasionally, another small flush in late summer or early fall. Weigelas are tolerant, growing well in town gardens and withstanding pollution. They suit clay soils and grow well in alkaline conditions. Most form a loose, rounded shrub 5–6ft. (1.5–2m) tall.

Recommended varieties of weigela include the following. **'Abel Carrière'** is free flowering with large, bright rose carmine flowers, flecked gold in the throat. **'Bristol Ruby'** is a vigorous and upright bush, free flowering with bright ruby red blooms; it is excellent planted against purple cotinus or red berberis. **'Carnaval'**, a French hybrid, bears pink and white bicolored flowers and clear pink flowers on a small, compact shrub. An old favorite, **'Eva Rathke'**, is compact and slow-growing, with bright red flowers with straw-colored anthers; it is a good choice for the smaller garden.

'Majestueux' is upright growing, with madder pink, carmine-flushed flowers early in the season. **'Bristol Snowflake'** is a white-flowered version of 'Bristol Ruby'. (See also pages 47, 54–55, 69.)

Prune weigelas straight after flowering, cutting out some of the stems that have flowered to allow new shoots to grow through. You do not need to do this every year. Pruning promotes sprays of flowers and an attractive habit.

Old weigelas are prone to thin foliage and growth of lichen on the branches; rejuvenate by hard pruning and feeding with a balanced, slow-release fertilizer.

MAINTAINING COLOR

Continuity of interest throughout the long summer months is a major goal in the garden. Use late-flowering summer shrubs such as buddleia and caryopteris to take over from early-flowering shrubs and herbaceous plants. *Buddleia* 'Lochinch' (z. 5–9) is a good planting partner for *Abutilon* 'Jermyns' (z. 9–11) (pictured left): when the abutilon finishes flowering, the buddleia is ready to bloom. *Caryopteris* × *clandonensis* 'Heavenly Blue' (z. 7–8) rekindles the sapphire of herbaceous geraniums that have been cut back after their summer display.

Early-flowering shrubs such as philadelphus and deutzia can be given a new lease on life with the addition of a light-growing, late-flowering clematis such as a *Clematis texensis* (z. 4–9) or *viticella* (z. 5–8).

Use the foliage backdrop of early shrubs to show off tall, later-blooming herbaceous plants, such as veronicastrum, helenium, and aster.

Plants for bees and butterflies

One of the greatest joys of the garden in summer is the sight of butterflies flitting from bloom to bloom, while the buzzing of bees is surely one of the season's most evocative sounds. The summer garden, particularly in the latter part of the season, is rich in nectar-laden flowers. Shrubs and herbaceous perennials join forces to attract bees, butterflies, and other beneficial insects.

There are numerous plants that attract insects. Favorites are those with flower heads made up of hundreds of tiny flowers, such as: buddleia, sedum, caryopteris, and verbena. These are easy-to-grow plants that thrive in an open, sunny position on any well-drained soil. All are excellent in most gardens, and will work their magic in attracting butterflies and bees in urban as well as rural situations.

Blue buddleias, such as the beautiful silver-leaved *Buddleia* **'Lochinch'** (z. 5–9) combine well with the tall, airy *Verbena* **bonariensis** (z. 8–9). The latter has a longer flowering season than the buddleia and will continue into autumn with its vivid heads of bright purple flowers with orange stamens. Both are irresistible to butterflies.

A blue caryopteris such as *Caryopteris × clandonensis* **'First Choice'** (z. 7–8) creates a classic, late-summer combination with the ever-popular *Sedum (Hylotelephium)* **'Autumn Joy'** (z. 3–8). The heads of sedums are attractive to bees and butterflies until they fade to a rich brown pink in the fall.

Hebes, with their bottlebrush flowers, bloom for a long period. The purple-leaved, blue-flowered *Hebe* **'Caledonia'** (z. 8–10), is the perfect planting partner for aromatic *Origanum laevigatum* **'Herrenhausen'** (z. 5–8). Both grow well on alkaline soils, and the hebe provides evergreen interest when the origanum dies back to ground level in winter.

OTHER SHRUBS GOOD FOR BEES AND BUTTERFLIES

Amelanchier	*Escallonia*	*Skimmia*
Berberis	*Helianthemum*	*Spiraea*
Ceanothus	*Hypericum*	*Syringa*
Chaenomeles	*Lavandula*	*Tamarix*
Cistus	*Nepeta*	*Thymus*
Cotoneaster	*Origanum*	*Weigela*
Cytisus	*Pyracantha*	
Daphne	*Ribes*	
Elaeagnus	*Rosmarinus*	

Fall

Autumn can be such a long season. Depending on zone, the first shades may start to appear before the end of summer; the last leaves fall in midwinter. That's up to four months, one-third of a year. With a little planning, fall can be a gloriously colorful time in the garden.

As the season progresses, the flat green of late summer is transformed into a rich backdrop for the blooms of dahlia, michaelmas daisy, and nerine. Without any competition from their deciduous partners, the evergreens begin to shine out, ready to take on their role as the stalwarts of the winter garden.

Fine days are spent gathering fallen leaves for the compost heap. Wet days are spent staring out of the window at the rain, lamenting the passing of another year. Suddenly some plants begin to come into their own in this more minimalist landscape. Falling leaves reveal the glories of the bark and berries that have developed under the heavy blanket of late-summer foliage.

It is trees that come to mind first for autumn color: think of beech, acer, liquidambar. They provide the most obvious changes in the landscape. However, much of the best color comes from shrubs, including European natives such as *Viburnum opulus* (zone 3–8), *Cornus mas* (zone 4–8), and *Euonymus europaeus* (zone 3–7), which oblige with a rich display.

Adding to the spectacle are the ripening fruits of the late-summer and autumn months. Plants need to effect seed disposal, and by making their fruit appetizing and attractive, some plants persuade animals and birds to do the work of distributing the species. Gardens glow with shiny rose hips and sealing-wax red haws, as well as the orange and scarlet berries of pyracantha and cotoneaster.

Some shrubs choose this season as their time to flower. Most start in late summer but continue through the mellow days of fall; in some cases the flowers are enhanced by the changing hues of the foliage.

Acer palmatum 'Osakazuki'

THE CHEMISTRY OF AUTUMN COLOR

Autumn color occurs when the components of photosynthesis are broken down in the leaf and nutrients, particularly nitrogen and phosphorus, are reabsorbed for winter storage. In the case of trees and shrubs, the food is stored in the woody stems.

Different pigments are responsible for different colors. The bright yellow colors are caused by carotenoids. These are present in the leaf throughout the year, but their yellow color becomes prevalent when chlorophyll, which is responsible for the green color, breaks down and is reabsorbed into the plant during the fall.

It is thought that the production of anthocyanins, responsible for the red shades of autumn, increases at this time. By screening the system from the effects of bright sunlight during the breakdown of photosynthetic compounds, anthocyanins enable a steady flow of energy to be maintained in the leaf, thus enabling complete breakdown and absorption.

While some evergreens do color, displaying red and orange shades rather than yellow, the phenomenon of autumn color occurs mainly in deciduous plants, which have a dormant season.

AUTUMN-FLOWERING SHRUBS

Abelia (zone 6–9) is not the most popular genus of shrubs, but it has much to offer the gardener, not least its ability to perform in the fall months. As young plants in pots, most varieties look ungainly and give little clue to the graceful, but robust, shrubs that they will make. (See also page 66.)

Abelia × *grandiflora* grows to a vigorous, arching, semi-evergreen shrub of medium size. The leaves are small, neat, dark, and glossy. The flowers start to appear in midsummer and continue well into early fall, white flushed pink, with a pink calyx that persists after the flower has fallen. This hybrid, originally raised in Italy, has been in cultivation since 1866. The cultivar *Abelia* × *grandiflora* 'Francis Mason' has variegated leaves with a golden margin; this variegation needs full sun if it is to develop properly.

Abelia schumannii is a small, very hardy shrub. The lilac-pink flowers are blotched orange and slightly fragrant. They are produced over a long period, from late summer through the fall.

Abelia 'Edward Goucher', a hybrid between *Abelia* × *grandiflora* and *Abelia parviflora*, was raised in the United States in 1911. It is a small evergreen shrub with bronze young foliage and profuse lilac-pink flowers in summer and fall.

Ceanothus 'Autumnal Blue'

With their graceful growth and pastel flowers, abelias make the perfect companion for some of our best autumn-flowering herbaceous plants, including echinacea, sedum, and aster, as well as any purple-leaved shrubs, such as berberis and elder.

It is not necessary to prune abelias, but if you need to reduce the size of the plant, cut out whole stems selectively; trimming will only ruin the graceful character of the plant.

The glorious blues of **Ceanothus** are not confined to spring (see page 140). The deciduous varieties perform in late summer and fall, albeit in a more subtle way than their evergreen cousins.

Ceanothus × *delileanus* 'Gloire de Versailles' (zone 7–10) is an attractive deciduous ceanothus, which has large

Ceratostigma willmottianum

panicles of powder blue flowers. Its light and open habit is perfect with late-summer herbaceous plants and the last blooms of the roses. As its name suggests, the evergreen *Ceanothus* 'Autumnal Blue' (zone 8–10) performs now. It has medium-sized, bright, glossy green leaves and sky blue flowers in late summer and fall. It often performs in spring, too.

Ceratostigma, the hardy plumbago, may well be regarded as a summer shrub because the most common form, *Ceratostigma willmottianum* (zone 8), starts flowering from midsummer.

Abelia 'Edward Goucher'

Hibiscus

Hibiscus syriacus (zone 5–8), the hardy hibiscus or shrubby mallow, is so late to break into leaf in spring, it is not surprising that it does not flower until late summer or fall. It makes a very upright shrub, with ascending branches of ash gray, and most varieties grow to 6–10ft. (2–3m). The leaves appear in late spring, pale yellow-green to start with, becoming medium-green. The flowers, which resemble individual hollyhock blossoms, appear from midsummer onward, but are usually at their best during early and mid-fall. Hibiscus thrive on well-drained soil and are good on limestone. Natives of eastern Asia, they are extremely hardy, but they do need full sun if they are to flower well.

Hibiscus syriacus was probably introduced to gardens in England as early as the 16th century. Today, there are a surprising number of varieties, some with single flowers, others with double flowers, and in a range of colors from white through pink and red to almost blue. They are useful, structural deciduous shrubs for the back of the border. They combine well with herbaceous perennials that bring interest earlier in the season, including Japanese anemones, achillea, and helenium. Hibiscus are often grown in pots, but because they are late to break into leaf and their season of interest is relatively short, their appeal as a permanent subject for a container is limited. There are other, better shrubs for pots.

Avoid pruning any hibiscus. They are not broad, spreading shrubs, and if they are topped in order to control height, their habit becomes ugly.

Hibiscus syriacus **'Oiseau Bleu'** (left), better known as **'Blue Bird'**, is the best-known and most widely planted cultivar. The single, violet-blue flowers have a darker eye. **'Marina'** is an improvement, with larger flowers of a clearer blue and a deep red eye.

Hibiscus syriacus **'Red Heart'** (left) has large white flowers with a deep red eye. The hybrid between this variety and 'Blue Bird', *Hibiscus syriacus* **'Russian Violet'**, has lilac-pink flowers with a deep red center.

Hibiscus syriacus **'Hamabo'**, one of the most reliable and attractive cultivars, has pale pink flowers with a crimson eye, clean and clear, and without the tired color of many varieties. **'Aphrodite'** has much larger flowers (up to 5in. [13cm] across), deeper pink, with a red eye.

OTHER GOOD HIBISCUS

Hibiscus syriacus **'Diana'**, the best white, with large single flowers with crinkly petals.

Hibiscus syriacus **'Pink Giant'**, large, feathered flowers, clear pink with a deep red eye.

Hydrangea paniculata 'Unique'

Hydrangea paniculata 'Kyushu'

Ceratostigma willmottianum (zone 8) grows to about 3ft. (1m); wiry stems carry neat, dark green leaves that tint with dark mahogany and red as fall progresses. This rich background is the perfect setting for the sapphire blue flowers that stud the plant like jewels. This is indeed a gem, introduced by plant collector Ernest Wilson in 1908. *Ceratostigma griffithii* (zone 7–10) is beautiful too, with deep blue flowers and foliage that turns particularly red in fall and persists well into winter.

Treat ceratostigmas in a similar way to hardy fuchsias: trim, or cut back to ground level, in late winter. The latter will make a more lush shrub but of lesser stature. In hard winters these plants may be cut back to the ground by frost, unless they are in a sheltered spot.

Ceratostigmas like dry, well-drained soil, and flower and color best in full sun. They are good plants for the base of a sunny wall and look stunning when planted with the sugar-pink *Nerine bowdenii* (zone 9–10), which flowers when the ceratostigma is at its best.

Hydrangea is a feature of summer and the prevalent shrub of gardens in many coastal areas. The "mophead" and "lacecap" hydrangeas develop their greenish red, mature shades as

summer turns to fall (see pages 156–57). Others have their heyday in the autumn.

One of the most breathtaking and showiest of large shrubs, *Hydrangea paniculata* **'Grandiflora'** (zone 3–8) cannot fail to grab attention as it erupts from the back of the border, with its large conical sprays of flowers resembling huge lilac blossoms. The flowers start in summer, pale green, then cream and, as they reach full size, pale cream strongly flushed pink in full sun.

There are many other cultivars of *Hydrangea paniculata* (zone 3–8). **'Unique'** is most spectacular, similar to 'Grandiflora' but with even larger flower heads, 16in. (40cm) or more in length. **'Tardiva'** is a late-flowering type, again with large flowers. **'Kyushu'** is upright in habit, and has dark glossy leaves and panicles of flowers with more, large ray florets. It is a native of Kyushu, Japan.

Hydrangea **'Preziosa'** (zone 5–7), a mophead, is a hybrid of *Hydrangea*

GOOD COMPANIONS

The dark purple leaves of *Sambucus nigra* f. *porphyrophylla* 'Gerda' ('Black Beauty') (1) (z. 5–7) complements *Abelia* × *grandiflora* (2) (z. 6–9).

A colorful autumn cameo: *Aster* × *frikartii* 'Mönch' (3) (z. 5–7) with *Clematis viticella* 'Royal Velours' (4) (z. 5–8) and *Hydrangea* 'Preziosa' (5) (z. 5–7).

Acer palmatum 'Sango-kaku'

PRUNING HYDRANGEA PANICULATA

Most hydrangeas do not need pruning, but if *Hydrangea paniculata* (z. 3–8) are left unpruned, growth can be lax and weak—a habit displayed in young plants, and perhaps one that puts some people off them. To display the magnificent flower panicles, *Hydrangea paniculata* need strong, upright branches. Once a strong base has been established, cut the plants back hard in late winter, to within 2–3in.(5–8cm) of the previous season's growth, ideally 2ft. (60cm) or so from the ground. This creates a pollarded effect.

---

macrophylla (zone 6–9) and *Hydrangea serrata* (zone 5–7). Reaching 5ft. (1.5m) in height, it has round heads of large rose pink florets, contrasting with its purple-tinged young leaves and the purple-red stems. The flowers change to deep red-purple as fall progresses, creating a bold, rich effect that suits the warm autumnal light. (See Good Companions, page 167.)

Hydrangea quercifolia (zone 5–9), the oak-leaved hydrangea, is one of the most underrated shrubs. Of medium size, it is an architectural plant, with its bold lobed leaves that resemble those of oak. Throughout the year, these are soft, felted green, turning in fall to a stunning orange red. The conical heads of large florets appear in late summer, but these are secondary to the foliage. A native of southeastern United States, there are several named cultivars, all easy to grow and shade tolerant. *Hydrangea quercifolia* 'Sike's Dwarf' is a compact variety that makes a small shrub, wider than it is tall—a good choice for the small garden.

Hydrangea quercifolia requires no pruning or maintenance once it is established; but it can take two or three seasons to get going so don't expect immediate results.

DECIDUOUS SHRUBS FOR AUTUMN COLOR

Acer palmatum (zone 6–8), the Japanese maples, are well known for their autumn colors. Versatile plants with numerous uses, they crop up in several sections of this book (see Plant Profile, pages 50–51). Their foliage is a feature throughout spring and summer, but the plants get a new lease on life with a glorious display of autumn color.

For the finest display of autumn color, plant acers in a sheltered spot, but one with good light and some direct sunshine; a woodland glade is the ideal, so the nearer the conditions are to this, the better. Autumn color is at its best on neutral to acid soil rich in organic matter. It is essential that the plants not dry out in summer. Drought causes the leaves to brown and shrivel from the ends. They may fall or simply die on the plant without coloring.

Red varieties look spectacular when the light shines through the leaves; take this into account when planting. The yellow forms work well against a dark background of bold evergreens.

Acer palmatum 'Bloodgood' (see page 51) has deep reddish purple foliage, which turns rich red in the fall. Mature plants produce attractive winged fruits to add to the effect.

Acer palmatum 'Seiryû'

Acer palmatum var. dissectum 'Inaba-shidare' (zone 6–8) is the best of the red Dissectum types for autumn color. The strong, purple, foliage turns crimson in fall. Its strong growth, and fine foliage are much less susceptible to summer drought than many of the varieties with finely cut leaves.

Acer palmatum 'Kamagata' (zone 6–8) is a smaller shrub, with bright green shoots and neat lobed leaves, red when young. The autumn color is a mix of brilliant yellow, orange and red.

Acer palmatum 'Ôsakazuki' (zone 6–8) is a green-leaved variety, with broader leaves than many. In fall the foliage turns fiery scarlet. This is one of the most brilliant maples for autumn color and is more scorch-resistant than most, being less susceptible to damage from wind and drought.

Acer palmatum 'Sango-kaku' ('Senkaki') (zone 6–8), the coral bark maple, is best known for its coral-red young branches in winter. The habit is upright and when young the plant is easily mistaken for a *Cornus alba*. The leaves turn soft yellow in fall, creating a pleasing effect with the coral stems.

Acer palmatum var. dissectum 'Seiryû' (zone 6–8) is the best of the green Dissectum types for autumn color, making a large, upright, graceful

shrub. The fresh green leaves are tinged red in summer, later turning orange yellow splashed with crimson.

Acer palmatum 'Yezo-Nishiki' (zone 6–8) is fast-growing, vigorous, with upright growth becoming arching as the plant matures. The red-purple foliage becomes brilliant red in fall.

Berberis may have declined in popularity, but it only takes the onset of fall to remind us of their value. The cultivars of *Berberis thunbergii* (zone 4–8) reliably reward with a brilliant display of autumn color on virtually any soil, regardless of the summer weather

conditions. On a dry site in full sun, their color is unbeatable. Their other great attribute is the length of the display. Those tough, round leaves hang on to the stems for several weeks; the color simply becomes more intense. Shining red berries are revealed by some varieties as their leaves thin. Note that in some zones, this plant may become invasive. For details, see the APWG website at www. nps.gov/plants/alien.

Most red-leaved varieties color well. Recommended fastigiate forms include *Berberis thunbergii* 'Helmond Pillar' and *Berberis thunbergii* 'Marshall

Acer palmatum 'Yezo-Nishiki'

Callicarpa bodinieri var. giraldii 'Profusion'

Cotinus 'Grace'

Euonymus alatus

red-brown summer hues to a climax of vivid scarlet by mid-fall. The sun shining through the round, delicate leaves makes a truly wonderful sight—bear this in mind when positioning the plant.

A hybrid between *Cotinus obovatus* and *Cotinus coggygria* 'Velvet Cloak', *Cotinus* 'Grace' was raised by Hillier propagator Peter Dummer in 1979. A tall, vigorous shrub, it often reaches a surprising 10ft. (3m) or more. It can be cut back hard in late winter and will reward with vigorous, graceful shoots carrying healthy foliage the next summer.

Cotinus 'Flame' (zone 4–8) is another hybrid of *Cotinus coggygria* and *Cotinus obovatus*. This is a large shrub, often treelike, with big round green leaves. Huge smoky plumes of pink flowers in summer are followed by a spectacular display of autumn color as the leaves turn brilliant orange-red.

The purple-leaved cotinus (see page 54) turn from purple to red as fall progresses. The variety, *Cotinus* 'Golden Spirit' (zone 4–8), colors extremely well, even in semi-shade. The colored foliage, a wonderful shade of coral orange, lasts well. (See page 45.)

Euonymus alatus (zone 3–8) is the most surprising of all the shrubs grown for their autumn color. A native of

Upright'. Their upright form makes a bold statement as the red-purple foliage of summer turns to burgundy-scarlet in fall. (See pages 52–53.)

Callicarpa, or beautyberry, conjures up an autumn cocktail of pastel colors. All summer the oval leaves are dull green, somewhat like those of a privet, then suddenly, as fall comes upon us, they turn to amber flushed with bronze purple, while pink and lilac-purple berries form clusters on the branches. The leaves exhaust their display and fall, leaving the berries: shining clusters of bright purple beads carried on fine, straight branches, creating an almost molecular display that lasts well into winter. The most commonly grown callicarpa, *Callicarpa bodinieri* var. *giraldii* 'Profusion' (zone 6–8), has bronze-purple young foliage. This is an upright, tall plant, ideal for a site where a green background shrub is needed behind herbaceous planting. In a more open situation, it is particularly effective underplanted with purple heucheras, such as *Heuchera* 'Amethyst Myst' (zone 4–8). The fruit often shrivels before maturing on young plants. Be patient:

this shrub has to be firmly established for several years before it performs well.

The virtues of **Cornus alba** (zone 2–8) are extolled in other parts of this book. Many cultivars of this versatile plant display superb autumn shades before they reveal their winter stems. They are a good choice for damp sites and clay, and for color on neutral to alkaline soils. (See pages 177–79).

The pleasing colors of **Cotinus 'Grace'** (zone 5–8) intensify from soft

Cotinus GOLDEN SPIRIT ('Ancot')

China and Japan, it is a dense, slow-growing shrub, reaching a maximum height of 5ft. (1.5m). The leaves appear in mid-spring and are unremarkable, until one fall day the bush is ablaze with color. The vivid coral-red leaves last well, falling to show attractive, green-winged stems. A mature plant may produce purple fruits that split to reveal bright orange seeds. Note that in some zones, this plant may become invasive. For details, see the APWG website at www.nps.gov/plants/alien.

Euonymus europaeus (spindle) (zone 3–7) is a European native. It sometimes makes a small tree with round green stems and good autumn color. The twigs and branches are very straight and were used as butchers' skewers,

many of the shrubs that provide good autumn color prefer acid soil.

Euonymus hamiltonianus (zone 4–8) is a larger-growing relative of *Euonymus europaeus*. *Euonymus hamiltonianus* ssp. *sieboldianus* 'Coral Charm' has pale pink fruits that split to reveal red seeds. *Euonymus hamiltonianus* 'October Fire' has spectacular reddish purple leaves in the fall. If your garden is large enough to accommodate a big, green deciduous shrub that has a moment of glory in the fall, you should consider one of these.

Parrotia persica (the iron tree) (zone 4–8) is a relative of hamamelis, resembling it in its growth habit, leaf shape, red flowers in winter, and its sensational autumn color. However, it differs from

brown, deep red, rich flame, and gold. Avoid pruning parrotias at all costs. This would rob them of their unique, open-centered and spreading shape. Do not underestimate the eventual size; in mixed planting, give them temporary partners that can be removed later.

Rhus typhina (stag's horn sumac) (zone 3–8) was an essential choice for gardens in the mid-20th century. Its reddish brown felty stems and flocked brown seed heads were widely seen, all the more noticeable in fall with the onset of the fiery autumn tints of the foliage. This is a large suckering shrub, which, once established, sends up offspring all over the garden, particularly if the roots are disturbed near the parent plant. Suckers were passed on from gardener

Euonymus europaeus 'Red Cascade'

Parrotia persica

Rhus typhina 'Dissecta' ('Laciniata')

hence another common name, skewer wood. Masses of scarlet seed capsules split to reveal orange seeds.

A selected form with rich, scarlet autumn color, **Euonymus europaeus 'Red Cascade'** is a large, light and airy shrub with masses of rosy red fruits on elegantly arching branches. It works particularly well with white-variegated evergreens such as *Rhamnus alaternus* 'Argenteovariegata' (zone 8–9) and *Pittosporum* 'Garnettii' (zone 9–10).

Euonymus alatus and *Euonymus europaeus* thrive on alkaline soil, which makes them especially useful when so

hamamelis in its tolerance of lime, on which it colors just as superbly as it does on acid soil. This is an excellent choice of large shrub for those who have alkaline soil and are looking for dramatic autumn effect.

Parrotias are superb shrubs, either for specimen planting in a lawn or as a striking backdrop for autumn-flowering herbaceous perennials, such as helenium and rudbeckia. The growth habit is architectural and spreading, the foliage deep green and shiny on the top surface. The autumn transformation is long-lasting, with shades of chestnut-

to gardener, and so the plant spread. Its invasive qualities and ability to sucker in the lawn has led to its fall from favor. Rhus are not appealing as young plants for sale in garden centers. However, they are interesting shrubs with a strong, architectural form and have the bonus of spectacular fall display. **Rhus typhina 'Dissecta' ('Laciniata')** is an excellent form, with the attractions of finely cut foliage, large brown seed heads and orange-yellow autumn color.

Rhus copallina (zone 4–9), the dwarf sumach, is a much more compact plant, native to North America. The leaves are shinier than those of *Rhus typhina*. The seed heads are not as spectacular, but the autumn color is a pleasing rich red or purple. This plant is a good choice for the smaller garden.

Rhus × pulvinata Autumn Lace Group 'Red Autumn Lace' (*Rhus glabra* 'Laciniata') (zone 3–9) is a large shrub with bold, fernlike leaves and deeply cut leaflets. The fruit clusters are red, set off by red, yellow, and orange autumn tints. The shoots are green, slightly hairy, and lack the "antler" bloom of the stag's horn sumac.

Viburnum opulus (zone 3–8), the guelder rose, resembles a maple, with pretty, white flowers in spring that look like lacecap hydrangeas. In fall the leaves turn rich and dark, plum purple and flame scarlet. At the same time the fruits ripen, bunches of them, translucent and bright red, like the most luscious redcurrants. The fruits, delicate though they look, persist long into the winter. This is plant is native to British woods and hedgerows, and grows well in wet situations. It deserves wider use in the garden. In rural situations and open areas, *Viburnum opulus* can be planted as hedging whips in groups of three or five. This is a good plant that will thrive in wet sites with *Cornus alba* and species of willow (See Good Companions, page 173.)

Nyssa sylvatica

Viburnum opulus 'Compactum'

Viburnum opulus 'Compactum' both flowers and fruits very freely and is a good cultivar for small gardens; sadly, it is hard to find. See page 147 for the snowball bush, *Viburnum opulus* 'Roseum' ('Sterile').

A number of the other deciduous and semi-evergreen viburnums display brilliant autumn color, but they are rarely planted for this purpose. *Viburnum lantana* (zone 3–7), the wayfaring tree, turns a deep wine color in the fall. The tiered horizontal branches of the frothy white beauty *Viburnum plicatum* f. *tomentosum* 'Mariesii' (zone 5–8) color well when the shrub is planted in good light. The compact, medium-sized *Viburnum × carlcephalum* (zone 6–9) is a shrub with round heads of fragrant flowers in spring and leaves that often color rich red brown in fall before they drop.

AUTUMN ON ACID SOIL

For owners of acid soil, **hamamelis** (see page 181) and **deciduous azaleas** (see page 104) are musts for autumn color as well as for their respective winter and spring displays of flowers. Colors vary according to variety but rich bronze and orange reign supreme. These plants are not related but have much in common; with their elegant branch framework and noble stature, both are excellent as feature shrubs planted in grass. The close relative of hamamelis, *Fothergilla major* (zone 4–8), is another good choice for autumn color (see page 111).

Eucryphia glutinosa, *Enkianthus campanulatus* and *Enkianthus perulatus*, described fully in the "Acid soils" section of this book, pages 110–11, are among the most spectacular and reliable of autumn-color shrubs.

Itea virginica 'Henry's Garnet' (zone 5–9) is a plant for neutral or acid soil originating in Pennsylvania. It is a small, upright, deciduous shrub that produces spikes of fragrant creamy flowers in July. The leaves turn rich red purple in fall, lasting into early winter.

Nyssa sylvatica (zone 3–9) is normally grown as a tree. Because it resents disturbance, it is transplanted when small, and so is usually seen for sale in garden centers in shrublike proportions. On a moist, lime-free soil, the autumn color is spectacular. *Nyssa sylvatica* 'Autumn Cascades' is an attractive new form, with a strongly weeping habit and good fall color.

The popularity of growing blueberries has led to wide cultivation of cultivars of the ericaceous shrub *Vaccinium corymbosum* (zone 8–9). These are

Leucothoe fontanesiana 'Rainbow'

Nandina domestica 'Fire Power'

not only productive but also highly decorative shrubs, with arching stems and bright green leaves that turn scarlet and bronze in fall. The summer fruits follow the clusters of pink and white flowers produced in May.

EVERGREENS THAT COLOR IN THE FALL

All evergreen shrubs and trees lose their leaves, but the process is a gradual one that takes place throughout the year, and not all in one season. After a hot summer, and particularly after dry conditions, many evergreens show some autumn color.

Leucothoe offer some attractive evergreen shrubs that are shade-tolerant but require lime-free soil. *Leucothoe fontanesiana* 'Rainbow', (zone 4–7) probably the best known, is a small spreading shrub with arching stems carrying leathery leaves variegated with cream, yellow, pink, and burgundy. There is some intensification, and change, in the plant's foliage color in fall and winter. However, *Leucothoe fontanesiana* 'Lovita' and 'Scarletta' are at their best during the fall and winter months. Raised in Ohio, they are extremely hardy, and have become popular for their robustness and suitability for pots. 'Lovita' is a compact, low-growing shrub with arching stems and slender, bright green, pointed leaves, flushed red when young. In fall and winter, leaves

color rich reddish purple. 'Scarletta' is similar but with finer, shorter stems and a more clump-forming habit. With the onset of cold weather, the foliage develops beautiful deep red shades, scarlet at the leaf tips.

Both plants make excellent ground cover in shade or semi-shade on acid soils. They are excellent for seasonal or permanent planting in containers. Because they survive in shade, they can bring color to areas where other winter container plants fail. For the best results, pot them in lime-free, loam-based soil mix.

The light, airy structure of *Nandina domestica* (zone 6–9), the sacred bamboo, is unlike that of any other

broad-leaved evergreen. As the plant's common name suggests, it resembles a bamboo, but it is in fact related to berberis. This is a medium-sized shrub with erect stems like canes, and large, spreading, fernlike leaves consisting of numerous leaflets. A native of China and Japan, it is hardy in many areas and grows on almost any well-drained soil. After the heat of summer, the small creamy white flowers turn into loose clusters of shining red berries at the top of the stems. The little pointed leaflets are tinged purplish red at the edges when the shrub is planted in sun. In spring and fall, the leaves become much more purplish red. On less fertile soils and in full sun this coloring can include shades of copper-orange and red.

Nandina domestica is a useful shrub for specimen planting in gravel, staying upright and neat. It looks attractive in a big oriental-style pot or against a light-colored wall. In mixed planting, it contributes the lightness and grace of a grass and the permanence and structure of an evergreen.

Nandina domestica 'Fire Power' is smaller, with a compact, rounded habit.

GOOD COMPANIONS

Nandina domestica (1) (z. 6–9) is a striking evergreen to plant with *Cornus sanguinea* 'Winter Beauty' (2) (z. 5–8), grown for winter stems.

An excellent group for a damp site: *Viburnum opulus* (3) (z. 3–8) with *Cornus alba* 'Elegantissima' (4) (z. 2–8) and *Salix alba* ssp. *vitellina* (5) (z. 2–9).

Hypericum × inodorum 'Rheingold'

Pyracantha 'Orange Glow'

The foliage is an unusual yellowish green in summer, turning orange red in fall and winter. (See Good Companions, page 173.)

AUTUMN BERRIES

Varieties of **Hypericum × inodorum** (zone 7–9) are now popular for floral decoration—not for their flowers but for their long-lasting autumn fruits. An upright shrub, *Hypericum × inodorum* flowers on wood produced the same season. The small yellow flowers are followed by conical, orange-red, or sometimes chestnut brown berries, trimmed with the neat green frill of the calyx. *Hypericum × inodorum* 'Rheingold' is an excellent cultivar that stays free of the rust and mildew that plague other varieties. To encourage long stems for cutting, prune hard at the end of

BERRIES FOR BIRDS

A plant produces berries as one way of getting its seeds dispersed—via birds and other animals that eat them. Plant berry-bearing shrubs and you will attract birds, surely the greatest joy of the winter garden.

winter. Strong new shoots follow during spring and summer; these will carry flowers and, in fall, fruit.

Pyracantha (firethorn) is a member of the rose family and a close relative of cotoneaster. It has a mass of hawthorn-like flowers in spring and colorful berries in fall. Pyracanthas are most commonly grown as wall shrubs, but many make excellent freestanding shrubs of loose, spreading habit. They are very hardy, evergreen, and easy to grow on almost any soil. Their main drawback is their susceptibility to disease, in particular fireblight and canker. It is best to choose one of the disease-resistant varieties.

Pyracantha 'Teton' (zone 6–9) is a hybrid between 'Orange Glow' and the yellow-berried *Pyracantha rogersiana* 'Flava'. This also fruits freely, with orange-yellow berries, and is very resistant to fireblight. The new Saphyr varieties are all very disease-resistant but may be hard to find. *Pyracantha* 'Kasan' (zone 6–9) is compact and cold hardy, a particularly good plant for hedging. *Pyracantha* 'Rutgers' (zone 6–9) is another red-fruited variety that is resistant to both scab and fireblight.

Whatever new varieties come along, *Pyracantha* 'Orange Glow' (zone 6–9) remains popular. A vigorous shrub that

makes a large dense mound, it is exceptionally free flowering and fruiting, with bright orange-red berries that hang on the branches well into winter. The once-popular cultivar 'Mohave' (zone 6–9) is rarely seen in some zones because it is susceptible to scab, a serious problem where the winters are mild and damp.

Pyracanthas grown as wall shrubs should be trimmed after flowering. Cut the new growth back to the flower clusters, so the autumn berries are not hidden by leaves. Apply the same technique to freestanding shrubs.

Pyracanthas are useful shrubs for bringing autumn color to plantings of plain evergreens. They also combine well with all the yellow-variegated shrubs, such as *Elaeagnus pungens* 'Maculata'.

Rosa rugosa (zone 2–7) is probably the easiest rose to grow. Large suckering shrubs, they require no pruning, apart from an occasional tidy-up in spring. They are disease resistant, with apple green foliage, and grow on almost any soil, including the poor sandy soils disliked by most roses. They have a long flowering season: from early summer to late fall. The flowers tend to be very fragrant, and the big tomato-like hips persist after the yellow-gold autumn leaves drop. Single-flowered forms are best for fruit: *Rosa rugosa* 'Alba' is a vigorous cultivar with fragrant, silky white, single flowers and exceptional fruits. *Rosa rugosa* 'Rubra' has wine crimson flowers and large, showy hips. For hips, do not deadhead *Rosa rugosa*.

Rosa rugosa

Cotoneaster

Cotoneaster is an essential genus in the garden. It includes shrubs of all proportions, from prostrate creepers to medium-sized and large shrubs or small trees. They are generally easy to grow on any soil. Some are evergreen and some deciduous, but all have at least two seasons of interest and are much appreciated by wildlife. The profuse, small, pink or white flowers in early summer are attractive to bees, and the berries, produced in fall, are attractive to birds.

The large cotoneasters are always loaded with clusters of autumn fruit weighing down the arching branches. Often semi-evergreen, these varieties have a much longer season of interest than do many small trees, such as prunus or malus varieties, and may well be worth considering as an alternative.

Many cotoneasters are invaluable for poor soil and difficult sites. Of the medium-sized shrubs, *Cotoneaster franchetii* (zone 5–7) and *Cotoneaster lacteus* (zone 6–8) are easy, effective, and thrive almost anywhere.

The ground-cover cotoneasters, such as *Cotoneaster dammeri* (zone 4–7), are excellent on banks or under other shrubs. Traditionally planted against a sunless wall of the house, *Cotoneaster horizontalis* is a low-growing, spreading shrub, with characteristic herringbone branches. Do not prune, as this robs the plant of the dramatic effect of its branch formation.

There are numerous other cotoneasters, some with yellow, cream, or salmon fruits, but the red-berried varieties are the showiest and the ones that best compete with the colors of autumn foliage.

Cotoneaster × *watereri* 'John Waterer' (left) (z. 5–7) and *Cotoneaster frigidus* 'Cornubia' (z. 7–9) are large, semi-evergreen shrubs or small trees, with arching branches and heavy clusters of red fruits.

Cotoneaster franchetii (left) (z. 5–7) is a graceful, medium-sized, semi-evergreen shrub with sage green leaves and orange-scarlet berries, larger and more oval than most. The small red berries of *Cotoneaster lacteus* (z. 6–8), an evergreen, color late but last until midwinter.

The tiny, shiny green leaves of *Cotoneaster horizontalis* (z. 6–8) are deciduous but color well before they fall, leaving the bright red berries that persist on the herringbone branches well into winter.

In fall, sealing-wax berries stud the shiny evergreen foliage of *Cotoneaster dammeri* (left) (z. 4–7) and *Cotoneaster procumbens* 'Queen of Carpets' (z. 6–9). Both are very good for ground cover and are also suitable for training over a frame.

Winter

Winter should on no account be regarded as a dead time in the garden. The lush green landscape and burgeoning borders that we associate with the traditional English-style garden take on a different persona during the coldest months. The low-level light and the lack of competing color alter the character of plants—even those that do not undergo a radical seasonal change.

A fall of snow transforms the garden scene, emphasizing shape and structure.

Woody plants can contribute to the winter garden in many ways: through their flowers and foliage, of course, but also through the color and texture of their stems and the framework of their branches. As the days become shorter and leaves fall, so deciduous trees and shrubs reveal hidden assets and take on a different dimension.

The blossoms of those plants that do flower during this season may not be the most spectacular in terms of size and color, but the majority of them are deliciously fragrant as they work hard to attract the few insects that are around on cold winter days.

Some winter-flowering shrubs make perfect subjects to plant near the house. There they can enjoy some shelter, and their beauty can easily be appreciated at a time of year when we may only rarely venture out into the garden. Many winter performers thrive happily in shade or semi-shade, situations where shrubs that bloom in summer so often struggle.

Abeliophyllum distichum (zone 5–8) is a hardy shrub from Korea, a member of the olive family and related to forsythia. It is sometimes called white forsythia, for the sake of giving it a common name, but it is more graceful and delicate than its yellow-flowered cousin. Although it is hardy, it needs a warm, sunny position to ripen the wood if it is to flower well. It is slow-growing and produces thin branches of dark purplish wood, which lose their leaves after some display of autumn color. The fragrant, fragile, pearl-white flowers open on the bare branches in February. In the wild, this plant is now rare and in danger of extinction. Hardly spectacular, it does have a delicate beauty, and is well worth preserving in our gardens.

Chimonanthus praecox (zone 7–9), known as wintersweet, lives up to its name when it comes to fragrance. This is not a conspicuous plant, but in flower, it cannot go unnoticed as it fills the garden with its delicious fragrance.

Abeliophyllum distichum

Chimonanthus praecox

Chimonanthus praecox (praecox means early) is a native of China and is a very hardy plant (zones 7–9). It is easy to grow, but needs a sunny spot to ripen for flowering; it is often grown against a sunny wall. This would not be the best choice of plant for a key position, as it is not particularly attractive: the foliage is ordinary—long, narrow, pointed leaves of medium green. It likes good drainage and is excellent on alkaline soil.

The species produces waxy, pale, translucent flowers stained purple in the center, carried on the bare branches in late winter. The form *Chimonanthus praecox* 'Grandiflorus' has larger flowers than the species, stained red, while those of *Chimonanthus praecox* var. *luteus* are clear, waxy yellow.

Long shoots can be cut back immediately after flowering, but any pruning later in the year reduces flowering potential. Flowers are rarely produced on young plants, so patience may be needed—but the winter fragrance is worth waiting for.

Cornus alba (zone 2–8), red-barked dogwood, boasts many cultivars that are very useful foliage plants in the summer garden. However, it is for the beauty of the winter stems that the plant is best known. *Cornus alba* makes a large shrub, a thicket of stems that layer themselves where they touch the ground. The winter stems of the species, exposed when the leaves fall after a fine display of autumn color, are rich red.

Cornus alba is one of the easiest shrubs to grow and succeeds on any soil, from dry to waterlogged. It grows in shade, but the stems need a bit of winter sun to show off their color. Originating in Siberia, Manchuria, and North Korea, it is extremely hardy. Its tough character, attractive stem color, and the ease with which it can be cultivated have led to its being used widely by commercial landscapers for mass planting. This makes it no less valuable as a garden plant.

Left unpruned, the more vigorous varieties of cornus make effective screening plants. They are useful on banks and sloping ground, where their suckering, layering habit successfully stabilizes the ground. For a particularly striking grouping, mix red- and yellow-stemmed varieties of winter dogwoods. They combine well with bold evergreens such as hollies and *Viburnum tinus* (see Good Companions, page 184).

The cultivar *Cornus alba* 'Sibirica' (also known as 'Atrosanguinea' or 'Westonbirt') is less robust than the species, but it displays very brilliant, crimson red winter shoots. *Cornus alba* 'Sibirica Variegata', the variegated form, is an excellent deciduous shrub and is suited to gardens of all sizes. The leaves, margined with creamy white and often flushed with pink, color superbly in the fall, and the stunning winter stems are no less vivid than those of the green-leaved form.

Cornus alba 'Kesselringii' has unusual black-purple stems. This is a subject for creative planting; put it where the stems show against a light background. It combines very well with the arching, white stems of *Rubus cockburnianus* 'Goldenvale' (zone 6–7).

Cornus alba 'Kesselringii'

GOOD COMPANIONS

For year-round interest, underplant *Corylus avellana* 'Contorta' (1) (z. 4–7) with *Ajuga reptans* 'Atropurpurea' (2) (z. 4–7) and *Hedera helix* 'Glacier' (3) (z. 4–9).

The dark plum purple flowers of *Vinca minor* 'Atropurpurea' (4) (z. 5–8) provide interest after *Daphne odora* 'Aureomarginata' (5) (z. 7–9) has finished flowering.

177

Cornus sanguinea 'Winter Beauty'

Cornus alba 'Sibirica'

PRUNING CORNUS FOR WINTER STEMS

The secret of success with cornus grown for their winter stems is correct pruning. After the end of winter, selectively cut back at least half the stems to ground level. Leave the others to provide structure through the following season, then cut them back at the end of the following winter. By that time, new shoots will have grown from the base to take their place. It is these new shoots, one year old, that display the best stem color. Light trimming will produce unattractive twiggy growth with poor color.

Alternatively, where space allows, plant winter dogwoods in groups and cut half the plants right back to ground level every winter, leaving the others to provide height through the summer months.

Cornus alba 'Elegantissima' (zone 2–8) is the popular white-variegated form, with pale green leaves edged and mottled white. This is a vigorous grower and is excellent where a large, light shrub is required. Slightly more upright in character and often less vigorous than *Cornus alba* 'Elegantissima', **Cornus alba 'Spaethii'** (zone 2–8) has golden-variegated leaves, frequently flushed red when the shrub is grown in full sun. *Cornus alba* 'Gouchaultii' (zone 2–8) is similar in habit to 'Spaethii' but its leaves are flushed pink. **Cornus alba 'Aurea'** (zone 2–8) deserves much wider planting. The leaves are a soft yellow (yellow lime when grown in shade) and the habit light and airy. It also has the bonus of the winter interest of the stems.

Cornus sanguinea (zone 5–8) is the British native common dogwood: green red-flushed stems with small white flowers followed by black fruits. This is not a noticeable plant for most of the year, but in fall is outstanding for its rich purple red leaf color. Various Dutch selections of this plant have become very popular for their outstanding stem color. **Cornus sanguinea 'Midwinter Fire'** and **Cornus sanguinea 'Winter Beauty'** have bright orange-yellow stems that turn orange red in winter. The leaves are pale green in summer, turning orange yellow in fall. This is a striking plant. In the nursery, the stock beds of container-grown plants positively glow in the winter sun.

All *Cornus sanguinea* cultivars can be more difficult to establish than other cornus ('Midwinter Fire' is the most vigorous). The roots are susceptible to frost damage in containers, so early winter planting is recommended.

Cornus sericea (previously known as *Cornus stolonifera*) is very similar to

Cornus sericea 'Flaviramea'

CORNUS IN THE HOUSE

The stems are attractive when cut and used for decoration in the house. A vaseful of brightly colored stems brings a surprisingly long-lasting touch of winter cheer. Long, flexible stems can be used to make wreaths and garlands for Christmas decorations.

Cornus alba; a rampant suckering shrub that grows up to 8ft. (2.5m) high. It is a native of North America, so equally hardy (zone 2–8) and just as easy to grow. The best-known cultivar is **Cornus sericea 'Flaviramea'**, whose yellow-green shoots combine well with the red-stemmed varieties of cornus. It thrives on wet sites. **Cornus sericea 'Budd's Yellow'** has bright yellow young shoots and is considered an improvement on 'Flaviramea'. **Cornus sericea 'Cardinal'** has scarlet shoots tipped orange, and makes a rather more vigorous alternative to *Cornus sanguinea* 'Midwinter Fire'.

Corylus avellana 'Contorta' (zone 4–7) is a form of the British native hazel, originally discovered growing wild in a hedgerow in Gloucestershire, England. Its greatest attribute is its twisted stems, which have given it the common name corkscrew hazel or Harry Lauder's walking stick. These are concealed in summer by a mass of green foliage that shares this distorted habit. It has to be said that in leaf this is not an attractive plant; it could easily be mistaken for one suffering from disease or pest infestation. However, when the leaves fall, it is a strikingly architectural shrub. What's more, the stems are adorned in late winter with long, yellow lambs' tails.

Corylus avellana 'Contorta' are propagated by grafting onto rootstocks of the common hazel, *Corylus avellana*. Suckering from the rootstock can occur; remove suckers as they appear, before the more vigorous rootstock takes over. This is a very easy plant to grow and thrives on any soil in sun or shade.

Growing *Corylus avellana* 'Contorta' in a container allows it to show off the branch structure and the catkins to advantage. The plant also looks good when grown as a specimen rising above low ground cover, such as hedera or ajuga, or when grown against a light fence or stone wall. (See Good Companions, page 177.)

Daphnes have been some of the most sought-after shrubs for many years. The genus contains around 50 species, both evergreen and deciduous, natives of Europe, Asia, and North Africa. Many are quite small, though some make substantial shrubs. The flowers are not spectacular, in some cases even insignificant, but many have the most divine fragrance, and it is for this quality that they are cherished.

Daphnes are poisonous plants and are left alone by rabbits and deer; for

Corylus avellana 'Contorta'

Daphne odora 'Aureomarginata'

Daphne bholua 'Jacqueline Postill'

this reason, they are excellent subjects for the country garden.

Daphne mezereum (zone 5–8) is a deciduous, small shrub with upright branches. It produces masses of purplish red flowers on the previous year's shoots in February and March; red berries often follow. The popularity of this plant has diminished, owing to a viral infection of stock. Affected plants will still flower, but look very poor in the garden for the rest of the year and grow reluctantly.

Daphne odora (zone 7–8) is a small rounded, evergreen shrub with glossy, dark green leaves. The slightly hardier form, and the most frequently grown, is *Daphne odora* 'Aureomarginata', (zone 6–8) which has a narrow, creamy yellow margin around the leaves. The starry, mauve-purple flowers are carried in clusters and are wonderfully fragrant. This plant does well in semi-shade and is an excellent choice to plant near the house, where its fragrance can be appreciated. It can be propagated from cuttings, best taken in late summer.

Daphne bholua (zone 8–9) is a much taller species, originating in the

DAPHNES IN THE HOUSE

Daphne flowers do not last well indoors if you pick the woody stems. The trick is to pick only the flower clusters, with a few leaves, and place them in water up to their necks.

PLANTING AND CARING FOR DAPHNES

Daphnes like good loamy soil; they like moisture but must have good drainage. They do well on lime as long as the other parameters are met. They are not ideal subjects for pots, and always thrive better in the open ground.

Many daphnes are reluctant rooters and difficult to propagate. They are often grafted and therefore more expensive than many other garden shrubs. On grafted daphnes such as *Daphne bholua* 'Jacqueline Postill', look out for vigorous suckers coming from the rootstock. Left alone, these can take over the plant.

Daphnes are not long-lived plants and often deteriorate after 10 or 15 years. *Daphne mezereum* and *Daphne odora*, in particular, manifest their decline by shedding leaves while still producing a few flowers. This means virus has taken its toll and it is time to buy a new plant.

Himalayas. It grows a bit like a leggy teenager, up to a height of 6ft. (2m). It is best described as a semi-evergreen, but the amount of leaf retention depends on the exposure of the site. It is narrow in habit and is ideal to plant close to the house, perhaps at the base of a climber that provides interest later in the year.

In 1982 Alan Postill, propagator at Hillier Nurseries in Britain, raised the

cultivar *Daphne bholua* 'Jacqueline Postill'. This is an excellent, robust form that no winter garden should be without. The many flowers are large and showy for a daphne and purplish pink in clusters. Their powerful fragrance carries widely on the cold winter air.

Garryas are inconspicuous plants for much of the year, with tough, dark leathery leaves. They are excellent to grow on a shady wall, tolerant of urban pollution and resistant to maritime exposure. Native to the southwestern United States, Mexico, and the West Indies, garryas are used to warm climes and can be hit by severe cold, despite their tough appearance, so they are not for cooler zones.

The main attribute of garryas is their catkins, which are produced during the winter months. These are most spectacular on the male. In fact, female plants are not worth growing, and it is essential to acquire a named male clone if you are to be certain of the performance of the plant.

Garrya elliptica 'James Roof' (illus. page 182) (zone 8–9) is the best known and deservedly the most popular choice among the garryas. The plant is draped with long, silvery gray-green catkins from early to late winter. As a relatively upright shrub, it lends itself to being grown against a wall, where it will also benefit from the extra protection. (Continued on page 182.)

Hamamelis

The genus Hamamelis is a small one, with a handful of species, but they are remarkably beautiful trees and shrubs, natives of North America, Japan, and China. In addition to their strangely delicate flowers, produced in the depths of winter, witch hazels contribute some of the best fall foliage color in the garden.

Ideal as freestanding small trees or large shrubs, hamamelis make architecturally beautiful specimens, with a spreading, irregular branch pattern and bowl-like form. Avoid pruning; these plants should be free spirits. All like a good, but not heavy, soil with plenty of organic matter. They color better on acid soils, and the cultivars of *Hamamelis mollis* (zone 5–8) prefer a low pH. They do not enjoy drought, and careful watering during establishment is essential. Hamamelis are hardy but enjoy the shelter of neighboring trees.

Site these plants so as to show off the wonderful flowers. Those with pale yellow flowers look better against a dark background; red-flowering cultivars should catch the low winter light. Buy witch hazels when they are in flower, so you can see what you are buying. Even the youngest shrub will flower, as most are grafted.

Hamamelis look stunning against the intense blue of a winter sky.

Hamamelis virginiana (zone 3–10), the Virginian witch hazel (whose branches settlers used as divining rods—a "magical" property that gave this plant the name witch hazel), is the commercial source of witch hazel lotion.

You can view native witch hazels (*Hamamelis vernalis*) and many other species, both native and introduced, at the United States National Arboretum, 3501 New York Avenue, NE Washington, D. C. 20002-1958. Many other regional arboretums offer the opportunity to see many trees and shrubs growing in beautiful settings, and are well worth a visit.

Hamamelis x *intermedia* **'Pallida'** (z. 5–8) is the most popular of the named x *intermedia* clones. Sulfur-yellow flowers cover the naked branches in midwinter. The autumn foliage color is yellow.

Hamamelis x *intermedia* **'Jelena'** (z. 5–8) is one of the best-loved of the exotic, red- and orange-flowered witch hazels. Autumn color is a late-season echo of the color of the blooms

Hamamelis x *intermedia* **'Diane'** (z. 5–8) is truly red, perhaps the best of the red-flowering hamamelis, with autumn foliage shades to match.

Hamamelis mollis (Chinese witch hazel) (z. 5–8) is the most popular variety. Its large flowers are sweetly fragrant, with broader ribbon-petals than on many witch hazels. The species is an excellent plant but, like all seed-raised plants, can be variable in flower quality.

Garrya elliptica 'James Roof'

Garrya × issaquahensis 'Glasnevin Wine'

***Garrya × issaquahensis* 'Glasnevin Wine'** (zone 7–9) is a broader shrub than *Garrya elliptica* but has similar, leathery foliage. The shoots are a more reddish purple, as are the long catkins; the total effect is most attractive.

Garryas benefit from pruning during their early years. Do this after the catkins fall. This creates a plant that is bushy at the base rather than one that becomes top-heavy.

Positioning garryas alongside light-variegated evergreens can lighten their heavy appearance, particularly after the catkins are over. *Pittosporum* 'Garnettii' (see page 64) is ideal for this purpose; the silvery quality of the foliage is the perfect complement to the pewter catkins of the garrya.

Lonicera × purpusii (zone 5–9) is one of the shrubby honeysuckles, a vigorous shrub, a hybrid between *Lonicera fragrantissima* and *Lonicera standishii*, both of which are winter-flowering, semi-evergreen species.

It has to be said that the plant is ordinary for most of the year, looking somewhat like a privet, with its plain, dark green foliage. The stems are arching and often layer themselves. This

enlarges the overall bulk of the shrub. Its appearance as a young container plant is deceiving; growth is initially weak and lax and belies its potential. It is an excellent subject for the back of a border, where the vigorous stems can be allowed to grow. This is an easy shrub to grow, tolerant of any soil or aspect.

Any pruning is done immediately after flowering, usually in late March. Ideally whole stems that have flowered should be cut back hard to allow new shoots to grow through and flower the following midwinter.

Lonicera × purpusii 'Winter Beauty'

The flowers are creamy white with cream stamens, carried in pairs at the leaf nodes. They are wonderfully fragrant, and the cultivar ***Lonicera × purpusii* 'Winter Beauty'** (zone 5–9) produces them freely over a long period. It was raised in 1966 by a Hillier foreman from a backcross of *Lonicera × purpusii* with *Lonicera standishii*.

In milder zones, this plant retains some of its foliage all year. This is an advantage, to some degree, but the leaves tend to obscure the flowers. If you bring stems into the house to enjoy the fragrance, remove the leaves.

Mahonias have long been among the more popular winter-flowering evergreens. With their stiff stems and strange leaf arrangement, they are somewhat awkward as young plants but acquire grace with maturity. Their leathery texture belies their delicate beauty and the delicious fragrance of the flowers. borne on long racemes.

Mahonia japonica (zone 6–9) is the best- known and arguably most beautiful species. This is a tolerant plant, grows on virtually any soil—even lime—and succeeds in shade. Although it is evergreen, on poor, shallow soils some leaves display rich scarlet and red shades that last well into the winter.

Mahonia aquifolium See page 90.

Mahonia japonica

Mahonia × media 'Underway'

Mahonia japonica (zone 6–9) has a more relaxed habit than that of many other mahonias.

Normally the foliage is a deep, shiny green, with hollylike leaflets arranged opposite each other down both sides of a rigid leaf stalk. These large leaves are held in whorls on tough upright stems. Like its cousin the berberis, this is a plant with armor; never pleasant to handle, it makes a good boundary plant where intruders are to be deterred. *Mahonia japonica* is one of the most fragrant mahonias. In midwinter the terminal rosettes of foliage produce a delightful posy of flowers that resemble lily-of-the-valley; the color is primrose yellow and the fragrance delicious.

Mahonia lomariifolia (zone 6–8) is an imposing, upright creature from Burma and western China. The leaves have more leaflets, of a narrower shape, than *Mahonia japonica*, and the magnificent sprays of showy yellow flowers are carried upright. However, outside the mildest zones, this plant can be hit by frost. Not only are the flowers affected; the desiccating effect of freezing wind can cause extensive leaf fall.

The hybrid **Mahonia × media** (zone 6–9) combines attributes of both species and has given rise to some of our most popular garden cultivars. These can reach a height of 10ft. (3m) and have a strong architectural quality, with racemes of bright yellow flowers. They may be an excellent alternative to a small tree in a limited space, particularly in shade.

There are several well-known named clones of *Mahonia × media*, including 'Lionel Fortescue' (named after the man who raised it), which has upright racemes, and **'Buckland'**, named after the Devonshire village where both were raised. Another × *media* clone, **'Charity'** has become very popular because of its robust nature and long

Mahonia × media 'Winter Sun'

flowering period, but, sadly, it is not especially fragrant; as with 'Buckland', its racemes are long and spreading. More compact forms of *Mahonia × media* include **'Underway'**, with upright racemes, and **'Winter Sun'**, which excels with its erect racemes of very fragrant flowers.

Sarcococcas (Christmas box) are charming dwarf evergreen shrubs. There are several popular species, all good on any fertile soil and especially happy on lime. They are slow-growing, rarely reach over 3ft. (1m) in height, and are remarkably tolerant, succeeding well in shade and under trees.

The evergreen foliage is valuable in its own right, but the delightful surprise comes in midwinter, when the tiny white, threadlike flowers open. Not conspicuous in color or showiness, the blooms cannot escape attention because of their wonderful fragrance.

PLANTING PARTNERS FOR MAHONIA

Mahonias are plants with strong, bold form; clever planting with yellow-variegated partners highlights their yellow flowers. The golden-variegated *Euonymus japonicus* 'Aureus' (z. 7–9) is an easy-to-grow plant that thrives in the same conditions as mahonias. For ground cover, choose the ever-popular *Euonymus fortunei* 'Emerald 'n' Gold' (z. 5–8); its small leaves lighten those of the mahonia. Where space allows, grow a large-leaved hedera as ground cover; *Hedera colchica* 'Sulfur Heart' (z. 6–9) is particularly effective. Nowadays mahonias start to flower early, often at the beginning of winter. Extend the season of interest by planting yellow narcissi alongside; the mahonia's bold green foliage makes the perfect backdrop.

Sarcococcas are very useful garden plants. There are few other hardy, dwarf evergreens that are as accommodating. They are superb for filling in at ground level under taller subjects. Their glossy, rich green foliage is an excellent background for early-spring-flowering bulbs. Plant them beside a path and near the entrance of the house, where their scent can be enjoyed even on cold winter days. They are good for cutting, both for the quality of the foliage and the fragrance of their flowers.

Sarcococca confusa (z. 6–8) has especially good glossy, rich green foliage and a graceful spreading habit. Once the plant becomes established, it tends to sucker and spread—not invasively but densely. Black berries follow the fragrant, creamy flowers.

Sarcococca confusa

Sarcococca hookeriana var. *digyna*

Sarcococca hookeriana var. *digyna* (z. 6–8) is a more upright shrub than *Sarcococca confusa*, with narrow leaves and a more open habit. The flowers appear thinner and sparser but are no less fragrant. **Sarcococca hookeriana var. *digyna* 'Purple Stem'** is attractive for its young stems and leaf stems, which are flushed purple. This shrub is a good backdrop for the red and purple *Helleborus orientalis* hybrids.

Sarcococca orientalis (z. 6–9) is upright and vigorous, with strong green stems. The leaves are larger than those of *Sarcococca confusa*, up to 3½in. (9cm) long, and the flowers are tinged pink. **Sarcococca ruscifolia** (z. 7–9) is uncommon in cultivation but is often confused with *Sarcococca confusa*. Look for **Sarcococca ruscifolia var. chinensis**; the rich green foliage is the perfect setting for dark red berries. This attractive plant forms a dense clump similar in appearance to butcher's broom, *Ruscus aculeatus* (see page 90).

Skimmias (z. 7–8) are shrubs that come to the fore as the days shorten and winter approaches. However, they look good all year round in the right situation. For many years they have been valued for their decorative qualities; frost hardy, they can withstand some freezing conditions.

Skimmias bring color and interest to winter containers and their dark green cut foliage, colorful flower buds or shiny red berries are used in seasonal flower decorations. But skimmias are more than seasonal decorations. Hailing from the Himalayas and eastern Asia, these excellent evergreen shrubs tolerate shade, maritime conditions, and urban pollution. They have a compact, bushy habit and dark green, glossy evergreen foliage. The leaves appear to be arranged in rosettes; they make an excellent background for the showy

GOOD COMPANIONS

For a winter group, plant *Viburnum tinus* (1) (z. 8–9) with red-stemmed *Cornus alba* 'Sibirica' (2) (z. 2–8) and a silvery *Ilex aquifolium* 'Ferox Argentea' (3) (z. 6–9).

Viburnum × *bodnantense* 'Dawn' (4) (z. 6–8) makes a good partner for the evergreen *Pittosporum* 'Garnettii' (5) (z. 9–10).

Underplant *Mahonia* × *media* 'Charity' (6) (z. 6–9) with *Hedera colchica* 'Sulphur Heart' (7) (z. 6–9); the ivy's yellow leaves set off the mahonia's flowers.

Skimmia japonica 'Rubella'

Skimmia japonica ssp.reevesiana

GETTING THE BEST OUT OF YOUR SKIMMIAS

Skimmias are plants for shade on well-drained soil. They enjoy a soil rich in organic matter and establish better when plenty of good compost or well-rotted manure is incorporated at the time of planting. The fibrous root system must be kept well watered until the plant is established. Skimmia is an easy shrub to grow and requires no special care and no pruning.

Planted in the open ground in full sun, skimmia has a tendency to go yellow, often leading to the conclusion that this plant is a lime-hater, and that this yellowing is a reaction to alkaline soil. Most skimmias are in fact happy on alkaline soils as well as acid, as long as they are planted in shade or semi-shade. In a hot, sunny position the yellowing can also be due to an infestation of red spider mite; use a biological control or a drench of systemic pest-killer.

If a plant fails to perform, does not flower, and refuses to berry, this is nearly always because it has been planted too deeply. Never plant deeper than the level of soil mix in the pot; otherwise the plant will sulk.

clusters of flowers and prominent berries produced by some varieties. Because of the fruiting season, they are sometimes used as a substitute for holly. Those that produce red flower buds in the winter are equally decorative.

Skimmia is a member of the family Rutaceae (other members include citrus and choisya), hence its aromatic foliage and fragrant flowers.

Skimmia japonica 'Rubella' (zone 7–8) is the best-known cultivar. This is a male clone, so does not produce berries. However, it is very free flowering and compensates with a profusion of red flower buds through fall into winter. In spring these open as fragrant, creamy flowers. This is an ideal subject for winter containers and temporary decoration, as well as for permanent planting.

Skimmia japonica ssp. *reevesiana* (zone 7–8) produces both male and female flowers. Self-pollinating, it produces sealing-wax red berries on dwarf plants that rarely grow to over 2ft. (60cm). The white flowers are fragrant. This plant is not good on lime. It is one of the more difficult skimmias to establish and is popular only because it berries as a young plant in a pot.

A female clone, *Skimmia japonica* 'Veitchii' ('Foremanii') (zone 7–8) produces berries of excellent quality if it has a male pollinator such as *Skimmia × confusa* 'Kew Green' (zone 7–8) to set the fruit. The male clones should not be regarded as inferior because of their lack of berries; the flowers are just as much of an attribute. 'Kew Green' has glossy, green foliage and large panicles of white, scented flowers. As its name implies, *Skimmia japonica* 'Fragrans' (zone 7–8) is also fragrant.

WINTER-FLOWERING BULBS TO PLANT UNDER WINTER SHRUBS

Crocus tommasinianus
Cyclamen coum
Eranthis hyemalis
Galanthus nivalis
Iris reticulata
Puschkinia scilloides

SKIMMIAS IN POTS

Because of their compact habit, skimmias make excellent shrubs for containers. Planted in a sensibly sized pot, more than 14in. (35cm) in diameter, a skimmia can be regarded as a permanent subject that will give years of pleasure in any situation out of full sun. Use loam-based mix for potting, and ensure that the container has good drainage.

The bold form and strong foliage of skimmia contrasts well with ferns and hostas, also good subjects for pots.

Skimmia × confusa 'Kew Green'

Viburnum

Of the 150 or more species of deciduous and evergreen viburnums, several are highly valued for their winter flowers. All are easy shrubs to grow on any soil, succeed in sun or shade, are frost-hardy, and make excellent structure plants.

Viburnum tinus (zone 8–9) originally known as *Laurustinus*, was introduced to English gardens in the 16th century from the Mediterranean region. Like many Mediterranean plants, it is a survivor, tolerant not only of inhospitable conditions and poor soil, but of the cold and wet of winter. It has many good qualities—low-maintenance, evergreen, free-flowering over a long period, and responsive to trimming. It copes well on the coast and seems resistant to urban pollution.

The species is a medium to large shrub, of dense and bushy habit, with masses of dark green, glossy oval leaves. The flattened heads of pink buds, opening to white flowers, are produced continuously from fall to late spring. Blue-black fruits often follow the flowers and are usually still present when the following season's flower buds are emerging.

With its evergreen mass, *Viburnum tinus* contributes bold, all-year-round form to any planting scheme. Its robust foliage and free-flowering habit make it easily compatible with any planting scheme, formal or informal.

Viburnum tinus survives in dry shade, even under oak trees. However, despite this, it has to get properly established before it can flourish. The secret of success is good soil preparation and watering—even in winter if conditions are dry.

Viburnum × *bodnantense* (zone 6–8) is one of the best-known winter-flowering shrubs. It has strong upright growth and clusters of pink buds, opening to pale pink, scented flowers. Usually unaffected by frost, these are produced freely from mid-fall onward.

A hybrid between two winter-flowering species, *Viburnum farreri* (often known as *Viburnum fragrans*) and

Viburnum tinus etched with frost.

Viburnum grandiflorum, *Viburnum* × *bodnantense* was raised at the Royal Botanic Garden, Edinburgh, and later at Bodnant, in Wales, after which it was named.

Viburnum × *bodnantense* makes a tall shrub, often in excess of 10ft. (3m), and is an excellent structure shrub for the back of the border, where it can be allowed to reach its potential. However, its eventual size is often underestimated, and it outgrows its allotted space. When grown in a sheltered position, *Viburnum* × *bodnantense* has a tendency to hang onto its foliage in winter, which spoils the effect of the flowers. For best effect, plant it in an open position.

TRIMMING AND TRAINING VIBURNUMS

All cultivars of *Viburnum tinus* respond well to trimming. Do this immediately after flowering in early spring, to give the plant time to produce mature growth on which to flower next winter. Pruning is necessary only to control size and shape; it is not essential. *Viburnum tinus* makes an excellent informal hedge or screen and is an interesting subject to train as a standard, cone, or ball—a softer and prettier alternative to the more traditional bay and box.

Because of the upright growth of *Viburnum* × *bodnantense*, poor pruning often spoils the shape and habit. Partially cutting back shoots, to reduce height, results in vigorous ugly growth at the top of the plant. Pruning is not essential; where it is necessary to control size, selectively remove whole branches to ground level, allowing new wood to come from the base.

Viburnum tinus 'Spirit' (zone 8–9) produces profuse white flowers, pink in bud, over a long period. Blue-black fruits follow reliably after the flowers. The foliage is excellent: lush and dark green, carried on deep red stems that add considerably to the overall effect of the plant. This will make a large shrub over 6ft. (2m) in height if left unpruned.

Viburnum × *bodnantense* 'Dawn' (above) (zone 6–8) was the first named form of the × *bodnantense* cross and is still popular. It is vigorous; its dark foliage is often tinted red brown later in the year. *Viburnum* × *bodnantense* 'Deben' (zone 6–8) has paler flowers.

Viburnum tinus 'French White' (above) (zone 8–9) is similar in stature to *Viburnum tinus* 'Spirit' and is one of the most widely planted forms. 'Purpureum' is a selection with darker foliage and bronze-tinged young growth. It has a looser habit than most viburnums, which makes it somewhat less solid—a useful attribute in mixed planting.

Viburnum tinus 'Eve Price' (above) (zone 8–9) is the most compact form, growing slowly to 5ft. (1.5m). The leaves are smaller than the type, and closer together. It produces masses of deep pink buds and pink-tinged flowers. It survives out of full sun and is a good evergreen for a large pot. 'Gwenllian' is another compact grower, with whiter, larger flowers.

Author's choice: top 20 performance shrubs

From the large selection of ornamental shrubs described in this book I have chosen 20 I consider to be excellent, easy-to-grow garden plants that have a long season of interest and will succeed on virtually any soil of reasonable fertility.

I have put these plants into four groups, two suitable for sun and two for shade. Between them, the plants in each combination give a pleasing variation in color, form, and texture, and achieve all-year-round appeal. All are tried and tested.

TALL SELECTION FOR A SUNNY POSITION—MAXIMUM HEIGHT 10FT. (3M)

 ***Buddleia* 'Lochinch'** (z. 5–9) (page 74) Silver foliage; lilac-blue, fragrant flowers in summer

 ***Ceanothus* 'Concha'** (z. 9–10) (page 140) Evergreen; fast-growing; blue flowers in late spring

 ***Choisya* 'Aztec Pearl'** (z. 8–10) (page 139) Evergreen; fragrant white flowers in late spring

 ***Sambucus nigra* f. *porphyrophylla* 'Eva'** ('Black Lace') (z. 5–7) (page 54) Plum-purple foliage; pink flowers in summer

 ***Weigela florida* 'Variegata'** (z. 5–9) (page 69) Variegated foliage; pink flowers in late spring

TALL SELECTION FOR SEMI-SHADE—MAXIMUM HEIGHT 6FT. (2M)

 ***Euonymus japonicus* 'Chollipo'** (z. 7–9) (page 59) Evergreen, gold-and-green variegated foliage

 Fatsia japonica (z. 8–9) (page 89) Evergreen, bold leaves; white flowers in early winter

 ***Hypericum* 'Hidcote'** (z. 6–7) (page 158) Golden-yellow flowers through summer and fall

 ***Osmanthus heterophyllus* 'Goshiki'** (z. 6–9) (page 43) Evergreen, golden-bronze variegated foliage

 ***Philadelphus coronarius* 'Aureus'** (z. 4–8) (page 45) Golden-yellow foliage; fragrant white flowers in early summer

SHORT SELECTION FOR A SUNNY POSITION—MAXIMUM HEIGHT 3FT. (1M)

 ***Cistus* ×*obtusifolius* 'Thrive'** (z. 8–10) (page 83) Evergreen; white flowers in summer

 ***Hebe* 'Red Edge'** (z. 8–10) (page 76) Evergreen, gray-green foliage, red-edged in winter

 Lavandula stoechas* ssp. *pedunculata (z. 7–8) (page 73) Gray-green aromatic leaves; mauve-blue flowers in summer

 ***Rosmarinus officinalis* 'Miss Jessopp's Upright'** (z. 8–10) (page 86) Evergreen, aromatic, culinary foliage; blue flowers in early spring

 ***Salvia officinalis* 'Purpurascens'** (z. 5–10) (page 49) Evergreen, purple-gray, aromatic, culinary foliage; blue flowers in summer

SHORT SELECTION FOR SHADE—MAXIMUM HEIGHT 3 FT. (1M)

 ***Cornus alba* 'Sibirica Variegata'** (z. 2–8) (page 177) White-and-green variegated leaves; red winter stems

 ***Euonymus fortunei* 'Silver Queen'** (z. 5–8) (page 59) Evergreen, cream-and-green variegated foliage

 Sarcococca confusa (z. 6–8) (page 90) Evergreen; fragrant white flowers in winter

 Viburnum davidii (z. 7–9) (page 37) Evergreen, bold foliage; small white flowers in summer

 ***Viburnum tinus* 'Eve Price'** (z. 8–9) (page 187) Evergreen; pink buds and white flowers in winter

Index

The letter *i* following a page number (for example 165*i*) refers to an illustration. A page number in **bold** type refers to a Plant Profile. The letter *z.* refers to USDA zones.